ERRATA

The National Diet and Nutrition Survey: adults aged 19 to 64 years.
Volume 1: Types and quantities of foods consumed.
Henderson L, Gregory J, Swan G. TSO (London, 2002).

ISBN   0 11 621566 6

Since its publication in December 2002, an error has come to light in the derivation of consumption data for the following food types:

Other cereals
Cream
Other milk
Beef, veal & dishes
Table sugar
Fruit juice
Concentrated soft drinks - not low calorie, as consumed
Concentrated soft drinks - low calorie, as consumed
Coffee, as consumed
Tea, as consumed
Other beverages, dry weight
Soup

The following tables have been revised to show correct consumption figures and are available at www.food.gov.uk/science/

Tables 2.10(a) and 2.10(b)
Tables 2.11(a), 2.11(b) and 2.11(c)
Tables 2.12(a) and 2.12(b)
Tables 2.13(a) and 2.13(b)
Table 2.14
Table 2.16(b)
Table 2.17(b)
Tables A2(a), A3(a), A4(a), A5(a), A6(a), A7(a) and A8.

Data on nutrient intakes are not affected by this error.

The National Diet and Nutrition Survey: young people aged 4 to 18 years.
Volume 1: Report of the diet and nutrition survey.
Gregory JR, Lowe S, Bates CJ, Prentice A, Jackson LV, Smithers G, Wenlock R, Farron M.
TSO (London, 2000).

ISBN   0 11 621265 9

The error noted above affects the consumption data for the following food types for the NDNS of young people aged 4 to 18 years:

Whole milk
Cream
Other milk
Concentrated soft drinks - not low calorie, as consumed
Concentrated soft drinks - low calorie, as consumed
Coffee, as consumed
Tea, as consumed
Other beverages, dry weight

Revised consumption figures for these food types are available at www.food.gov.uk/science/

Office for National Statistics
June 2003

Volume 3

The National Diet & Nutrition Survey: adults aged 19 to 64 years

Vitamin and mineral intake and urinary analytes

Lynne Henderson
Karen Irving
Jan Gregory
Office for National Statistics

with **Christopher J Bates**
Ann Prentice
Jayne Perks
*Medical Resource Council
Human Nutrition Research*

Gillian Swan
Melanie Farron
Food Standards Agency

A survey carried out in Great Britain on behalf of the Food Standards Agency and the Departments of Health by the Social Survey Division of the Office for National Statistics and Medical Research Council Human Nutrition Research

London: TSO

ISBN 0 11 621568 2

Contact points

For enquiries about this publication, contact
Lynne Henderson
Tel: **020 7533 5385**
E-mail: **lynne.henderson@ons.gov.uk**

To order this publication, call TSO
on **0870 600 5522**. See also inside back cover.

For general enquiries, contact the National Statistics
Customer Enquiry Centre on **0845 601 3034**
(minicom: 01633 812399)
E-mail: **info@statistics.gov.uk**
Fax: 01633 652747
Letters: Room D.115, Government Buildings,
Cardiff Road, Newport NP10 8XG

You can also find National Statistics on the Internet
at **www.statistics.gov.uk**

About the Office for National Statistics

The Office for National Statistics (ONS) is the government
agency responsible for compiling, analysing and disseminating
many of the United Kingdom's economic, social and
demographic statistics, including the retail prices index, trade
figures and labour market data, as well as the periodic census of
the population and health statistics. The Director of ONS is also
the National Statistician and the Registrar General for England
and Wales, and the agency administers the statutory registration
of births, marriages and deaths there.

This report has been produced by the Social Survey Division of
the Office for National Statistics in accordance with the Official
Statistics Code of Practice.

Contents

Foreword

This survey, of a national sample of adults aged 19 to 64 years, is one of a programme of national surveys with the aim of gathering information about the dietary habits and nutritional status of the British population. The results of the survey will be used to develop nutrition policy and to contribute to the evidence base for Government advice on healthy eating.

This report, covering intakes of vitamins and minerals and levels of urinary analytes, is the third in a series on the findings of this survey. The first report, covering foods consumed, was published in December 2002, and the second, covering intakes of energy and macronutrients, in June 2003. A further report covering nutritional status will be published later this year and a summary report will complete the series.

The work described in this series of reports results from a successful collaboration between the Food Standards Agency and the Department of Health, who jointly funded the collection of the survey data, with the Office for National Statistics and the Medical Research Council Human Nutrition Research.

We warmly welcome this third report of the latest survey in the National Diet and Nutrition Survey programme and express our thanks to all the respondents who took part.

Sir John Krebs
Chairman
Food Standards Agency

Hazel Blears
Minister for Public Health
Department of Health

Authors' acknowledgements

We would like to thank everyone who contributed to the survey and the production of this report:

- the respondents without whose co-operation the survey would not have been possible;

- the interviewers of Social Survey Division of ONS (SSD) who recruited the respondents and carried out all the fieldwork stages of the survey;

- colleagues in Social Survey Division of ONS in the Sampling Implementation Unit, Field Branch, Business Solutions, Methodology Unit and Project Support Branch, in particular, Amanda Wilmot, Jo Bacon, Jacqueline Hoare, Bev Botting, Goli Lashkari, Ann Whitby, Michaela Pink, Caroline Ojemuyiwa, Michael Staley, Glenn Edy, Andrew Tollington, Dave Elliot, Jeremy Barton and Tracie Goodfellow;

- the ONS nutritionists, namely Debbie Hartwell, Michaela Davies, Sui Yip, Laura Hopkins, Jessica Ive, Sarah Oyston, Claire Jaggers and Robert Anderson;

- the ONS editors, namely Angela Harris, Carole Austen, Mike Donovan, Nina Hall, Sue Heneghan, Sarah Kelly, Dave Philpot, Colin Wakeley, Carol Willis and Heather Yates;

- staff of the Medical Research Council Human Nutrition Research (HNR), particularly staff of the Micronutrient Status Laboratory, namely: Steve Austin, Shailja Nigdikar, Filomena Liuni, Karen Giddens, Hanneke Schippers, Neal Matthews, Glynn Harvey, Laura Wang, Richard Carter, Helen Martindale, Clare Kitchener, Jason Swain; and staff of the Survey Office, namely: Jolieke van der Pols, Robert Quigley, Roberta Re, Lucy Winter, Elaine Proud, Carmen Treacy, Kathleen Edwards, Gemma Bramwell, Michael Garratt, Ansar Malik;

- Dr Maureen Birch, the survey doctor, for her input into the design, conduct and interpretation of the survey, in particular for her negotiations with NHS Local Research Ethics Committees;

- the phlebotomists and local laboratory personnel who were recruited by HNR to take the blood samples, and process and store the blood specimens;

- Professor Elaine Gunter, Chief, National Health and Nutrition Examination Survey (NHANES) Laboratory, Centres for Disease Control and Prevention, Atlanta, USA, for an independent review of the methodology for the blood and urine collection and laboratory analyses;

- Professor Angus Walls for his contribution to the oral health component and briefing the interviewers on the procedures for the self-tooth and amalgam-filling count;

- Professor Chris Skinner and Dr David Holmes at the University of Southampton for an independent review of response to this NDNS and an assessment of non-response bias;

- David Marker at Westat for an independent review of NDNS methodology and procedures;

- the professional staff at the Food Standards Agency and the Department of Health, in particular Jamie Blackshaw, Susan Church, Michael Day, Hannah Green, Miguel Goncalves, Tom Murray, Dr John Pascoe, Dr Roger Skinner and Alette Weaver of the Food Standards Agency; Richard Bond, Tony Boucher, Ian Cooper, Dr Sheela Reddy and Robert Wenlock of the Department of Health.

Notes to the tables

Tables showing percentages

In general, percentages are shown if the base is 30 or more. Where a base number is less than 30, actual numbers are shown within square brackets.

The row or column percentages may add to 99% or 101% because of rounding and weighting.

The varying positions of the bases in the tables denote the presentation of different types of information. Where the base is at the foot of the table, the whole distribution is presented and the individual percentages add to between 99% and 101%. Where the base is given in a column, the figures refer to the proportion of respondents who had the attribute being discussed, and the complementary proportion, to add to 100%, is not shown in the table.

In tables showing cumulative percentages the row labelled 'All' is always shown as 100%. The proportion of cases falling above the upper limit of the previous band can be calculated by subtracting from 100 the proportion in the previous band. Actual maximum values are not shown in tables of cumulative percentages, since they could vary for different subgroups being considered within the same tables.

Unless shown as a separate group, or stated in the text or a footnote to a table, estimates have been calculated for the total number of respondents in the subgroup, excluding those not answering. Base numbers shown in the tables are the total number of respondents in the subgroup, including those not answering.

The total column may include cases from small subgroups not shown separately elsewhere on the tables, therefore the individual column bases may not add to the base in the total column.

Conventions

The following conventions have been used in the tables:

..	data not available
-	category not applicable; no cases
0	values less than 0.5%
[ ]	numbers inside square brackets are the actual numbers of cases, when the base is fewer than 30.

Tables showing descriptive statistics – mean, percentiles, standard deviation

These are shown in tables to an appropriate number of decimal places.

Significant differences

Differences commented on in the text are shown as being significant at the 95% or 99% confidence levels ($p < 0.05$ and $p < 0.01$). Throughout this volume, the terms 'significant' and 'statistically significant' are used interchangeably. Where differences are shown or described as being 'not statistically significant' or 'ns' this indicates $p > 0.05$. The formulae used to test for significant differences are given in Appendix A, pages 137–140.

As a general indication of those groups showing the largest differences, the differences between all pairs of groups were tested for statistical significance. Because of this 'trawling' approach, real statistical significance levels are lower than indicated here and some of the reported significant differences are likely to be spurious. However, these significance tests can still be validly used for testing hypotheses suggested by earlier work.

Where differences between subgroups are compared for a number of variables, for example differences between respondents in different age groups in mean daily calcium intake, the significance level shown ($p<0.05$ or $p<0.01$) applies to all comparisons, unless otherwise stated.

Standard deviations

Standard deviations for estimates of mean values are shown in the tables and have been calculated for a simple random sample design. In testing for the significant difference between two sample estimates, proportions or means, the sampling error calculated as for a simple random design was multiplied by an assumed design factor of 1.5, to allow for the complex sample design. The reader is referred to Appendix A for an account of the method of calculating true standard errors and for tables of design factors for the main variables and subgroups used throughout this volume. In general, design factors were below 1.5. Therefore although not commented on in the text, there will be some differences in sample proportions and means, that are significantly different, at least at the $p<0.05$ level.

Weighting

Unless otherwise stated, all proportions and means presented in the tables in the substantive chapters in this volume are taken from data weighted to compensate for the differential probabilities of selection and non-response. Base numbers are presented weighted. All base numbers are given in italics. *See* Appendix B for unweighted base numbers, and Appendix D of the Technical Report online for more details on the weighting: accessible at http://www.food.gov.uk/science.

1 Background, research design and response

This volume presents findings on vitamin and mineral intakes and urinary analytes from a survey of the diet and nutrition of adults aged 19 to 64 years living in private households in Great Britain, carried out between July 2000 and June 2001. It is the third volume in a series that covers food and nutrient intake data derived from the analyses of dietary records, and data on nutritional status from physical measurements including anthropometric data, blood pressure, physical activity and the analyses of blood and urine samples[1]. This first chapter of this volume describes the background to the National Diet and Nutrition Survey (NDNS) of adults aged 19 to 64 years, its main aims, research designs and methodologies and response. Chapters 2 and 3 report on average daily intakes of vitamins and minerals, respectively, from food sources alone and from all sources, that is including any dietary supplements being taken. Throughout both chapters actual intakes are compared with UK dietary reference values, where appropriate. Chapter 4 presents results from analysis of the 24-hour urine collection. Differences are considered by age, sex, region and household receipt of benefits. Where appropriate comparisons are made between this survey and the Dietary and Nutritional Survey of British Adults aged 16 to 64 years carried out in 1986/87[2].

A Technical Report containing the methodological chapters and appendices is available online[3]. Like previous surveys in the NDNS programme, following publication of the final summary volume, a copy of the survey database, containing the full data set will be deposited with The Data Archive at the University of Essex. Independent researchers who wish to carry out their own analyses should apply to the Archive for access[4].

1.1 The National Diet and Nutrition Survey Programme

The survey forms part of the National Diet and Nutrition Survey programme, which was set up jointly by the Ministry of Agriculture, Fisheries and Food[5] and the Department of Health in 1992 following the successful Dietary and Nutritional Survey of British Adults aged 16 to 64 years carried out in 1986/87 (1986/87 Adults Survey)[2]. MAFF's responsibility for the NDNS programme has now transferred to the Food Standards Agency.

The NDNS programme aims to provide comprehensive, cross-sectional information on the dietary habits and nutritional status of the population of Great Britain. The results of the surveys within the programme are used to develop nutrition policy at a national and local level, and to contribute to the evidence base for Government advice on healthy eating.

The NDNS programme is intended to:

- provide detailed quantitative information on the food and nutrient intakes, sources of nutrients and nutritional status of the population under study as a basis for Government policy;

- describe the characteristics of individuals with intakes of specific nutrients that are above and below the national average;

- provide a database to enable the calculation of likely dietary intakes of natural toxicants, contaminants, additives and other food chemicals for risk assessment;

- measure blood and urine indices that give evidence of nutritional status or dietary biomarkers and to relate these to dietary, physiological and social data;

- provide height, weight and other measurements of body size on a representative sample of individuals and examine their relationship to social, dietary, health and anthropometric data as well as data from blood analyses;

- monitor the diet of the population under study to establish the extent to which it is adequately nutritious and varied;

- monitor the extent of deviation of the diet of specified groups of the population from that recommended by independent experts as optimum for health, in order to act as a basis for policy development;

- help determine possible relationships between diet and nutritional status and risk factors in later life;

- assess physical activity levels of the population under study; and

- provide information on oral health in relation to dietary intake and nutritional status.

The NDNS programme consists of a planned programme of cross-sectional surveys of representative samples of defined age groups of the population. The surveys of older adults, pre-school children, and young people have been published[6,7,8]. The last national survey of diet and nutrition in adults was the 1986/87 Adults Survey[2].

1.2 The sample design and selection

A nationally representative sample of adults aged 19 to 64 years living in private households was required. The sample was selected using a multi-stage random probability design with postal sectors as first stage units. The sampling frame included all postal sectors within mainland Great Britain; selections were made from the small users' Postcode Address File. The frame was stratified by 1991 Census variables. A total of 152 postal sectors was selected as first stage units, with probability proportional to the number of postal delivery points, and 38 sectors were allocated to each of four fieldwork waves. The allocation took account of the need to have approximately equal numbers of households in each wave of fieldwork and for each wave to be nationally representative.

From each postal sector 40 addresses were randomly selected[9].

Eligibility was defined as being aged between 19 and 64 and not pregnant or breastfeeding at the time of the doorstep sift[10]. Where there was more than one adult between the ages of 19 and 64 years living in the same household, only one was selected at random to take part in the survey[11]. A more detailed account of the sample design is given in Appendix D of the Technical Report[3]. In keeping with Social Survey Division of ONS (SSD) normal fieldwork procedures, a letter was sent to each household in the sample in advance of the interviewer calling, telling them briefly about the survey (see Appendix A of the Technical Report[3]).

As in previous surveys in the NDNS series, fieldwork covered a 12-month period, to cover any seasonality in eating behaviour and in the nutrient content of foods; for example, full fat milk. The 12-month fieldwork period was divided into four fieldwork waves, each of three months duration[12]. The fieldwork waves were:

Wave 1: July to September 2000

Wave 2: October to December 2000

Wave 3: January to March 2001

Wave 4: April to June 2001

Feasibility work carried out between September and December 1999 by the SSD and the Medical Research Council Human Nutrition Research (HNR) tested all the components of the survey and made recommendations for revisions for the mainstage. For a subgroup of the feasibility study sample, the validity of the dietary recording methodology was tested using the doubly labelled water methodology to compare energy expenditure against reported energy intake. Further details of the design and results of the feasibility study are summarised in Appendix C of the Technical Report[3].

Ethics approval was gained for the feasibility and mainstage survey from a Multi-centre Research Ethics Committee (MREC), and National Health Service Local Research Ethics Committees covering each of the 152 sampled areas (see Appendix N of the Technical Report[3]).

1.3 The components of the survey

The survey design included: an interview to provide information about the socio-demographic circumstances of the respondent and their household, medication and eating and drinking habits; a weighed dietary record of all food and drink consumed over seven consecutive days; a record of bowel movements for the same seven days; a record of physical activity over the same seven days; physical measurements of the respondent (height, weight, waist and hip circumferences); blood pressure measurements; and a request for a sample of blood and a 24-hour urine collection. Respondents were also asked to do a self-count of the number of teeth and amalgam fillings they had, and provide a sample of tap water from the home for analysis of fluoride. Results of the self-tooth and amalgam filling count are not reported in any of the four volumes of this NDNS.

1.3.1 The dietary and post-dietary record interview

The interview comprised two parts. An initial face-to-face interview using computer-assisted personal interviewing methods (CAPI) to collect information about the respondent's household, their usual dietary behaviour, consumption of artificial sweeteners, herbal teas and other drinks; any foods that were avoided and the reasons for doing so, including vegetarianism and dieting behaviours; the use of salt at the table and in cooking; and the use of fluoride preparations and dietary supplements. Information was also collected on: the respondent's health status; their smoking and drinking habits; socio-economic characteristics; and, for women in defined age groups, the use of the contraceptive pill, menopausal state and use of hormone replacement therapy.

There was also a short interview, using CAPI, conducted at the end of the seven dietary recording days (post-dietary record interview). Respondents were asked about any problems they experienced in keeping the diary, whether their consumption of specific foods had changed during the seven days and whether they had been unwell at all during the recording period. Respondents were also asked to complete an eating restraint questionnaire, using computer assisted self-interviewing (CASI) or on paper. Information was also collected on prescribed medications taken during the seven days.

The interview questionnaire is reproduced in Appendix A of the Technical Report[3].

1.3.2 The dietary record

The survey used a weighed intake methodology since its main aims were to provide detailed quantitative information on the range and distribution of intakes of foods and nutrients for respondents aged 19 to 64 years in Great Britain,

and to investigate relationships between nutrient intakes, physical activity levels and various nutritional status and health measures. The advantages and disadvantages of this method and the factors affecting the choice are discussed in Appendix F of the Technical Report[3].

In deciding to use a weighed intake methodology, the period over which to collect information needed to be long enough to give reliable information on usual food consumption, balanced against the likelihood of poor compliance if the recording period was lengthy. The doubly labelled water study carried out as part of the feasibility study to assess the validity of the seven-day weighed intake method indicated a level of under-reporting that is typical of this method but no evidence of differential bias by age or sex. The feasibility study concluded that it was possible to collect dietary information for a seven-day period from respondents and that the quality of information would be acceptable (see Appendix C of the Technical Report[3]).

Information which would be of use to the interviewer when checking the dietary record was also collected: for example, on respondents' usual eating pattern on weekdays and at weekends; and on the types of certain common food items eaten, such as milk, bread and fat. This information was recorded on a paper form rather than in the CAPI program, so that the interviewer could use it to check diary entries during the recording period (see F7, Appendix A of the Technical Report[3]).

Respondents were asked to keep a weighed record of all food and drink they consumed, both in and out of the home, over seven consecutive days. Each respondent was issued with a set of accurately calibrated Soehnle Quanta digital food scales and two recording diaries; the 'Home Record' diary for use when it was possible for foods to be weighed, generally foods eaten in the home; and a smaller 'Eating and Drinking Away From Home' diary (the 'Eating Out' diary) for use when foods could not be weighed, generally foods eaten away from home. The respondent was also issued with a pocket-sized notebook for recording any of this information in circumstances where they were reluctant or it was inappropriate to carry the 'Eating Out' diary. The instruction and recording pages from these documents relating to the dietary information are included in Appendix A of the Technical Report[3].

The respondent, together with any other household member who might be involved in keeping the diary, for example their spouse or partner, was shown by the interviewer how to use the scales to weigh food and drinks, how to weigh and record leftovers, and how to record any food that was spilt or otherwise lost and so could not be re-weighed.

The 'Home Record' diary was the main recording and coding document. For each item consumed over the seven days a description of the item was recorded, including the brand name of the product and, where appropriate, the method of preparation. Also recorded was the weight served and the weight of any leftovers, the time food was eaten, whether it was eaten at home or elsewhere, and whether fruit and vegetables were home grown, defined as being grown in the household's own garden or allotment. The person who did the weighing, the respondent or someone else, was also recorded for each food item and, for each day, the respondent was asked to indicate whether they were 'well' or 'unwell'.

Respondents who completed a full seven-day dietary record were given a £10 gift voucher by the interviewer, as a token of appreciation. It was made clear that receiving the voucher was not dependent on co-operation with any other component of the survey, in particular, consenting to provide a blood sample.

Respondents started to record their consumption in the diaries as soon as the interviewer had explained the procedure and left the home, although the seven-day recording period started from midnight. The interviewer called back approximately 24 hours after placing the diaries in order to check that the items were being recorded correctly, to give encouragement and to re-motivate where appropriate. Everything consumed by the respondent had to be recorded, including medicines taken by mouth, vitamin and mineral supplements, and drinks of water. Respondents were encouraged to weigh everything they could, including takeaway meals brought into the home to eat. Where a served item could not be weighed, respondents were asked to record a description of the portion size, using standard household measures, or to describe the size of the item in some other way. Each separate item of food in a served portion needed to be weighed separately in order that the nutrient composition of each food item could be calculated. In addition, recipes for all home-made dishes were collected.

The amount of salt used either at the table or in cooking was not weighed, however questions on the use of salt in the cooking of the respondent's food and their use of salt at the table were asked at the dietary interview. All other sauces, pickles and dressings were recorded.

Vitamin and mineral supplements and artificial sweeteners were recorded as units consumed: for example, one Boots Vitamin C tablet 200mg, one teaspoon of Canderel Spoonful.

A large amount of detail needed to be recorded in the dietary record to enable similar foods prepared and cooked by different methods to be coded correctly, as such foods will have different nutrient compositions. Information could also be needed on cooking method, preparation and packaging as well as an exact description of the item before it could be accurately coded. Details on the recording of leftovers and spillage are given in Appendix F of the Technical Report[3]. An aide-memoire on using the scales and recording in the 'Home Diary' was left with respondents (see W1 and W2, Appendix A of the Technical Report[3]).

The 'Eating Out' diary was intended to be used only when it was not possible to weigh the food items. In such cases, respondents were asked to write down as much information as possible about each food item consumed, particularly the portion size and an estimate of the amount of any left over. Prices, descriptions, brand names, place of purchase, and the time and place where the food was consumed were all recorded. In certain circumstances, interviewers were allowed to purchase duplicate items which they would then weigh.

Where the respondent consumed food or drink items provided by their workplace or college, the interviewer was required to visit the workplace/college canteen to collect further information from the catering manager about, for example, cooking methods, portion sizes and types of fats used. The information was recorded on a 'catering questionnaire' which included standard questions on portion sizes and cooking methods, and had provision for recording information on specific items that the respondent had consumed (see Appendix A of the Technical Report[3]).

At each visit to the household, interviewers checked the diary entries with the respondent to ensure that they were complete and all the necessary detail had been recorded. Reasons for any apparent omission of meals were probed by the interviewers and noted on the diaries. If the interviewers probing uncovered food items that had been consumed but not recorded, these were added to the diary at the appropriate place. Before returning the coded diaries to ONS headquarters, interviewers were asked to make an assessment of the quality of the dietary record, in particular the extent to which they considered that the diary was an accurate reflection of the respondent's actual diet.

Interviewers were trained in and responsible for coding the food diaries so they could readily identify the level of detail needed for different food items and probe for missing detail at later visits to the household. A food code list, giving code numbers for about 3,500 items and a full description of each item, was prepared by nutritionists at the Food Standards Agency and the ONS, for use by the interviewers. As fieldwork progressed, further codes were added to the food code list for home-made recipe dishes and new products found in the dietary record. A page from the food code list is reproduced in Appendix A of the Technical Report[3].

Brand information was collected for all food items bought pre-wrapped, as some items, such as biscuits, confectionery and breakfast cereals, could not be food coded correctly unless the brand was known. Brand information was only coded for artificial sweeteners, bottled waters, herbal teas and herbal drinks, and soft drinks and fruit juices, to ensure adequate differentiation of these items. Food source codes were also allocated to each meal in order to identify food obtained and consumed outside the home. The contribution to total nutrient intake by foods from different sources could then be calculated.

After the interviewers had coded the entries in the dietary records, ONS headquarters coding and editing staff checked the documents. ONS nutritionists carried out initial checks for completeness of the dietary records, dealt with specific queries from interviewers and coding staff, and advised on and checked the quality of coding, with advice from Food Standards Agency nutritionists. They were also responsible for converting descriptions of portion sizes to weights, and checking that the appropriate codes for recipes and new products had been used. Computer checks for completeness and consistency of information were run on the dietary and questionnaire data. Following completion of these checks and calculations, the information from the dietary record was linked to the nutrient databank; nutrient intakes were thereby calculated from quantities of food consumed. This nutrient databank, which was compiled by the Food Standards Agency, holds information on 56 nutrients for each of the 6,000 food codes. Further details of the nutrient databank are provided in Appendix H of the Technical Report[3]. Each food code used was also allocated to one of 115 subsidiary food groups; these were aggregated into 57 main food groups and further aggregated into 11 food types (*see* Appendix G of the Technical Report[3]).

1.3.3 24-hour urine collection

The relationship between dietary intakes of sodium, present in salt (sodium chloride), and other dietary components and blood pressure has been investigated in relation to the established association between hypertension and cardiovascular disease. The Scientific Advisory Committee on Nutrition in its recent report on salt and health concluded that reducing the average population salt intake would proportionally lower population average blood pressure levels and confer significant public health benefits by contributing to a reduction in the burden of cardiovascular disease[13]. It was considered important therefore that this survey obtained information on both sodium intakes and blood pressure[14].

It is not possible to obtain accurate estimates of dietary intake of sodium from weighed food intake information, mainly because it is not possible to assess accurately the amount of salt added to food in cooking or at the table. Estimates of sodium and potassium intakes can be obtained by measuring their urinary excretion, assuming the body is in balance for these minerals.

Since the rate of excretion of both sodium and potassium varies with intake, the best estimate of intake is obtained from the analysis of a urine sample taken from a complete 24-hour collection, which allows for the fluctuations in intake over the collection period. A spot urine sample is not sufficiently representative to provide a valid long-term estimate of intakes, and hence excretion, of sodium and potassium. There were some concerns about the acceptability of a 24-hour collection among this population following the response in the feasibility study for the NDNS of adults aged 65 or over[6]. However, the feasibility study for this NDNS found the 24-hour collection method to be acceptable to respondents (*see* Appendix C of the Technical Report[3]).

The aim was to have a complete collection of urine over a 24-hour period from as many of the respondents as possible, and to analyse a sample from the complete collection for sodium, potassium, creatinine, urea and fluoride.

The collection of a complete 24-hour urine sample is a demanding task, and previous experience has shown that samples are frequently incomplete. Therefore, an additional procedure, 'PABA-check', has been devised. This is designed to monitor the completeness of the collection by asking respondents to take three 80mg tablets of para-aminobenzoic acid (PABA) at intervals during the

24-hour collection period. Measurement of the PABA concentration and total volume of the collected sample permits the calculation of the percentage recovery of the administered PABA, which in turn is a measure of completeness of the 24-hour urine collection. The taking of PABA required signed consent from the respondents.

The use of this procedure in this survey was approved by the Multi-centre and Local Research Ethics Committees and was successfully piloted in the feasibility study. It was included in part of Wave 1 of the mainstage survey. One respondent in Wave 1 exhibited an acute allergic reaction with generalised urticaria and periorbital oedema soon after taking the three PABA doses. Although this occurrence may have been a chance association, the survey doctor decided, after seeking external advice, to recommend the discontinuation of the PABA-check procedure as a precaution[15]. From part-way through Wave 1 until the end of the survey, all subsequent 24-hour urine collections were made without PABA-check[16].

Respondents were provided with an explanation of the procedures for making the 24-hour urine collection and the purpose of this (see L2 and L5, Appendix K of the Technical Report[3]). They were also provided with instructions (W3) on how to take the subsamples of the urine, under supervision by the interviewer, and a form (M3A) on which to record the date of collection, times of taking the PABA tablets and any problems with the urine collection or PABA procedures.

During Wave 1 when PABA was used, interviewers first checked whether the respondent had a history of allergy or regular use of drugs that would contraindicate the taking of PABA. If there were no contraindications, interviewers asked the respondent to sign the consent for the taking of PABA (see Z8, Appendix K of the Technical Report[3]). Respondents were provided with the following equipment:

- a blister pack of three 80mg tablets of PABA;

- a safety-pin to be attached to an item of under-clothing as a reminder for urine collection;

- a 5-litre plastic bottle for the urine, containing approximately 5g boric acid as a preservative;

- an empty 2-litre plastic bottle for urine collections made outside the home, together with a plastic carrying bag;

- a 1-litre plastic jug for initial collection of each urine sample before transfer to the 5 or 2-litre

bottles. All urine was to be transferred to the 5-litre bottle as soon as possible after each collection and swirled to mix in the preservative;

The usual (suggested) procedure was for the respondent to take the first PABA tablet at breakfast time and then to begin the urine collection after breakfast, and continue collecting it until just before breakfast the following day. The other two PABA tablets were usually taken at lunchtime and suppertime, respectively.

On the day after starting the collection the interviewer paid another visit to the respondent to weigh the collection and take the sub-samples. The following items were provided:

- protective disposable gloves;

- an electronic balance weighing up to 10kg in 0.01kg divisions;

- four 10ml Sarstedt[17] syringe-type urine containers without preservative, plus extension tubes;

- disposable absorbent paper and mats;

- pre-printed cryo-labels with the respondent's serial number and barcode; plus a cryo-pen to add the date to these;

- postal containers consisting of four plastic screw-cap containers with absorbent paper liners, inside a cardboard box, inside a padded 'Jiffy' bag;

- parcel tape and scissors;

Once the 24-hour collection was completed, the urine collection was thoroughly mixed. The interviewer weighed the total collection twice and recorded both measurements on form M3B (see Appendix K of the Technical Report[3]). The respondent was then asked to take four aliquots, each 10ml, from the total collection using Sarstedt syringes. If the respondent was unable, or unwilling, to take the aliquots themselves, the interviewers were asked to take the subsamples if they were happy to do so. If the collection was tainted with blood no subsamples were taken. The interviewer added the pre-printed cryo-labels to the aliquots, added the date to these, and then transferred all four to the postal plastic containers. These were then placed in the cardboard box and then in the Jiffy bag along with completed forms M3A and M3B. The Jiffy bag was sealed with parcel tape and posted to HNR.

If the respondent failed to make a full 24-hour collection, no repeat collection was attempted. Aliquots were still taken, from the incomplete collection, and a note made of the reasons why a full collection had not been made. Samples were sent by first class post to HNR where they were analysed. On arrival at HNR the samples were stored at –40°C or lower.

The procedure without PABA was essentially the same, except that all of the equipment, forms and procedural elements that were specific to the PABA-check procedure, were omitted. More detailed information was collected on M3A about missed collections.

1.4 Response and weighting

Table 1.1 shows response to the dietary interview and dietary record overall and by fieldwork wave. Of the 5,673 addresses[18] (see Chapter 2 of the Technical Report[3]) issued to the interviewers, 35% were ineligible for the survey. This high rate of ineligibility is mainly due to the exclusion of those aged under 19 years and those aged 65 or over. Just over one-third of the eligible sample, 37%, refused outright to take part in the survey. Only 2% of the eligible sample were not contacted. Overall, 61% of the eligible sample completed the dietary interview, including 47% who completed a full seven-day dietary record. Overall, 77% of those who completed the dietary interview completed a full seven-day dietary record.

Table 1.2 shows the proportion of respondents who consented to making a 24-hour urine collection and the proportion of cases where a sample was obtained[19]. Overall, 66% of the responding sample and 83% of the diary sample consented to making a 24-hour urine collection. A urine sample was obtained for 98% of those who consented to making the 24-hour urine collection (65% of the responding and 81% of the diary samples).

While there has been a general fall in response to government social surveys over the last decade[20], the level of refusal to this NDNS was higher than expected. Steps were taken at an early stage to improve response, and included reissuing non-productive cases[21], developing the interviewer training to address further response issues, providing general guidance on approaching and explaining the survey to respondents, and increased support to the interviewers and their managers. This met with some success so that in Wave 4 a higher proportion of the eligible sample, 67%, completed the dietary interview compared

with previous waves, 56% to 60%. However, the proportions of the responding sample from whom a urine sample was obtained were lower in Waves 3 and 4, 59% and 61% respectively, than in Waves 1 and 2, 70% and 73%.

Those who completed the dietary record had a similar demographic profile, by sex, age and social class of the Household Reference Person as those who completed the dietary interview (see also Chapter 2 of the Technical Report[3]). However, a urine sample was obtained from a significantly lower proportion of men aged 19 to 24 years, 51% of the responding sample, and 25 to 34 years, 58% than from those aged 35 to 49 years, 70% (p<0.05).

The potential for bias in any dataset increases as the level of non-response increases. Assessing bias is particularly difficult when there is little or no information on particular subgroups within the study population. An independent evaluation of the potential impact of non-response bias in this survey was undertaken by the University of Southampton[22]. The authors concluded that there was no evidence to suggest serious non-response bias, although this should be interpreted with caution as bias estimates were based upon assumptions about the total refusals and non-contacts for whom there was very little information. The authors recommended population-based weighting by sex, age and region. Indeed, without weighting for the differential response effect, estimates for different groups would be biased estimates because, in particular, they under-represent men and the youngest age group. To correct for this, the data presented in this volume and the other volumes of this survey have been weighted using a combined weight, based on differential sampling probabilities and differential non-response. Bases in tables are weighted bases scaled back to the number of cases in the responding and diary samples. Unweighted bases are given in Appendix B on page 149. Further details of the weighting procedures are given in Appendix D of the Technical Report[3].

In summary, the estimates presented in this report result from weighting the data as effectively as possible using the available information. However, results should be interpreted with caution, particularly where the sample sizes are low. The reader should note that the sample size in Scotland is particularly low and therefore standard errors may be large (see Appendix A, pages 137-140, for further details on standard errors).

(Tables 1.1 and 1.2)

References and endnotes

[1] The other volumes in this series are:

(i) Henderson L, Gregory J, Swan G. *National Diet and Nutrition Survey: adults aged 19 to 64 years. Volume 1: Types and quantities of foods consumed.* TSO (London, 2002);

(ii) Henderson L, Gregory J, Irving K, Swan G. *National Diet and Nutrition Survey: adults aged 19 to 64 years. Volume 2: Energy, protein, carbohydrate, fat and alcohol intake.* TSO (London, 2003);

(iii) Nutritional status (blood pressure, anthropometry, blood analytes and physical activity), to be published in autumn 2003;

(iv) Summary report, providing a summary of the key findings from the four volumes, to be published in autumn 2003.

[2] Gregory J, Foster K, Tyler H, Wiseman M. *The Dietary and Nutritional Survey of British Adults.* HMSO (London, 1990).

[3] The Technical Report is available online at http//:www.food.gov.uk/science.

[4] For further information about the archived data contact:

The Data Archive
University of Essex
Wivenhoe Park
Colchester
Essex CO4 3SQ
United Kingdom
Tel: (UK) 01206 872001
Fax: (UK) 01206 872003
E-mail: archive@essex.ac.uk
Website: www.data-archive.ac.uk

[5] Responsibility for this survey and the National Diet and Nutrition Survey programme transferred from the Ministry of Agriculture, Fisheries and Food to the Food Standards Agency on its establishment in April 2000.

[6] Finch S, Doyle W, Lowe C, Bates CJ, Prentice A, Smithers G, Clarke PC. *National Diet and Nutrition Survey: people aged 65 years and over. Volume 1: Report of the diet and nutrition survey.* TSO (London, 1998).

[7] Gregory JR, Collins DL, Davies PSW, Hughes JM, Clarke PC. *National Diet and Nutrition Survey: children aged 1 1/2 to 4 1/2 years. Volume 1: Report of the diet and nutrition survey.* HMSO (London, 1995).

[8] Gregory JR, Lowe S, Bates CJ, Prentice A, Jackson LV, Smithers G, Wenlock R, Farron M. *National Diet and Nutrition Survey: young people aged 4 to 18 years. Volume 1: Report of the diet and nutrition survey.* TSO (London, 2000).

[9] Initially 30 addresses were selected within each postal sector. Results from Wave 1 indicated a higher level of age-related ineligibles than expected and a much lower response rate. In order to increase the actual number of diaries completed and to give interviewers enough work an extra 10 addresses were selected for Waves 2, 3 and 4.

[10] The diet and physiology of pregnant or breastfeeding women is likely to be so different from those of other similarly aged women as possibly to distort the results. Further, as the number of pregnant or breastfeeding women identified within the overall achieved sample of 2000 would not be adequate for analysis as a single group, it was decided that they should be regarded as ineligible for interview.

[11] Selecting only one eligible adult per household reduces the burden of the survey on the household and therefore reduces possible detrimental effects on co-operation and data quality. It also reduces the clustering of the sample associated with similar dietary behaviour within the same household and improves the precision of the estimates.

[12] As in some cases fieldwork extended beyond the end of the three-month fieldwork wave, or cases were re-allocated to another fieldwork wave, cases have been allocated to a wave for analysis purposes as follows. Any case started more than four weeks after the end of the official fieldwork wave has been allocated to the actual quarter in which it started. For example, all cases allocated to Wave 1 and started July to October 2000 appear as Wave 1 cases. Any case allocated to Wave 1 and started in November 2000 or later appears in a subsequent wave; for example a case allocated to Wave 1 which started in November 2000 is counted as Wave 2. All cases in Wave 4 (April to June 2001) had been started by the end of July 2001.

[13] Scientific Advisory Committee on Nutrition. *Salt and Health.* TSO (London, 2003).

[14] The relationship between urinary sodium and blood pressure is examined in Chapter 3 of Volume 4.

[15] The respondent was offered the opportunity of a additional test under medical supervision to ascertain any allergic reaction. This challenge test was performed in July 2001 and concluded that PABA was not the cause of the respondent's allergic symptoms.

[16] Subsequent to the removal of the PABA check a decision was made to use plasma creatinine to provide the basis for the calculation of an indicator of the completeness of the 24-hour urine collection (as described on page 128).

[17] Sarstedt Ltd, 68 Boston Road, Beaumont Leys, Leicester LE4 1AW: 'Urine Monovette without stabiliser'.

[18] Initially 1,140 addresses were issued per wave. This was increased in Wave 2 to 1,520 addresses, 40 in each quota of work. In Wave 3, 27 addresses were withdrawn. These were unapproachable due to access restrictions in place because of the foot-and-mouth disease outbreak.

[19] Response rates are based on those who consented to making a 24-hour urine collection, and those for whom a sample was obtained. Samples were taken from the full 24-hour collection. Not all the samples were analysed - some were damaged, or deteriorated in transit. Details of the numbers of urine samples analysed and reported on are given in Chapter 4.

[20] Martin J and Matheson J Responses to declining response rates on government surveys. *Survey Methodology Bulletin* 1999; **45**: 33–7.

[21] Non-productive cases are those where the interviewer was unable to make contact with the selected household or respondent (non-contacts) and where the household or selected respondent refused to take part in the survey (refusals). Addresses that were returned to the office coded as refusals or non-contacts were considered for reissue. Where it was thought that a non-productive case might result in at least a dietary interview (for example, where the selected respondent had said they were too busy at the time of the original call but would be available at a later date) these addresses were issued to interviewers working in subsequent waves of fieldwork.

[22] Skinner CJ and Holmes D (2001) *The 2000–01 National Diet and Nutrition Survey of Adults Aged 19–64 years: The Impact of Non-response.* University of Southampton. Reproduced as Appendix E of the Technical Report (*see* note 3).

Table 1.1

Response to the dietary interview and seven-day dietary record by wave of fieldwork*

Unweighted data   Numbers and percentages

| | Wave of fieldwork | | | | | | | | All | |
| | Wave 1: July–September | | Wave 2: October–December | | Wave 3: January–March | | Wave 4: April–June | | | |
	No.	%	No.	%	No.	%	No.	%	No.	%
Set sample = 100%	1098	100	1397	100	1450	100	1728	100	5673	100
Ineligible	382	35	514	37	515	36	558	32	1969	35
Eligible sample = 100%	716	100	883	100	935	100	1170	100	3704	100
Non-contacts	12	2	24	3	23	2	30	3	89	2
Refusals	271	38	369	42	364	39	360	31	1364	37
Co-operation with:										
dietary interview	433	60	490	56	548	59	780	67	2251	61
seven-day dietary record	325	45	385	44	429	46	585	50	1724	47

Note: * For productive cases, fieldwork wave is defined as the wave (quarter) in which the dietary interview took place; for unproductive cases, fieldwork wave is the wave in which the case was issued (or reissued).

Table 1.2

Co–operation with the 24-hour urine collection by wave of fieldwork, sex and age of respondent and social class of household reference person

Unweighted data

Numbers and percentages

	Consent obtained:			Samples obtained*:			
	No.	% responding sample	% diary sample	No.	% responding sample	% diary sample sample	% consenting sample
Fieldwork wave							
Wave 1	306	71	88	301	70	87	98
Wave 2	363	74	89	357	73	88	98
Wave 3	335	61	76	325	59	74	97
Wave 4	491	63	80	476	61	77	97
Sex and age of respondent							
Men aged (years):							
19–24	46	54	75	44	51	72	96
25–34	131	60	76	127	58	74	97
35–49	283	72	89	126	70	87	98
50–64	211	68	84	209	68	83	99
All	671	66	84	656	65	82	98
Women aged (years):							
19–24	67	62	74	62	57	69	92
25–34	179	65	81	175	63	80	98
35–49	332	68	83	324	66	81	98
50–64	246	66	82	242	65	82	98
All	824	66	82	803	65	80	98
Social class of household reference person							
Non-manual	843	68	83	824	66	81	98
Manual	624	66	83	605	64	81	97
All	1495	66	83	1459	65	81	98

Note: * This includes respondents who reported making a partial collection, that is, recorded missing at least one collection during the 24 hours, but a sample was obtained and analysed.

2 Vitamins

2.1 Introduction

Vitamins are organic compounds, which are required in small amounts for growth and metabolism. They are essential substances which, with the exception of vitamin D, cannot be synthesised in the body and are therefore required in the diet.

This chapter presents data on the daily intakes of vitamins and some precursors, for example carotene, which were derived from the quantities of food being consumed and from the intake of dietary supplements. No attempt has been made to adjust the intakes to take account of under-reporting.

Dietary supplements may have a marked impact on the intakes of some vitamins; 40% of women and 29% of men who completed a seven-day dietary record recorded intakes of dietary supplements. In this chapter data are therefore presented for intakes both from *all sources* (that is, including supplements) and *food sources* (excluding supplements) for the 1,724 respondents who completed a seven-day dietary record.

For those vitamins where UK Reference Nutrient Intake values (RNIs) and Lower Reference Nutrient Intake values (LRNIs) have been published for adults in the appropriate sex and age groups, the proportion of respondents with intakes below the LRNIs are shown and mean daily intakes are compared with current RNIs. Current LRNIs and RNIs for vitamins are shown in Table 2.1[1]. Table 2.2 shows the proportion of respondents with intakes below the LRNIs for those vitamins where LRNIs have been published.

(Tables 2.1 and 2.2)

2.1.1 Reference Nutrient Intake (RNI) and Lower Reference Nutrient Intake (LRNI)

The RNI for a vitamin or mineral is an amount of that nutrient that is sufficient, or more than sufficient, for about 97% of the people in that group. If the average intake of the group is at the RNI, then the risk of deficiency in the group is judged to be very small. However, if the average intake is lower than the RNI then it is possible that some of the group will have an intake below their requirement. This is even more likely if a proportion of the group have an intake below the Lower Reference Nutrient Intake (LRNI). The LRNI for a vitamin or mineral is the amount of that nutrient that is enough for only the few people in a group who have low needs. For further definitions of the RNI and LRNI see Department of Health (1991)[1,2].

2.2 Vitamin A (retinol and carotene)

Vitamin A as pre-formed retinol is only available from animal products, especially liver, kidneys, oily fish and dairy products. However a number of carotenoids can be converted to retinol in the body, and these are primarily found in the yellow and orange pigments of vegetables; carrots and dark green vegetables are rich sources. Carotene is also added to margarine and fat spreads.

2.2.1 Pre-formed retinol

Table 2.3 shows the average daily intake of pre-formed retinol from food sources and all sources, for men and women in different age groups.

Mean daily intake of pre-formed retinol from food sources was 571mg for men and significantly lower for women, 352mg (medians 327mg and 241mg) (p<0.01). The two youngest groups of men had significantly lower mean daily intakes of pre-formed retinol than the oldest group of men (25 to 34: p<0.05; 19 to 24: p<0.01). For example, men aged 19 to 24 years had a mean daily intake of 315mg compared with 735mg for those aged 50 to 64 years. In addition, men aged 19 to 24 years had a significantly lower mean pre-formed retinol intake than those aged 35 to 49 years (p<0.05). Mean daily intake of pre-formed retinol was significantly lower for women aged 19 to 24 years, 251mg, than for those aged 50 to 64 years, 449mg (p<0.01).

The range of intakes within age and sex groups was wide and the distributions skewed, reflecting the limited distribution of pre-formed retinol in foods[3]. Median intakes were between 20% and 50% lower than mean values.

Dietary supplements providing pre-formed retinol increased the mean daily intake from food sources alone for men by 18%, from 571mg to 673mg, and for women by 34%, from 352mg to 472mg.

(Table 2.3)

2.2.2 Total carotene (β-carotene equivalents)

Total carotene is expressed as β-carotene equivalents, that is the sum of β-carotene and half the amount of α-carotene and β-cryptoxanthin, which have approximately half the activity of β-carotene.

Table 2.4 shows mean daily intake of total carotene from food sources was 2041µg for men and 1914µg for women (ns). The youngest group of men had significantly lower mean daily intakes of total carotene than men aged 35 to 64 years, and the youngest group of women significantly lower intakes than all other age groups (women 19 to 24 years compared with 25 to 34: p<0.05; all others: p<0.01). For example, mean daily total carotene intake was 1469µg for men and 1294µg for women aged 19 to 24 years compared with 2459µg for men and 2205µg for women aged 50 to 64 years. In addition, men and women aged 25 to 34 years had significantly lower intakes than those aged 50 to 64 years (p<0.01).

The distribution of intakes was skewed, with median intakes 1716µg for men and 1583µg for women, about 16% lower than mean intakes[3]. There was a wide range of intakes of total carotene within each sex/age group.

The contribution of dietary supplements to intakes of total carotene was negligible.

(Table 2.4)

Food sources of total carotene

Men and women obtained over half their mean daily total carotene intake, 59% and 66% respectively, from vegetables (excluding potatoes) (p<0.05). Cooked carrots were the largest single provider accounting for 30% of intake for both men and women; raw carrots provided 5% of intake overall.

Meat & meat products provided a further 12% of the carotene intake overall, mainly from vegetables added to meat dishes.

Overall, drinks provided 4% of mean intake of total carotene, nearly all of which came from the consumption of soft drinks; β-carotene is often used as colour in orange-coloured drinks.

(Table 2.5)

2.2.3 β-carotene, α-carotene and β-cryptoxanthin

β-carotene, α-carotene and β-cryptoxanthin are all carotenoids with vitamin A activity. Only a few of the more than 100 carotenoids have structures that enable them to serve as precursors of vitamin A; β-carotene is the most important of these. α-carotene and β-cryptoxanthin have approximately half the activity of β-carotene on a weight-for-weight basis.

Table 2.6 shows that mean daily intake of β-carotene from food sources was 1836µg for men and 1719µg for women (medians 1560µg and 1424µg) (ns). As with total carotene, the youngest group of men had significantly lower mean daily intakes of β-carotene than men aged 35 to 64 years, and the youngest group of women significantly lower intakes than all other age groups (women 19 to 24 years compared with 25 to 34: p<0.05; all others: p<0.01). For example, mean daily intake of β-carotene was 1341µg for men and 1170µg for women aged 19 to 24 years compared with 2201µg and 1977µg for men and women, respectively, aged 50 to 64 years. In addition, men and women aged 25 to 34 years had significantly lower intakes than those aged 50 to 64 years (both: p<0.01).

Tables 2.7 and 2.8 show the mean daily intake of α-carotene and β-cryptoxanthin respectively, for men and women in different age groups. Mean daily intake of α-carotene from food sources was 342μg for men and 320μg for women (medians 248μg and 227μg), and for β-cryptoxanthin, 66μg and 68μg respectively (medians 44μg for both men and women). Intake of α-carotene was significantly lower for men and women in the youngest age group than for those in the two oldest age groups (women 19 to 24 compared with 35 to 49: p<0.05; all others: p<0.01). For example, mean daily intake for men aged 19 to 24 years was 197μg compared with 444μg for those aged 50 to 64 years. In addition, men and women aged 25 to 34 years had significantly lower mean daily intakes of α-carotene than those aged 50 to 64 years (women: p<0.05; men: p<0.01). Mean intakes of β-cryptoxanthin for women were significantly lower for the youngest age group than for all other age groups (25 to 34: p<0.05; all others: p<0.01). There were no significant differences in mean intakes of β-cryptoxanthin by age for men.

The increase in mean daily intakes of all three carotenoids with age reflects age patterns in fruit and vegetable consumption, where the youngest group of men and women consumed a significantly lower mean number of portions of fruit and vegetables, 1.3 and 1.8 respectively, than men and women aged 50 to 64 years, 3.6 and 3.8 portions respectively (see Volume 1, Chapter 2, section 2.4.5[4]).

For all three carotenoids there was a wide range of intakes within sex and age groups, and some respondents had zero intakes of some carotenoids during the seven-day dietary recording period. Overall, 2% of men and 1% of women had zero intakes of α-carotene, and 3% of both men and women had zero intakes of β-cryptoxanthin from food sources.

The contribution of dietary supplements to intakes of β-carotene, α-carotene and β-cryptoxanthin was negligible.

(Tables 2.6 to 2.8)

2.2.4 Vitamin A (retinol equivalents)

The total vitamin A content of the diet is usually expressed as retinol equivalents; 1μg retinol equivalent is equal to 1μg retinol or 6μg total carotene (β-carotene equivalents).

Table 2.9 shows the mean daily intake of vitamin A from food and all sources for respondents in the survey. Mean daily intake of vitamin A from food sources was 911μg for men and, significantly lower, 671μg for women (p<0.01) (medians 660μg and 549μg).

The two youngest groups of men, and the youngest group of women, had significantly lower mean daily intakes of vitamin A from food sources than the two oldest groups of men and women (men 25 to 34 compared with 35 to 49: p<0.05; all others: p<0.01). For example, mean daily intake of vitamin A was 560μg for men and 467μg for women aged 19 to 24 years compared with 1145μg and 816μg respectively, for the oldest group of men and women. In addition, women aged 25 to 34 years had significantly lower mean daily intakes of vitamin A than women aged 50 to 64 years (p<0.05).

The distribution of intakes was skewed, with median intakes between 11% and 32% lower than mean intakes depending on sex and age[3]. The range of intakes of vitamin A from food sources, like those for pre-formed retinol, α-and β-carotene and β-cryptoxanthin, was very large.

Dietary supplements containing pre-formed retinol or carotene increased mean daily intake of vitamin A overall by 12% for men, from 911μg to 1017μg, and by 19% for women, from 671μg to 800μg. However, the contribution of supplements to mean intakes differed by age for men and women. For example, supplements increased mean intakes from food sources alone by 3% for men aged 19 to 24 years, but by 18% for those aged 25 to 34 years. For women, the increase in mean intake ranged from 8% for those aged 25 to 34 years to 26% for those aged 19 to 24 years.

Table 2.1 shows the current UK RNI and LRNI values for vitamin A for adults for two age groups, 19 to 50 years and 51 to 64 years. Table 2.10 shows average daily intake of vitamin A as a percentage of the RNI[5]. Mean daily intake of vitamin A from food sources was 130% of the RNI for men and 112% for women. Men aged 19 to 24 years and women aged 19 to 24 years and 25 to 34 years were the only age groups where mean intake of vitamin A from food sources was below the RNI. Dietary supplements increased mean intakes of vitamin A to above the RNI for women aged 25 to 34 years.

Table 2.2 shows the proportion of respondents with average daily intakes of vitamin A below the LRNI. Seven per cent of men and 9% of women had intakes of vitamin A from food sources which were below the LRNI (ns). The proportion with intakes below the LRNI ranged from 4% and 5% of the oldest group of men and women to 16% of men and 19% of women aged 19 to 24 years (men: ns;

women: p<0.05). Dietary supplements had little effect on the proportion of men or women with intakes below the LRNI.

(Tables 2.9, 2.10 and 2.2)

Food sources of vitamin A

Table 2.11 shows that the main food groups contributing to mean daily intake of vitamin A were meat & meat products, contributing 28% overall, vegetables (excluding potatoes), 27%, milk & milk products, 14%, and fat spreads, 10%.

Meat & meat products accounted for a significantly higher proportion of vitamin A intake for men than for women, 34% compared with 22% (p<0.01). The contribution from this food group came mainly from liver, liver products & liver dishes, accounting for 26% of intake for men and 15% for women (p<0.01).

Meat & meat products accounted for a significantly lower proportion of vitamin A intake for men aged 19 to 24 years, 16%, than for men aged 35 to 64 years, 38% (p<0.01). In addition, men aged 25 to 34 years obtained a significantly lower proportion of their vitamin A intake from meat & meat products than those aged 35 to 49 years (p<0.05). There were no significant differences in the contribution of meat & meat products to vitamin A intake for women by age. However, the contribution made by liver, liver products & dishes increased significantly with age for both sexes, from 6% for the youngest group of men and 9% for the youngest group of women to 32% and 21% respectively for the oldest group of men and women (women: p<0.05; men: p<0.01).

Men derived about one quarter, 23%, and women one third, 32%, of their vitamin A intake from vegetables (excluding potatoes) (p<0.01), about half of which came from carrots.

Overall, milk & milk products contributed a further 14% of the vitamin A intake, including 6% which came from cheese. Fat spreads contributed 10% to the mean daily vitamin A intake.

(Table 2.11)

2.3 B vitamins

2.3.1 Thiamin (vitamin B$_1$)

Mean daily intake of thiamin from food sources was 2.00mg for men, and for women, significantly lower, 1.54mg (p<0.01). Men aged 19 to 24 years had a significantly lower mean daily intake of thiamin, 1.60mg, than men aged 35 to 49 years, 2.04mg, and those aged 50 to 64 years, 2.07mg

(35 to 49: p<0.05; 50 to 64: p<0.01). There were no significant differences by age for women.

Dietary supplements providing thiamin taken by respondents in the survey increased mean intake from that from food sources alone by 11% for men, from 2.00mg to 2.22mg, and by 26% for women, from 1.54mg to 1.94mg.

Table 2.13 shows that average daily intakes of thiamin from food sources alone were well above the RNIs for men and women in each age group[5]. Overall, mean intakes from food sources were 214% and 193% of the RNI for men and women respectively. One per cent of both men and women had an average daily intake of thiamin below the LRNI (*see* Table 2.2). Dietary supplements made no difference to the proportion of men and women with intakes below the LRNI.

(Tables 2.12, 2.13 and 2.2)

Food sources of thiamin

Most breakfast cereals are fortified with thiamin and cereals & cereal products were the main dietary source of thiamin for respondents in the survey, providing a third of mean daily intake, 34% overall. Within this group the major contributors were breakfast cereals, providing 14% of thiamin intake overall, and white bread which contributed 9%.

Meat & meat products provided a further 21% of thiamin intake, a third of which, 7%, came from bacon & ham. Vegetables (excluding potatoes) provided 15% of the thiamin intake overall, and potatoes & savoury snacks provided a further 13%.

(Table 2.14)

2.3.2 Riboflavin (vitamin B$_2$)

Table 2.15 shows the mean daily intake of riboflavin from food sources and all sources for men and women in different age groups. The mean daily intake of riboflavin from food sources was 2.11mg for men and, significantly lower, 1.60mg for women (p<0.01). The youngest group of men had significantly lower mean riboflavin intakes than men in any other age group (25 to 34: p<0.05; all others: p<0.01). For example, mean daily intake of riboflavin was 1.68mg for men aged 19 to 24 years compared with 2.20mg for men aged 50 to 64 years. For women, the two youngest age groups had significantly lower mean intakes than the two oldest groups of women (19 to 24 compared with 35 to 49: p<0.05; all others: p<0.01).

Dietary supplements increased mean riboflavin intakes from food sources alone by 10% for men, from 2.11mg to 2.33mg, and by 26% for women, from 1.60mg to 2.02mg. For men and women the contribution of supplements to mean intake was most marked for the oldest age group, where intake of riboflavin from all sources was 14% and 42% higher than from food sources alone for men and women respectively.

Table 2.16 shows the mean daily intake of riboflavin as a percentage of RNI. Mean riboflavin intake from food sources was 162% of the RNI for men and 146% for women, and was above the RNI for all sex/age groups[5]. Table 2.2 shows that, overall, 3% of men and a significantly higher proportion of women, 8%, had a riboflavin intake from food sources alone which was below the LRNI (p<0.01). Fifteen per cent of women aged 19 to 24 years and 10% of women aged 25 to 34 years had a mean intake of riboflavin from food sources which was below the LRNI. Dietary supplements had little effect on the proportion of men and women with intakes below the LRNI.

(Tables 2.15, 2.16 and 2.2)

Food sources of riboflavin

Table 2.17 shows the percentage contribution of food types to mean daily intake of riboflavin. The main source of riboflavin was milk & milk products providing a third, 33%, of intake. Within this group semi-skimmed milk contributed 16% overall. Just under one quarter, 24%, of the mean daily intake of riboflavin came from cereals & cereal products, mainly from breakfast cereals, many of which are fortified with riboflavin.

Meat & meat products contributed a further 15% to mean riboflavin intake overall. Drinks contributed 12% to riboflavin intake for men and 6% for women, including 7% for men and 1% for women which came from beer & lager (men compared with women, drinks and beer & lager: p<0.01).

(Table 2.17)

2.3.3 Niacin equivalents

Niacin is a B vitamin, which can be obtained pre-formed from the diet or can be made in the body from the amino acid, tryptophan. Niacin intake is expressed as niacin equivalents, defined as the total amount of niacin plus one sixtieth of the weight, in mg, of tryptophan.

As Table 2.18 shows the mean daily intake of niacin equivalents from food sources was 44.7mg for men and significantly lower for women, 30.9mg (p<0.01). Mean daily intake was significantly lower for women than men in each age group (p<0.01). Men aged 19 to 24 years had a significantly lower mean daily intake than men in any other age group (35 to 49: p<0.05; all others: p<0.01). For example, mean daily intake of niacin equivalents was 39.4mg for men aged 19 to 24 years compared with 46.2mg for men aged 25 to 34 years. Women aged 25 to 34 years had a significantly lower mean intake than women aged 35 to 64 years (35 to 49: p<0.05; 50 to 64: p<0.01).

Supplements contributed very little to niacin intake and thus mean and median intakes from all sources were close to intakes from food sources alone.

Mean daily intake of niacin equivalents from food sources alone was over 200% of the RNI for men and women in each age group[5]. Table 2.2 shows that, overall, less than 0.5% of men and 1% of women had intakes of niacin equivalents from food sources alone that were below the LRNI.

(Tables 2.18, 2.19 and 2.2)

Food sources of niacin equivalents

The main source of niacin was meat and meat products, providing about one third, 34%, of mean daily intake overall, about half of which came from chicken, turkey & dishes, including coated chicken.

A further 27% of intake came from consumption of cereals & cereal products, just over a third of which came from breakfast cereals, which are often fortified with niacin. Drinks provided a further 12% of intake for men and 5% for women, including 9% for men and 2% for women which came from beer & lager (men compared with women, drinks and beer & lager: p<0.01).

(Table 2.20)

2.3.4 Vitamin B_6

The mean daily intake of vitamin B_6 from food sources for men was 2.9mg, significantly higher than the mean intake for women, 2.0mg (p<0.01). Men had a significantly higher vitamin B_6 intake than women in each age group (p<0.01). There were no significant differences in mean daily intake for men by age. However, for women, those aged 25 to 34 years had a significantly lower mean intake of vitamin B_6 than those aged 50 to 64 years, 1.9mg and 2.1mg respectively (p<0.05).

Dietary supplements providing vitamin B_6 increased mean intake from food sources alone by 14% for men, from 2.9mg to 3.3mg, and by 45% for women, from 2.0mg to 2.9mg.

Table 2.22 shows the average daily intake of vitamin B_6 as a percentage of the RNI[5]. For both men and women mean daily intake of vitamin B_6 from food sources alone was well above the RNI for each age group. Table 2.2 shows the proportion of respondents with intakes of vitamin B_6 below the LRNI. Overall, one per cent of men and 2% of women had an average daily intake of vitamin B_6 which was below the LRNI. Five per cent of women aged 19 to 24 years had a mean intake below the LRNI. Dietary supplements providing vitamin B_6 made very little difference to the proportions of respondents with intakes below the LRNI.

(Tables 2.21, 2.22 and 2.2)

Food sources of vitamin B_6

Table 2.23 shows the percentage contribution of food types to mean daily intake of vitamin B_6. The three main sources of vitamin B_6 in the diets of respondents were cereals & cereal products, meat & meat products and potatoes & savoury snacks, each providing about 20% of the mean intake. Within cereals & cereal products the main contributor was breakfast cereals, many of which are fortified with vitamin B_6. The contribution from meat & meat products came mainly from chicken, turkey & dishes, including coated chicken, which provided 8% of vitamin B_6 intake overall. The contribution from potatoes & savoury snacks came mainly from potato chips, 7%.

Men derived a further 15%, and women 6%, of their vitamin B_6 intake from drinks; almost entirely from beer & lager, 13% for men and 3% for women (men compared with women, drinks and beer & lager: $p<0.01$).

(Table 2.23)

2.3.5 Vitamin B_{12}

Mean daily intake of vitamin B_{12} from food sources was 6.5µg for men and, significantly lower, 4.8µg for women ($p<0.01$). Mean daily intake of vitamin B_{12} was significantly lower for men aged 19 to 24 years than for any other age group ($p<0.01$). In addition, men aged 25 to 49 years had significantly lower intakes than those aged 50 to 64 years ($p<0.05$). For women, mean daily intake was significantly lower for those aged 19 to 34 years compared with those aged 35 to 64 years (19 to 24 compared with 35 to 49: $p<0.05$; all others: $p<0.01$). For example, women aged 19 to 24 years had a mean daily intake of vitamin B_{12} of 4.0µg compared with 5.7µg for those aged 50 to 64 years. Additionally, women aged 35 to 49 years had significantly lower intakes than those aged 50 to 64 years ($p<0.05$).

Dietary supplements increased the mean daily intake of vitamin B_{12} from that from food sources alone by 5% for men, from 6.5µg to 6.8µg, and 6% for women, from 4.8µg to 5.1µg.

As Table 2.25 shows, mean daily intakes of vitamin B_{12} from food sources were well in excess of the RNI, 431% of the RNI for men and 316% of the RNI for women[5]. Less than 0.5% of men and 1% of women had a mean daily intake of vitamin B_{12} below the LRNI (see Table 2.2).

(Tables 2.24, 2.25 and 2.2)

Food sources of vitamin B_{12}

Vitamin B_{12} is found only in animal products and in microorganisms including yeast. Table 2.26 shows that the main contributor to vitamin B_{12} intake for respondents in the survey was milk & milk products, providing 36% of intake overall, half of which, 18%, came from semi-skimmed milk. Meat & meat products provided 34% of mean daily intake for men and 24% for women ($p<0.01$). The contribution from meat & meat products came mainly from liver, liver products & dishes and from beef, veal & dishes. The percentage contribution of liver, liver products & dishes to vitamin B_{12} intake increased significantly with age for men from 1% for those aged 19 to 24 years to 13% for those aged 50 to 64 years ($p<0.01$).

The only other major contributor to vitamin B_{12} intake was fish & fish dishes, which accounted for 16% of mean daily intake for men and 22% for women ($p<0.05$). Nearly three-fifths of the contribution made by fish & fish dishes came from oily fish. The contribution from oily fish increased significantly with age for men, from 2% for those aged 19 to 24 years to 12% for those aged 50 to 64 years ($p<0.01$).

(Table 2.26)

2.3.6 Folate

The mean daily intake of folate from food sources for men was significantly higher than for women, 344µg and 251µg respectively ($p<0.01$). Men had significantly higher mean folate intakes than women in each age group ($p<0.01$). For both sexes, mean daily intake of folate increased significantly with age, from 301µg for men and 229µg for women aged 19 to 24 years to 361µg and 268µg for men and women aged 50 to 64 years, respectively ($p<0.05$). In addition, women aged 25 to 34 years had significantly lower mean intakes than those aged 35 to 64 years (35 to 49: $p<0.05$; 50 to 64: $p<0.01$). The significant increase in mean daily intake of folate with age reflects age patterns in fruit and vegetable consumption (*see* Volume 1, Chapter 2, section 2.4.5[4]).

Dietary supplements providing folate increased mean intakes from food sources alone by 4% for men, from 344μg to 359μg, and by 16% for women, from 251μg to 292μg. The contribution from supplements was most marked for women aged 50 to 64 years, where dietary supplements increased intake from food sources alone by 34%, from 268μg to 359μg.

As can be seen from Table 2.28, mean daily intakes of folate from food sources were above the appropriate RNI for each sex and age group, providing 172% and 125% of the RNI for men and women respectively[5]. Dietary supplements providing folate increased mean intake as a percentage of the RNI to 180% for men and 146% for women. Overall less than 0.5% of men and, a significantly higher proportion of women, 2%, had an intake of folate below the LRNI, 100μg/day (*see* Table 2.2). The Department of Health currently recommend that those women who could become pregnant take a supplement of 400μg folic acid per day prior to conception and until the twelfth week of pregnancy in order to minimise the risk of neural tube defects (NTD)[6]. In this survey, 86% of women aged 19 to 24 years, 92% of those aged 25 to 34 years and 84% of women aged 35 to 49 years had an intake of folate from all sources, including supplements, of less than 400μg/day.

(Tables 2.27, 2.28 and 2.2)

Food sources of folate

Table 2.29 shows the percentage contribution of food types to the mean daily intake of folate for men and women in the survey. The main source of folate in the diets of respondents was cereals & cereal products which provided 33% of mean daily intake overall, of which just under half, 15%, came from breakfast cereals, many of which are fortified with folate.

Vegetables (excluding potatoes) contributed 15% to the mean daily intake of folate, and potatoes & savoury snacks provided a further 12%.

Drinks contributed 18% and 9% to the mean daily folate intake for men and women respectively, 11% of folate for men and 3% for women came from beer & lager (men compared with women, drinks and beer & lager: p<0.01).

There were no significant age differences for either sex in the contribution of food groups to average daily intake of folate.

(Table 2.29)

2.3.7 Biotin and pantothenic acid

Tables 2.30 and 2.31 show the average daily intake of biotin and pantothenic acid respectively, from food sources and all sources, for men and women in different age groups.

Mean daily intake of *biotin* from food sources was 41mg for men and, significantly lower, 29μg for women (p<0.01). Mean daily intake of biotin was significantly lower for men aged 19 to 24 years than for men in any other age group (p<0.01). For example, mean daily intake was 30μg for the youngest group of men compared with 44μg for men aged 35 to 49 years. The two youngest age groups of women had significantly lower mean intakes of biotin than the two oldest age groups (p<0.01).

Dietary supplements providing biotin increased mean intake from food sources alone by 7% for men, from 41μg to 44μg, and by 14% for women, from 29μg to 33μg.

The mean daily intake of *pantothenic acid* from food sources was 7.2mg for men, significantly higher than the mean intake for women, 5.4mg (p<0.01). Differences in mean daily intake of pantothenic acid by age and sex were the same as for biotin: the youngest group of men had significantly lower intakes than men in any other age group and the youngest two groups of women had significantly lower intakes than the two oldest groups of women (men aged 19 to 24 compared with 25 to 34, women aged 19 to 24 compared with 35 to 49: p<0.05; all others: p<0.01). For example, mean daily pantothenic acid intake was 5.9mg for men and 4.8mg for women aged 19 to 24 years compared with 7.5mg and 5.9mg, respectively, for those aged 50 to 64 years.

Dietary supplements increased intakes of pantothenic acid from food sources alone, by 8% for men, from 7.2mg to 7.8mg, and by 18% for women, from 5.4mg to 6.4mg. The most marked increase was among the oldest group of women where mean intake from all sources was 34% higher than that from food sources alone, 7.9mg compared with 5.9mg.

There are no DRVs set for either biotin or pantothenic acid. However intakes for biotin within the range 10mg to 200mg are considered safe and adequate, as are intakes for pantothenic acid in the range of 3mg to 7mg[1]. Mean intakes of biotin were within the range of 10μg to 200μg, as were intakes at both the lower and upper 2.5 percentiles. Less than 0.5% of men and 2% of women had mean intakes of biotin below 10μg. For pantothenic acid, 2% of men and a significantly higher proportion of women, 8%, had intakes below 3mg (p<0.01). Fifty-one per cent of men and 23% of women had intakes of pantothenic acid, including dietary supplements, at or above 7.0mg (men compared with women: p<0.01). A significantly higher proportion of men and women aged 50 to 64 years had intakes of pantothenic acid at or above 7.0mg than those aged 19 to 24 years (p<0.01).

(Tables 2.30 and 2.31)

2.4 Vitamin C

Mean daily intakes of vitamin C from food sources were 83.4mg for men and 81.0mg for women (medians 70.7mg and 68.7mg) (ns). Men aged 19 to 34 years and women aged 19 to 49 years, had significantly lower mean vitamin C intakes than those aged 50 to 64 years (women 35 to 49 compared with 50 to 64: p<0.05; all others: p<0.01). For example, mean daily intakes of vitamin C increased from 64.9mg for men and 67.9mg for women aged 19 to 24 years to 94.5mg for men and 94.5mg for women aged 50 to 64 years. In addition, men aged 19 to 24 years had significantly lower vitamin C intakes than those aged 35 to 49 years (p<0.05).

The distribution of intakes was skewed with median intakes between 10% and 21% lower than mean intakes depending on sex and age[3].

Dietary supplements providing vitamin C increased mean intake from food sources alone by 22% for men, from 83.4mg to 101.4mg, and by 38% for women, from 81.0mg to 112.0mg. For men the effect of supplements on mean intake was most marked for those aged 50 to 64 years where intake of vitamin C from all sources was 32% higher than from food sources alone, 125.0mg and 94.5mg respectively. For women, the effect was most marked for those aged 35 to 49 years, where intake from all sources was 54% higher, 123.1mg, than from food sources alone, 80.0mg.

Mean daily intake of vitamin C from food sources was above the RNI for each sex and age group, and as Table 2.33 shows, provided 209% of the RNI for men and 202% of the RNI for women[5]. Dietary supplements increased mean daily intake as a percentage of RNI to 253% for men and 280% for women. As Table 2.2 shows, overall, less than 0.5% of men and women had an average daily intake of vitamin C below the LRNI.

(Tables 2.32, 2.33 and 2.2)

Food sources of vitamin C

Over one quarter, 27%, of the mean daily intake of vitamin C came from drinks in the form of fruit juice, 19%, and soft drinks, 8%. Soft drinks may be fortified with vitamin C or include vitamin C as an antioxidant. The proportion of vitamin C intake accounted for by drinks was significantly higher for women aged 19 to 24 years than for women aged 50 to 64 years, 40% and 21% respectively (p<0.05).

Overall, vegetables (excluding potatoes) contributed 22% to mean daily intake of vitamin C, and potatoes & savoury snacks a further 15%. Men derived a significantly lower proportion of their vitamin C intake from fruit & nuts than women, 16% compared with 22% (p<0.05). Fruit & nuts accounted for a significantly lower proportion of vitamin C intake for men aged 19 to 24 years than for men aged 35 to 64 years, and for women aged 19 to 34 years compared with women aged 50 to 64 years (both: p<0.05).

(Table 2.34)

2.5 Vitamin D

Most of the body's requirement for vitamin D can be synthesised by the skin in the presence of sufficient sunlight of the appropriate wavelength, that is, between April and October in England. Adequate summer exposure provides sufficient vitamin D stores throughout winter. Food sources are therefore particularly important for those who do not receive adequate sunlight. No RNIs have been set for vitamin D for adults aged 19 to 64 years. Vitamin D is found naturally in some animal products, including oily fish. Some foods, such as margarine and fat spreads and some breakfast cereals, are fortified with vitamin D.

Table 2.35 presents data on the average daily intake of vitamin D from food and all sources. Mean daily intake from food sources for men was 3.7μg and for women, 2.8μg (ns) (medians 3.1μg and 2.3μg). Mean daily intake of vitamin D was significantly lower for men aged 19 to 24 years, 2.9μg, than for men aged 35 to 49 years, 3.7μg, and men aged 50 to 64 years, 4.2μg (35 to 49: p<0.05; 50 to 64: p<0.01). In addition, men aged 25 to 34 years had significantly lower intakes than those aged 50 to 64 years (p<0.05). Women aged 19 to 49 years had significantly lower mean vitamin D intakes than the oldest group of women (p<0.01).

The distribution of intakes of vitamin D for both men and women was skewed, with median intakes being between 3% and 20% lower than mean intakes depending on sex and age[3].

Overall, supplements providing vitamin D increased mean intakes from food sources alone by 14% for men, from 3.7µg to 4.2µg, and by 32% for women, from 2.8µg to 3.7µg. Mean daily intake of vitamin D for women aged 50 to 64 years, increased by 46%, from 3.5µg to 5.1µg, when dietary supplements were included.

(Table 2.35)

Food sources of vitamin D

The main sources of vitamin D in the diets of respondents in the survey were fish & fish dishes, meat & meat products, cereals & cereal products and fat spreads[7]. Fish & fish dishes contributed 21% and 30% respectively to the mean daily intake of vitamin D for men and women (p<0.01), nearly all of which came from oily fish, which is a rich source of vitamin D. Men aged 19 to 24 years obtained 3% of their vitamin D intake from fish & fish dishes, a significantly lower proportion than for any other age group (25 to 34: p<0.05; all others: p<0.01). In addition, men aged 25 to 34 years obtained a significantly lower proportion of their vitamin D intake from fish & fish dishes than the oldest group of men (p<0.05). Fish & fish dishes accounted for a significantly lower proportion of vitamin D intake for women aged 19 to 24 years, 21%, and 25 to 34 years, 22%, than for those aged 50 to 64 years, 37% (p<0.05).

Meat & meat products contributed 24% and 18% respectively to the vitamin D intake for men and women (p<0.05). Cereals & cereal products provided a further 21% of vitamin D intake overall. Within this group breakfast cereals contributed 13% of the intake of vitamin D. Some breakfast cereals are fortified with vitamin D.

Overall, fat spreads contributed 17% to the mean daily intake of vitamin D. About half the contribution made by fat spreads, 8%, came from reduced fat spreads. Vitamin D is required by law to be added to margarine and is also added to most reduced and low fat spreads.

(Table 2.36)

2.6 Vitamin E

The vitamin E data is expressed as α-tocopherol equivalents. Vitamin E in food is present as various tocopherols and tocotrienols, each having a different level of vitamin E activity. In most animal products the α-form is the only significant form present, but in plant products, especially seeds and their oils, γ-tocopherol and other forms are present in significant amounts.

Table 2.37 shows the mean daily intake of vitamin E from all sources and food sources for men and women in different age groups. Men had a significantly higher mean daily intake of vitamin E from food sources, 10.6mg than women, 8.1mg (p<0.01). There were no significant differences in mean daily intakes of vitamin E for men or women by age.

Supplements providing vitamin E increased mean daily intakes from food sources alone by 26% for men, from 10.6mg to 13.4mg, and by 85% for women, from 8.1mg to 15.0mg. For both sexes, there were marked differences in the contribution of supplements between age groups; for example, supplement taking increased mean intakes by 3% for men and 19% for women aged 19 to 24 years, but by 38% for men and 183% for women aged 50 to 64 years.

There are no DRVs set for vitamin E. However, intakes above 4mg/d for adult men and above 3mg/d for adult women are considered safe[1]. Mean intakes for men and women in each age group were above these levels. Overall, 3% of men had a mean daily intake of vitamin E below 4mg, and 3% of women had an intake of less than 3mg.

(Table 2.37)

Food sources of vitamin E

Table 2.38 presents data on the percentage contribution of food types to mean daily intake of vitamin E. The main contributor was fat spreads, providing 18% of vitamin E intake overall, over half of which, 11%, came from polyunsaturated reduced and low fat spreads.

Cereals & cereal products provided 17% of vitamin E intake, a third of which, 5%, came from breakfast cereals, and a further third, 5%, from biscuits, buns, cakes & pastries.

Overall, potatoes & savoury snacks contributed 13% to the vitamin E intake. Within this food group, potato chips and savoury snacks were the main contributors, where vitamin E was provided by the oil used in cooking and frying. Vegetables (excluding potatoes) contributed a further 13% of intake.

Meat & meat products provided 11% of vitamin E intake overall, of which 5% came from chicken, turkey & dishes, including coated chicken.

(Table 2.38)

2.7 Variations in vitamin intake

In this section, the variation in the average daily intake of vitamins from *food sources* and *all sources* in relation to the region[8] in which the respondent lives and household receipt of benefits[9] is considered. Variation in mean daily intake from food sources and all sources as a percentage of the RNI, and in the proportion of respondents with intakes below the LRNI is also considered.

Caveat

Inter-relationship between the main classificatory variables need to be borne in mind when interpreting these results. For example, there is significant variation in the age distribution of respondents by household benefit status and any variation associated with this characteristic may be partly accounted for by variation by age (or equally variation with age could be accounted for by variation with this characteristic)[10].

2.7.1 Region

Table 2.39 shows mean daily intake of vitamins from food sources and all sources for men and women by region.

There were very few significant regional differences in vitamin intakes from food sources for men or women. Men living in the Northern region and in Central and South West regions of England and in Wales had a significantly lower mean daily intake of vitamin C than men in London and the South East, 77.1mg and 79.4mg compared with 93.8mg (p<0.05).

Women living in London and the South East had a significantly higher mean daily intake of total carotene, 2206µg, than those living in Central and South West regions of England and in Wales, 1815µg, and in the Northern region, 1741µg (p<0.05). In addition, women in London and the South East had a significantly higher mean daily intake of vitamin E, 8.7mg, than those in the Northern region, 7.7mg (p<0.05), and a higher intake of vitamin D, 3.3µg compared with women in Scotland, 2.4µg, and those in Central and South West regions of England and in Wales, 2.6µg (p<0.01).

When dietary supplements are included the only remaining significant differences are for women in the London and the South East, who had significantly higher intakes of total carotene compared with women in the Northern region (p<0.05), and significantly higher intakes of vitamin D compared with women in Scotland (p<0.05) and

in Central and South West regions of England and in Wales (p<0.01)[11].

Table 2.40 shows mean daily intakes of vitamins from food sources and all sources as a percentage of the RNI and the proportion of men and women with intakes below the LRNI by region. For all vitamins, mean daily intake from food sources was above the RNI for men and women in each of the four regions. There were no significant regional differences in the proportion of men or women with intakes from food sources below the LRNI for any of the vitamins. This remained the case when dietary supplements were included. The inclusion of intakes from dietary supplements had little effect on the proportions with intakes below the LRNI, except for vitamin A intakes in Scotland. Dietary supplements reduced the proportion of men and women with vitamin A intakes below the LRNI in Scotland from 7% of both men and women to 4% of men and 3% of women.

(Tables 2.39 and 2.40)

2.7.2 Household receipt of benefits

Table 2.41 shows that mean daily intakes from food sources for the majority of vitamins were significantly lower for men and women living in benefit households compared with those in non-benefit households. For both men and women, intakes from food sources of riboflavin, vitamin B_6, vitamin B_{12}, folate, vitamin C and vitamin E were significantly lower for those living in benefit households than for those in non-benefit households (men, vitamin B_{12} and vitamin E: p<0.05; all others: p<0.01). For example, mean daily intake of vitamin C from food sources was 62.7mg for men and 60.4mg for women living in benefit households compared with 86.6mg for men and 85.1mg for women in non-benefit households. In addition, men in benefit households had a significantly lower mean daily intake of thiamin from food sources, and women in benefit households significantly lower intakes of vitamin A, total carotene and vitamin D, than those in non-benefit households (p<0.01).

When dietary supplements are included, significant differences in mean intakes by household benefit status remain for vitamin B_{12} and vitamin C for men and women, for folate for men and for vitamin A, total carotene and vitamin D for women[11].

As noted in section 2.3.6, the Department of Health currently recommends a folate intake of 400µg/day for women who could become pregnant. In this survey, 93% of women aged 19 to 24 years, 99% of women aged 25 to 34 years, and 85% of women aged 35 to 49 years, living in benefit households had an mean daily folate intake less than 400µg/day (table not shown).

Table 2.42 shows average daily intake of vitamins from food sources and all sources as a percentage of the RNI and the proportion with intakes below the LRNI by sex and household benefit status. For most vitamins mean daily intakes from food sources as a percentage of the RNI were lower for men and women living in benefit households compared with those in non-benefit households. However, mean intakes from food sources for benefit households were above the RNI for all vitamins except for vitamin A for women which was 84% of the RNI. Dietary supplements increased intakes of vitamin A for women in benefit households to 97% of the RNI.

A significantly higher proportion of women in benefit households had intakes of vitamin A and riboflavin from food sources below the LRNI, 22% and 19%, respectively, than women in non-benefit households, 6% and 5% (p<0.01). Six per cent of women in benefit households had an intake of folate below the LRNI, 100µg/day, compared with 1% of women in non-benefit households (ns). Dietary supplements made a negligible difference to the proportions of men or women in benefit and non-benefit households with intakes below the LRNI.

(Tables 2.41 and 2.42)

2.8 Comparison of vitamin intakes between 1986/87 Adults survey and present NDNS

Tables 2.43(a) and (b) and 2.44(a) and (b) compare vitamin intakes from food sources and all sources in the present survey of adults with corresponding data from the Dietary and Nutritional Survey of British Adults aged 16 to 64 years carried out in 1986/87 (1986/87 Adults Survey)[12]. Tables 2.43(a) and 2.43(b) present data on vitamin intakes from food sources alone for the two sets of survey data for men and women by age respectively. Tables 2.44(a) and 2.44(b) present data on vitamin intakes from all sources for men and women respectively. Comparisons are made between comparable age groups in the two surveys; no attempt is made to use the data to undertake cohort analysis[13]. It should be noted that in the 1986/87 Adults Survey the youngest age group was adults aged 16 to 24 years, while in the current NDNS the youngest age group is adults aged 19 to 24 years. This should be borne in mind where there are differences between these groups. A summary of the methodology and findings from

the 1986/87 Adults Survey is given in Appendix S of the Technical Report[14]. Data are presented on absolute intakes from food sources and all sources, and comparisons do not take into account differences in energy intake.

The following discussion focuses on differences between the two surveys in intakes of vitamins from food sources alone. The effect of dietary supplements on intakes between the two surveys is then commented on. Data on mean daily intakes of total carotene from food sources alone were not available for the 1986/87 Adults Survey.

For seven of the thirteen vitamins presented, intakes from food sources were significantly higher for men and women overall in the present survey compared with the 1986/87 Adults Survey. This was true for thiamin, niacin equivalents, vitamin B_6, folate, pantothenic acid, vitamin C and vitamin E (men, vitamin E: p<0.05; all others: p<0.01). In addition, intakes of vitamin D were significantly higher for women in the present survey than in the 1986/87 Adults Survey (p<0.05). The increase in intakes of vitamin D for women seen in the present survey is likely to be attributable in part to the revision of vitamin D values in poultry and meat and meat products[7].

Men aged 25 to 64 years had significantly higher mean daily intakes of niacin equivalents and vitamin B_6, and those aged 35 to 64 years significantly higher intakes of thiamin, pantothenic acid and vitamin C in the present survey than the equivalent age groups in the 1986/87 Adults Survey (thiamin for 35 to 49 years and niacin equivalents for 25 to 34 years: p<0.05; all others: p<0.01). In addition, the oldest group of men had significantly higher intakes of folate and vitamin E in the present survey (p<0.01).

Women in all age groups in the current survey had significantly higher mean daily intakes of vitamin B_6, and those from the age of 25 years significantly higher mean daily intakes of folate, vitamin C and thiamin than those in equivalent age groups in the 1986/87 Adults Survey (thiamin and folate for 25 to 34 years: p<0.05; all others: p<0.01). In addition, women from the age of 35 years had significantly higher intakes of niacin equivalents and pantothenic acid, and the oldest group of women significantly higher mean biotin, vitamin D and vitamin E intakes compared with women in equivalent age groups in the earlier survey (niacin equivalents for 35 to 49 years, biotin and vitamin D for 50 to 64 years: p<0.05; all others: p<0.01).

Intakes of vitamin A and pre-formed retinol were significantly lower for both men and women in the present survey (p<0.01). This fall in assessed intakes is largely due to revised data for retinol levels in liver and milk becoming available since the 1986/87 Adults Survey.

In all age groups, men and women had significantly lower mean daily intakes of vitamin A and pre-formed retinol in the present survey than the equivalent age groups in the 1986/87 Adults Survey (men aged 25 to 34 years vitamin A: p<0.05; all others: p<0.01). In addition, men aged 19 to 24 years in the present survey had significantly lower mean daily intakes of vitamin B_{12} than men aged 16 to 24 years in the earlier survey, 4.4µg and 6.2µg respectively (p<0.01).

For both sexes and all age groups there were no significant differences between the two sets of survey data for mean daily intakes from food sources of riboflavin.

In the 2000/01 NDNS, 41% of women and 30% of men who completed the dietary record reported taking dietary supplements, this compares with 17% of women and 9% of men in the 1986/87 Adults Survey. Many of the differences in mean daily intakes from food sources between the two sets of survey data are still evident when dietary supplements are included (see Tables 2.44(a) and 2.44(b))[11]. When dietary supplements are included significant differences between the two sets of survey data remain, overall, for both men and women for intakes of vitamin A, pre-formed retinol, niacin equivalents, folate, pantothenic acid and vitamin C, for men for intakes of vitamin B_6 and for women for intakes of vitamin D and vitamin E. In addition, when dietary supplements are included men and women in the present survey had a significantly higher mean intake of biotin, and men, but not women a significantly lower mean intake of total carotene than those in the 1986/87 Adults Survey. There are no consistent patterns by age for men or women in the significant differences that remain when dietary supplements are included.

The extent to which these differences reflect changes in the diets of adults over the period is not clear. Many factors contribute to any differences, including changes in nutrient composition and, as noted previously, new analytical methods[7], increase in fortification practices, changes in food consumption patterns and increased use of dietary supplements.

(Tables 2.43(a), 2.43(b), 2.44(a) and 2.44(b))

References and endnotes

[1] Department of Health. Report on Health and Social Subjects: 41. *Dietary Reference Values for Food Energy and Nutrients for the United Kingdom.* HMSO (London, 1991).

[2] Department of Health. *Dietary Reference Values. A Guide.* HMSO (London, 1991).

[3] For each sex and age group the distribution of data was evaluated using the skewness statistic in SPSS. If the skewness statistic was less than twice the standard error of the statistic then data were considered to be normally distributed.

[4] Henderson L, Gregory J, Swan G. *National Diet and Nutrition Survey: adults aged 19 to 64 years. Volume 1: Types and quantities of foods consumed.* TSO (London, 2002).

[5] Intakes as a percentage of the RNI were calculated for each respondent, taking the appropriate RNI for each sex/age groups. The values for all respondents in each age group were then pooled to give a mean, median and standard deviation.

[6] Department of Health. Report on health and social subjects: 50. *Folic acid and the prevention of disease: report of the Committee on Medical Aspects of Food and Nutrition Policy.* TSO (London, 2000).

[7] Measurable amounts of vitamin D and its metabolites have now been found in meats as a result of new analytical methods.

[8] The areas included in each of the four analysis 'regions' are given in the response chapter, Chapter 2 of the Technical Report, online at http://www.food.gov.uk/science. Definitions of 'regions' are given in the glossary (*see* Appendix C).

[9] Households receiving benefits are those where someone in the respondent's household was currently receiving Working Families Tax Credit or had, in the previous 14 days, drawn Income Support or (Income-related) Job Seeker's Allowance. Definitions of 'household' and 'benefits (receiving)', are given in the glossary (*see* Appendix C).

[10] Chapter 2 of the Technical Report includes information on inter-relationships between the main socio-economic variables and gives tables of distributions for household benefit status by sex and age of respondent (Table 2.23). The Technical report is available online at http://www.food.gov.uk/science.

[11] Where there are no longer significant differences once dietary supplements are included this does not necessarily mean that dietary supplements reduce differences between sub-groups, as the inclusion of dietary supplements is likely to increase the variance and skew the distribution.

[12] Gregory J, Foster K, Tyler H, Wiseman M. *The Dietary and Nutritional Survey of British Adults.* HMSO (London, 1990).

[13] Due to the number of years between the two surveys it would only be possible to undertake cohort analysis for those who were aged 16 to 40 years in the 1986/87 Adults Survey. The numbers available to undertake this form of analysis are therefore limited.

[14] The Technical Report is available online at http://www.food.gov.uk/science.

Table 2.1

Reference Nutrient Intakes (RNIs) and Lower Reference Nutrient Intakes (LRNIs) for vitamins*

RNI and LRNI by age (years)** and sex		Vitamins							
		Vitamin A	Thiamin***	Riboflavin	Niacin***	Vitamin B$_6$****	Vitamin B$_{12}$	Folate	Vitamin C
Men		μg/d	mg/d	mg/d	mg/d	mg/d	μg/d	μg/d	mg/d
19 to 50	RNI	700	1.0	1.3	17	1.4	1.5	200	40
	LRNI	300	0.6	0.8	11	1.0	1.0	100	10
51 to 64	RNI	700	0.9	1.3	16	1.4	1.5	200	40
	LRNI	300	0.5	0.8	10	1.0	1.0	100	10
Women									
19 to 50	RNI	600	0.8	1.1	13	1.2	1.5	200	40
	LRNI	250	0.4	0.8	9	0.8	1.0	100	10
51 to 64	RNI	600	0.8	1.1	12	1.2	1.5	200	40
	LRNI	250	0.4	0.8	8	0.8	1.0	100	10

Note: * Source: Department of Health. Report on Health and Social Subjects: 41. Dietary Reference Values for Food Energy and Nutrients for the United Kingdom. HMSO (London, 1991).

** The age groups presented represent those for which different RNI and LRNI values are calculated.

*** Calculated values based on Estimated Average Requirements (EARS) for energy; calculated values from quoted LRNIs mg/1000kcal.

**** Based on protein providing 14.7% of the EAR for energy . Calculated values from quoted LRNIs μg/g protein.

Table 2.2

Proportion of respondents with average daily intakes of vitamins below the Lower Reference Nutrient Intake (LRNI) by sex and age of respondent

Percentages

Vitamins	% with average daily intake below the LRNI									
	Men aged (years):				All men	Women aged (years):				All women
	19–24	25–34	35–49	50–64		19–24	25–34	35–49	50–64	
	%	%	%	%	%	%	%	%	%	%
All sources										
Vitamin A	16	5	5	3	6	15	10	6	4	8
Thiamin	2	0	0	1	1	-	2	1	1	1
Riboflavin	7	1	2	2	2	13	10	5	5	7
Niacin equivalents	-	-	0	0	0	2	-	1	0	1
Vitamin B$_6$	-	0	1	1	1	5	1	2	2	2
Vitamin B$_{12}$	1	-	0	0	0	1	1	1	0	1
Folate	2	-	0	-	0	3	2	1	2	2
Vitamin C	-	0	-	-	0	1	-	0	0	0
Base	108	219	253	253	833	104	210	318	259	891
Food sources										
Vitamin A	16	7	5	4	7	19	11	8	5	9
Thiamin	2	0	0	1	1	-	2	1	1	1
Riboflavin	8	1	2	3	3	15	10	5	6	8
Niacin equivalents	-	-	0	0	0	2	-	1	0	1
Vitamin B$_6$	-	0	2	1	1	5	1	2	2	2
Vitamin B$_{12}$	1	-	0	0	0	1	1	1	0	1
Folate	2	-	0	-	0	3	2	2	2	2
Vitamin C	-	0	-	-	0	1	-	0	0	0
Base	108	219	253	253	833	104	210	318	259	891

Table 2.3

Average daily intake of pre-formed retinol (μg) by sex and age of respondent

Cumulative percentages

Pre-formed retinol (μg)	Men aged (years):				All men	Women aged (years):				All women
	19–24	25–34	35–49	50–64		19–24	25–34	35–49	50–64	
	cum %	cum %	cum %	cum %	cum %	cum %	cum %	cum %	cum %	cum %
(a) Intakes from *all sources*										
Less than 100	10	1	2	1	3	15	10	7	4	8
Less than 150	18	6	10	6	9	25	21	18	11	18
Less than 200	25	19	15	12	16	50	36	27	24	31
Less than 250	45	33	26	21	29	68	49	41	32	43
Less than 300	55	43	37	27	38	74	64	54	42	55
Less than 350	65	52	45	36	47	75	78	61	52	64
Less than 400	76	61	56	43	56	77	83	69	55	70
Less than 500	86	71	73	60	70	78	90	76	65	76
Less than 600	91	76	76	65	75	86	92	80	69	81
Less than 800	95	82	83	72	81	90	94	83	72	83
Less than 1000	98	89	85	75	85	97	98	88	80	89
Less than 2000	98	96	94	92	94	99	99	97	95	97
All	100	100	100	100	100	100	100	100	100	100
Base	*108*	*219*	*253*	*253*	*833*	*104*	*210*	*318*	*259*	*891*
Mean (average value)	334	551	721	877	673	341	341	462	645	472
Median	280	332	367	444	363	201	257	285	331	277
Lower 2.5 percentile	51	123	106	117	100	44	36	59	80	60
Upper 2.5 percentile	906	3079	4024	5168	3922	1790	944	2130	3194	2122
Standard deviation	305	647	1350	1278	1095	402	668	541	800	654
	cum %	cum %	cum %	cum %	cum %	cum %	cum %	cum %	cum %	cum %
(b) Intakes from *food sources*										
Less than 100	11	2	4	1	3	17	10	8	5	9
Less than 150	18	7	12	7	10	29	22	21	15	21
Less than 200	25	21	17	13	18	57	40	34	32	38
Less than 250	49	37	31	24	33	77	53	51	44	53
Less than 300	60	51	41	34	44	85	70	65	57	66
Less than 350	73	62	50	44	54	88	84	74	71	77
Less than 400	80	70	62	54	64	90	89	83	76	83
Less than 500	92	80	80	71	79	93	95	90	85	90
Less than 600	94	84	84	78	84	95	97	94	90	93
Less than 800	96	91	89	85	89	97	98	95	92	95
Less than 1000	98	93	91	87	91	99	99	96	92	96
Less than 2000	98	97	95	92	95	99	99	98	96	98
All	100	100	100	100	100	100	100	100	100	100
Base	*108*	*219*	*253*	*253*	*833*	*104*	*210*	*318*	*259*	*891*
Mean (average value)	315	424	643	735	571	251	302	339	449	352
Median	252	297	350	380	327	187	230	248	267	241
Lower 2.5 percentile	51	108	82	111	81	44	36	49	78	54
Upper 2.5 percentile	906	2078	4024	5168	3659	954	674	1381	3190	1498
Standard deviation	296	435	1327	1221	1034	323	654	445	726	584

Table 2.4

Average daily intake of total carotene (β-carotene equivalents) (μg) by sex and age of respondent

Cumulative percentages

Total carotene (β-carotene equivalents) (μg)	Men aged (years):				All men	Women aged (years):				All women
	19–24	25–34	35–49	50–64		19–24	25–34	35–49	50–64	
	cum %	cum %	cum %	cum %	cum %	cum %	cum %	cum %	cum %	cum %
(a) Intakes from all sources										
Less than 300	4	2	0	2	2	7	3	3	2	3
Less than 600	23	12	6	7	10	18	17	9	6	11
Less than 900	33	25	13	12	18	40	29	23	14	24
Less than 1200	43	39	28	19	30	62	43	35	26	37
Less than 1500	55	51	37	29	40	70	52	43	37	47
Less than 1800	68	62	49	43	53	81	60	51	45	55
Less than 2100	82	70	62	54	64	87	70	61	52	63
Less than 2400	84	77	69	62	71	89	76	69	59	70
Less than 2700	89	82	76	68	77	91	84	76	69	78
Less than 3000	90	84	81	70	80	91	86	82	76	82
Less than 3300	96	89	85	73	84	92	92	88	82	88
Less than 3500	96	90	90	76	86	94	93	89	86	90
All	100	100	100	100	100	100	100	100	100	100
Base	108	219	253	253	833	104	210	318	259	891
Mean (average value)	1470	1806	2088	2514	2063	1498	1754	2047	2222	1964
Median	1392	1474	1853	1936	1716	1054	1428	1753	2019	1608
Lower 2.5 percentile	275	307	427	302	322	145	288	261	371	275
Upper 2.5 percentile	4281	4989	5750	6676	5774	4283	5797	6280	5275	5275
Standard deviation	970	1258	1276	1965	1524	1936	1357	1710	1395	1591
	cum %	cum %	cum %	cum %	cum %	cum %	cum %	cum %	cum %	cum %
(b) Intakes from food sources										
Less than 300	4	2	1	2	2	7	3	3	2	3
Less than 600	23	12	6	7	10	18	17	9	6	11
Less than 900	33	25	13	12	19	41	28	23	14	24
Less than 1200	43	39	28	19	30	63	43	35	26	37
Less than 1500	55	51	37	29	41	71	52	44	38	47
Less than 1800	68	62	49	43	53	82	60	51	47	56
Less than 2100	82	70	63	55	65	88	70	61	53	64
Less than 2400	84	78	69	63	71	90	76	70	60	71
Less than 2700	89	82	77	69	77	92	84	77	69	78
Less than 3000	90	85	81	71	80	92	86	82	76	83
Less than 3300	96	89	85	73	84	93	92	88	82	88
Less than 3500	96	90	89	76	86	95	93	89	86	90
All	100	100	100	100	100	100	100	100	100	100
Base	108	219	253	253	833	104	210	318	259	891
Mean (average value)	1469	1801	2077	2459	2041	1294	1712	2015	2205	1914
Median	1392	1474	1853	1936	1716	1045	1426	1741	1991	1583
Lower 2.5 percentile	258	307	422	302	322	145	270	261	371	267
Upper 2.5 percentile	4281	4989	5750	6676	5750	4283	5193	6280	5275	5186
Standard deviation	971	1253	1267	1741	1431	966	1231	1522	1397	1392

Table 2.5

Percentage contribution of food types to average daily intake of total carotene (β-carotene equivalents) by sex and age of respondent

Percentages

Type of food	Men aged (years):				All men	Women aged (years):				All women	All
	19–24	25–34	35–49	50–64		19–24	25–34	35–49	50–64		
	%	%	%	%	%	%	%	%	%	%	%
Cereals & cereal products	8	5	3	3	4	6	5	3	3	4	4
Milk & milk products	3	3	3	2	3	3	3	2	2	2	3
Eggs & egg dishes	0	0	0	0	0	0	0	0	1	0	0
Fat spreads	5	4	3	3	4	3	3	2	3	3	3
Meat & meat products	16	16	14	11	14	11	11	11	9	10	12
Fish & fish dishes	1	0	2	1	1	0	1	1	2	1	1
Vegetables (excluding potatoes)	47	56	60	63	59	60	64	66	68	66	62
of which:											
raw carrots	*3*	*5*	*4*	*6*	*5*	*9*	*5*	*7*	*4*	*6*	*5*
other salad vegetables	*2*	*4*	*4*	*4*	*4*	*3*	*5*	*5*	*4*	*5*	*4*
raw tomatoes	*3*	*5*	*5*	*5*	*5*	*5*	*6*	*6*	*6*	*6*	*5*
carrots – not raw	*26*	*28*	*30*	*32*	*30*	*26*	*24*	*28*	*35*	*30*	*30*
Potatoes & savoury snacks	1	1	1	1	1	1	1	1	0	0	1
Fruit & nuts	1	1	2	2	2	2	1	3	4	3	2
Sugars, preserves & confectionery	0	0	0	0	0	0	0	0	0	0	0
Drinks*	13	4	5	3	5	7	5	4	3	4	4
of which:											
fruit juice	*0*	*1*	*0*	*1*	*1*	*1*	*1*	*2*	*1*	*1*	*1*
soft drinks, including low calorie	*12*	*3*	*4*	*2*	*4*	*7*	*3*	*2*	*2*	*3*	*3*
Miscellaneous**	6	8	6	9	8	6	7	6	7	7	7
Average daily intake (μg)	**1469**	**1801**	**2077**	**2459**	**2041**	**1294**	**1712**	**2015**	**2205**	**1914**	**1975**
Total number of respondents	**108**	**219**	**253**	**253**	**833**	**104**	**210**	**318**	**259**	**891**	**1724**

Note: * Includes soft drinks, alcoholic drinks, tea, coffee and water.

    ** Includes powdered beverages (except tea and coffee), soups, sauces, condiments and artificial sweeteners.

Table 2.6

Average daily intake of β-carotene (μg) by sex and age of respondent

Cumulative percentages

β-carotene (μg)	Men aged (years):				All men	Women aged (years):				All women
	19–24	25–34	35–49	50–64		19–24	25–34	35–49	50–64	
	cum %	cum %	cum %	cum %	cum %	cum %	cum %	cum %	cum %	cum %
(a) Intakes from *all sources*										
Less than 200	2	1	-	1	1	3	1	2	0	1
Less than 400	9	6	2	5	5	12	8	4	3	5
Less than 600	25	12	6	8	10	22	20	12	8	14
Less than 800	33	22	12	11	17	35	27	22	14	22
Less than 1200	45	43	31	23	34	65	45	38	30	41
Less than 1600	66	62	48	41	52	76	61	52	45	55
Less than 2000	84	72	65	58	67	86	73	65	54	66
Less than 2400	89	81	76	69	77	90	84	75	70	77
Less than 2800	90	85	83	72	81	90	89	85	80	85
Less than 3200	96	90	89	79	87	94	93	90	86	90
Less than 3600	96	91	92	84	90	94	95	92	91	93
All	100	100	100	100	100	100	100	100	100	100
Base	*108*	*219*	*253*	*253*	*833*	*104*	*210*	*318*	*259*	*891*
Mean (average value)	1342	1633	1875	2255	1858	1374	1579	1842	1995	1770
Median	1282	1346	1669	1774	1560	972	1307	1551	1801	1464
Lower 2.5 percentile	208	301	417	290	301	142	274	252	334	262
Upper 2.5 percentile	3840	4341	4802	5760	5031	3722	5204	5405	4609	4676
Standard deviation	881	1108	1102	1770	1354	1888	1221	1540	1223	1444
	cum %	cum %	cum %	cum %	cum %	cum %	cum %	cum %	cum %	cum %
(b) Intakes from *food sources*										
Less than 200	2	1	-	1	1	3	1	2	0	1
Less than 400	9	6	2	5	5	11	8	4	3	6
Less than 600	25	12	6	8	10	22	20	12	8	14
Less than 800	33	22	12	11	17	36	27	22	14	22
Less than 1200	45	43	31	24	34	67	46	38	31	41
Less than 1600	66	62	48	41	52	77	61	52	47	55
Less than 2000	84	72	65	59	68	87	73	65	56	67
Less than 2400	89	82	77	69	78	91	84	76	71	78
Less than 2800	90	86	83	73	82	91	89	85	80	85
Less than 3200	96	90	90	80	88	95	93	90	86	90
Less than 3600	96	91	92	85	90	95	96	92	91	93
All	100	100	100	100	100	100	100	100	100	100
Base	*108*	*219*	*253*	*253*	*833*	*104*	*210*	*318*	*259*	*891*
Mean (average value)	1341	1627	1864	2201	1836	1170	1538	1810	1977	1719
Median	1282	1346	1669	1774	1560	956	1304	1539	1746	1424
Lower 2.5 percentile	208	301	411	290	301	142	253	252	334	255
Upper 2.5 percentile	3840	4341	4802	5692	5031	3678	4536	5405	4609	4568
Standard deviation	882	1103	1093	1514	1248	837	1076	1349	1224	1225

Table 2.7

Average daily intake of α-carotene(µg) by sex and age of respondent

Cumulative percentages

α-carotene (µg)	Men aged (years):				All men	Women aged (years):				All women
	19–24	25–34	35–49	50–64		19–24	25–34	35–49	50–64	
	cum %	cum %	cum %	cum %	cum %	cum %	cum %	cum %	cum %	cum %
(a) Intakes from *all sources*										
Zero	5	3	1	0	2	1	1	2	1	1
Less than 10	19	16	6	9	11	21	13	9	8	11
Less than 25	30	20	13	13	17	27	18	13	12	16
Less than 50	34	27	15	16	21	33	23	18	15	20
Less than 75	38	32	19	17	24	38	28	23	19	25
Less than 150	42	45	31	26	35	61	45	35	32	39
Less than 300	72	66	57	49	59	76	67	58	51	60
Less than 400	94	74	69	61	71	87	74	70	59	69
Less than 500	96	80	81	68	79	88	82	77	70	78
Less than 600	96	85	84	74	83	94	85	85	78	84
Less than 700	98	90	89	78	87	94	91	89	85	89
All	100	100	100	100	100	100	100	100	100	100
Base	*108*	*219*	*253*	*253*	*833*	*104*	*210*	*318*	*259*	*891*
Mean (average value)	198	282	352	444	342	203	275	336	383	320
Median	181	189	263	303	248	117	174	259	294	227
Lower 2.5 percentile	0	0	3	2	1	0	1	1	2	1
Upper 2.5 percentile	713	1275	1611	1693	1363	1163	1022	1307	1331	1176
Standard deviation	181	315	379	461	381	263	292	358	350	335
	cum %	cum %	cum %	cum %	cum %	cum %	cum %	cum %	cum %	cum %
(b) Intakes from *food sources*										
Zero	5	3	1	0	2	1	1	2	1	1
Less than 10	19	16	6	9	11	21	13	9	8	11
Less than 25	31	20	13	13	17	27	18	13	12	16
Less than 50	34	27	15	16	21	33	23	18	15	20
Less than 75	38	32	19	17	24	38	28	23	19	25
Less than 150	42	45	31	26	35	61	45	35	32	39
Less than 300	72	66	57	49	59	76	67	58	51	60
Less than 400	94	74	69	61	71	87	74	70	59	69
Less than 500	96	80	81	68	79	88	82	77	70	78
Less than 600	96	85	84	74	83	94	85	85	78	84
Less than 700	98	90	89	78	87	94	91	89	85	89
All	100	100	100	100	100	100	100	100	100	100
Base	*108*	*219*	*253*	*253*	*833*	*104*	*210*	*318*	*259*	*891*
Mean (average value)	197	282	352	444	342	203	275	336	383	320
Median	181	189	263	303	248	117	174	259	294	227
Lower 2.5 percentile	0	0	3	2	1	0	1	1	2	1
Upper 2.5 percentile	713	1275	1611	1693	1363	1163	1022	1307	1331	1176
Standard deviation	182	315	379	461	381	263	292	357	350	335

Table 2.8

Average daily intake of β-cryptoxanthin (μg) by sex and age of respondent

Cumulative percentages

β-cryptoxanthin (μg)	Men aged (years):				All men	Women aged (years):				All women
	19–24	25–34	35–49	50–64		19–24	25–34	35–49	50–64	
	cum %	cum %	cum %	cum %	cum %	cum %	cum %	cum %	cum %	cum %
(a) Intakes from *all sources*										
Zero	-	3	2	3	2	3	2	4	3	3
Less than 10	19	11	9	14	12	16	12	16	11	14
Less than 30	44	43	33	34	38	44	35	36	33	36
Less than 60	68	62	61	62	62	78	65	62	61	64
Less than 90	76	76	75	78	76	89	77	75	75	77
Less than 120	91	89	83	85	86	95	83	83	84	85
Less than 150	93	92	90	90	91	97	87	88	87	89
Less than 180	95	95	95	92	94	97	90	91	91	91
All	100	100	100	100	100	100	100	100	100	100
Base	*108*	*219*	*253*	*253*	*833*	*104*	*210*	*318*	*259*	*891*
Mean (average value)	57	62	71	69	66	43	71	72	69	68
Median	37	37	51	46	44	34	44	46	48	44
Lower 2.5 percentile	1	0	2	0	1	0	2	0	0	0
Upper 2.5 percentile	248	290	270	330	290	195	290	350	254	271
Standard deviation	63.0	64.9	92.8	77.5	77.9	41.0	92.1	86.0	71.6	79.9
	cum %	cum %	cum %	cum %	cum %	cum %	cum %	cum %	cum %	cum %
(b) Intakes from *food sources*										
Zero	1	3	2	3	3	3	2	4	3	3
Less than 10	19	11	9	14	14	16	12	16	11	14
Less than 30	44	43	33	34	34	44	35	36	33	36
Less than 60	68	62	61	62	62	78	65	62	61	64
Less than 90	76	76	75	78	78	89	77	75	75	77
Less than 120	91	89	83	85	85	95	83	83	84	85
Less than 150	93	92	90	90	90	97	87	88	87	89
Less than 180	95	95	95	92	92	97	90	91	91	91
All	100	100	100	100	100	100	100	100	100	100
Base	*108*	*219*	*253*	*253*	*833*	*104*	*210*	*318*	*259*	*891*
Mean (average value)	57	62	71	69	66	43	71	72	69	68
Median	37	37	51	46	44	34	44	46	48	44
Lower 2.5 percentile	1	0	2	0	1	0	2	0	0	0
Upper 2.5 percentile	248	290	270	330	290	195	290	350	254	271
Standard deviation	63.0	64.9	92.8	77.5	77.9	41.0	92.1	86.0	71.6	79.9

Table 2.9

Average daily intake of vitamin A (retinol equivalents) (µg) by sex and age of respondent

Cumulative percentages

Vitamin A (retinol equivalents) (µg)	Men aged (years):				All men	Women aged (years):				All women
	19–24	25–34	35–49	50–64		19–24	25–34	35–49	50–64	
	cum %	cum %	cum %	cum %	cum %	cum %	cum %	cum %	cum %	cum %
(a) Intakes from *all sources*										
Less than 250	9	3	2	1	3	15	10	6	4	8
Less than 300	16	5	5	3	6	24	17	11	5	12
Less than 400	35	20	11	9	16	46	33	20	11	24
Less than 600	60	46	34	25	38	70	62	46	34	49
Less than 700	72	58	49	36	50	71	75	57	44	59
Less than 800	84	65	58	45	59	82	82	65	53	67
Less than 1000	90	75	72	57	71	92	89	76	65	77
Less than 1200	96	83	80	66	79	93	93	82	72	83
Less than 1400	99	87	84	73	83	97	97	89	80	89
Less than 1600	99	90	88	80	88	97	98	93	87	93
Less than 1800	99	92	90	83	90	97	99	95	91	95
Less than 2000	99	94	93	85	92	97	99	96	93	96
All	100	100	100	100	100	100	100	100	100	100
Base	*108*	*219*	*253*	*253*	*833*	*104*	*210*	*318*	*259*	*891*
Mean (average value)	579	852	1069	1296	1017	590	634	803	1015	800
Median	489	643	715	865	697	418	534	624	754	606
Lower 2.5 percentile	166	242	241	295	221	127	132	173	226	173
Upper 2.5 percentile	1230	3477	4287	5382	4286	2712	1461	2534	3769	2635
Standard deviation	361	711	1380	1339	1151	595	718	629	838	729
	cum %	cum %	cum %	cum %	cum %	cum %	cum %	cum %	cum %	cum %
(b) Intakes from *food sources*										
Less than 250	9	4	3	2	4	19	11	8	5	9
Less than 300	16	7	5	4	7	29	18	13	5	14
Less than 400	38	23	12	10	18	53	35	24	15	27
Less than 600	62	51	39	30	42	81	68	54	47	59
Less than 700	74	65	54	42	56	85	81	67	58	70
Less than 800	86	73	65	52	66	90	86	76	70	78
Less than 1000	93	83	80	66	78	97	92	87	84	88
Less than 1200	96	89	85	76	85	99	96	92	89	93
Less than 1400	99	92	88	82	89	99	99	94	92	95
Less than 1600	99	93	90	87	91	99	99	97	93	96
Less than 1800	99	95	92	88	93	99	99	97	94	97
Less than 2000	99	97	94	90	94	99	99	98	95	97
All	100	100	100	100	100	100	100	100	100	100
Base	*108*	*219*	*253*	*253*	*833*	*104*	*210*	*318*	*259*	*891*
Mean (average value)	560	724	989	1145	911	467	587	675	816	671
Median	489	585	670	789	660	393	510	571	635	549
Lower 2.5 percentile	162	219	235	271	219	127	132	170	222	171
Upper 2.5 percentile	1218	2412	4287	5382	4124	1076	1270	1878	3713	2103
Standard deviation	351	525	1353	1269	1083	347	692	507	766	633

Table 2.10

Average daily intake of vitamin A (retinol equivalents) as a percentage of Reference Nutrient Intake (RNI) by sex and age of respondent

Percentages

Sex and age of respondent	Average daily intake as % of RNI*							
	(a) All sources			Base	(b) Food sources			Base
	Mean	Median	sd		Mean	Median	sd	
Men aged (years):								
19–24	83	70	51.6	108	80	70	50.2	108
25–34	122	92	101.6	219	103	84	74.9	219
35–49	153	102	197.1	253	141	96	193.3	253
50–64	185	124	191.2	253	164	112	181.3	253
All	145	100	164.4	833	130	94	154.7	833
Women aged (years):								
19–24	98	70	99.1	104	78	66	57.8	104
25–34	106	90	119.6	210	98	85	115.4	210
35–49	134	104	104.8	318	112	95	84.5	318
50–64	169	126	139.6	259	136	106	127.6	259
All	133	101	121.5	891	112	92	105.5	891

Note: * Intake as a percentage of RNI was calculated for each respondent. The values for all respondents in each age group were then pooled to give a mean, median and sd.

Table 2.11

Percentage contribution of food types to average daily intake of vitamin A (retinol equivalents) by sex and age of respondent

Percentages

Type of food	Men aged (years):				All men	Women aged (years):				All women	All
	19–24	25–34	35–49	50–64		19–24	25–34	35–49	50–64		
	%	%	%	%	%	%	%	%	%	%	%
Cereals & cereal products	13	9	6	5	7	11	10	7	7	8	7
of which:											
pizza	6	3	1	1	2	3	2	1	1	1	2
buns, cakes & pastries	3	3	2	2	2	1	3	3	3	3	2
Milk & milk products	15	17	14	12	14	19	16	15	13	15	14
of which:											
whole milk	1	3	2	2	2	4	3	3	2	2	2
reduced fat milk	4	3	3	2	3	3	3	4	3	3	3
cheese	9	8	6	5	6	8	8	6	5	6	6
Eggs & egg dishes	6	5	4	4	5	5	4	5	5	5	5
Fat spreads	16	11	9	10	10	9	9	9	9	9	10
of which:											
butter	6	3	4	4	4	3	3	4	4	4	4
soft margarine, not polyunsaturated	2	2	1	1	1	1	1	1	1	1	1
polyunsaturated low fat spread	2	2	1	1	1	1	2	1	1	1	1
polyunsaturated reduced fat spread	2	1	1	1	1	0	1	1	1	1	1
other reduced fat spread	3	3	2	1	2	3	1	2	1	1	2
Meat & meat products	16	25	38	38	34	16	18	21	26	22	28
of which:											
beef, veal & dishes	6	3	3	2	3	4	3	3	2	3	3
chicken, turkey & dishes including coated	2	3	2	1	2	2	3	3	2	2	2
liver, liver products & dishes	6	15	31	32	26	9	11	13	21	15	21
Fish & fish dishes	1	1	1	1	1	1	1	1	2	1	1
Vegetables (excluding potatoes)	21	24	22	23	23	28	32	33	31	32	27
of which:											
raw carrots	1	2	2	2	2	4	3	3	2	3	2
raw tomatoes	1	2	2	2	2	2	3	3	3	3	2
carrots - not raw	12	12	10	11	11	12	12	14	16	14	12
Potatoes & savoury snacks	1	1	1	1	1	1	1	1	0	1	1
Fruit & nuts	0	1	1	1	1	1	1	1	2	1	1
Sugars, preserves & confectionery	1	0	0	0	0	1	0	0	0	0	0
Drinks*	6	2	2	1	2	4	2	2	1	2	2
Miscellaneous**	3	4	3	4	4	3	5	4	4	4	4
Average daily intake (µg)	560	724	989	1145	911	467	587	675	816	671	787
Total number of respondents	108	219	253	253	833	104	210	318	259	891	1724

Note: *   Includes soft drinks, alcoholic drinks, tea, coffee and water.
       ** Includes powdered beverages (except tea and coffee), soups, sauces, condiments and artificial sweeteners.

Table 2.12

Average daily intake of thiamin (mg) by sex and age of respondent

Cumulative percentages

Thiamin (mg)	Men aged (years):				All men	Women aged (years):				All women
	19–24	25–34	35–49	50–64		19–24	25–34	35–49	50–64	
	cum %	cum %	cum %	cum %	cum %	cum %	cum %	cum %	cum %	cum %
(a) Intakes from *all sources*										
Less than 0.70	3	0	2	1	1	5	6	6	4	5
Less than 0.80	12	2	5	3	5	14	17	10	9	12
Less than 1.00	26	11	9	8	11	26	27	23	20	24
Less than 1.30	32	20	20	16	20	51	47	37	31	39
Less than 1.50	36	34	25	24	28	67	61	48	44	52
Less than 1.70	51	47	35	38	41	73	71	63	56	64
Less than 1.90	67	55	49	46	52	82	81	76	67	75
Less than 2.10	81	65	61	56	63	85	86	81	73	80
Less than 2.30	88	71	74	64	72	88	89	86	80	85
Less than 2.50	93	76	79	74	79	89	92	89	83	88
Less than 2.70	95	81	86	81	84	90	93	92	87	91
Less than 3.00	100	87	91	85	89	91	95	94	91	93
All		100	100	100	100	100	100	100	100	100
Base	*108*	*219*	*253*	*253*	*833*	*104*	*210*	*318*	*259*	*891*
Mean (average value)	1.62	2.32	2.26	2.35	2.22	1.58	1.62	1.97	2.33	1.94
Median	1.67	1.78	1.92	1.96	1.86	1.29	1.36	1.52	1.62	1.46
Lower 2.5 percentile	0.64	0.90	0.78	0.84	0.82	0.47	0.53	0.54	0.64	0.56
Upper 2.5 percentile	2.75	5.87	5.28	5.38	5.38	5.31	5.70	3.81	6.64	5.17
Standard deviation	0.570	2.624	2.551	3.132	2.615	0.961	1.344	5.688	6.560	4.958
	cum %	cum %	cum %	cum %	cum %	cum %	cum %	cum %	cum %	cum %
(b) Intakes from *food sources*										
Less than 0.70	3	0	2	2	2	5	6	6	4	5
Less than 0.80	12	2	5	4	5	18	18	11	10	13
Less than 1.00	26	11	10	10	12	30	30	26	22	26
Less than 1.30	32	21	21	18	22	55	49	40	35	43
Less than 1.50	36	36	26	26	30	71	64	53	53	58
Less than 1.70	52	51	36	41	44	78	75	71	69	72
Less than 1.90	72	60	51	50	56	87	85	85	79	84
Less than 2.10	82	71	64	61	67	90	89	91	86	89
Less than 2.30	89	79	78	69	77	94	92	95	91	93
Less than 2.50	96	84	84	78	84	95	94	97	93	95
Less than 2.70	97	89	90	85	89	95	95	98	94	96
Less than 3.00	100	92	95	91	93	95	96	98	96	97
All		100	100	100	100	100	100	100	100	100
Base	*108*	*219*	*253*	*253*	*833*	*104*	*210*	*318*	*259*	*891*
Mean (average value)	1.60	2.08	2.04	2.07	2.00	1.45	1.55	1.52	1.60	1.54
Median	1.67	1.69	1.89	1.89	1.78	1.25	1.32	1.47	1.44	1.40
Lower 2.5 percentile	0.64	0.90	0.78	0.77	0.79	0.47	0.53	0.54	0.63	0.54
Upper 2.5 percentile	2.74	5.12	3.59	4.99	4.00	4.11	4.40	2.59	3.82	3.90
Standard deviation	0.555	2.263	1.620	1.263	1.638	0.781	1.288	0.970	0.864	1.007

Table 2.13

Average daily intake of thiamin as a percentage of Reference Nutrient Intake (RNI) by sex and age of respondent

Percentages

Sex and age of respondent	Average daily intake as % of RNI*							
	(a) All sources			Base	(b) Food sources			Base
	Mean	Median	sd		Mean	Median	sd	
Men aged (years):								
19–24	162	167	57.0	108	160	167	55.5	108
25–34	232	178	262.4	219	232	178	262.4	219
35–49	226	193	255.1	253	204	189	162.0	253
50–64	261	218	347.9	253	230	211	140.4	253
All	230	191	275.1	833	214	188	181.5	833
Women aged (years):								
19–24	198	161	120.2	104	181	157	97.6	104
25–34	202	170	167.9	210	194	165	160.9	210
35–49	246	190	711.0	318	190	183	121.2	318
50–64	291	203	820.0	259	200	180	107.9	259
All	243	182	619.8	891	193	175	125.9	891

Note: * Intake as a percentage of RNI was calculated for each respondent. The values for all respondents in each age group were then pooled to give a mean, median and sd.

Table 2.14

Percentage contribution of food types to average daily intake of thiamin by sex and age of respondent

Percentages

Type of food	Men aged (years):				All men	Women aged (years):				All women	All
	19–24	25–34	35–49	50–64		19–24	25–34	35–49	50–64		
	%	%	%	%	%	%	%	%	%	%	%
Cereals & cereal products	37	33	35	34	35	32	32	34	35	34	34
of which:											
white bread	12	9	10	9	10	10	8	8	7	8	9
wholemeal bread	1	2	2	3	2	1	2	2	3	2	2
soft grain bread and other bread	3	3	3	4	3	3	3	3	3	3	3
whole grain and high fibre breakfast cereals	5	8	8	8	8	6	5	9	11	8	8
other breakfast cereals	8	5	6	5	6	7	7	6	5	6	6
Milk & milk products	4	5	5	5	5	6	6	7	7	7	6
Eggs & egg dishes	1	1	1	1	1	1	1	1	1	1	1
Fat spreads	0	0	0	0	0	0	0	0	0	0	0
Meat & meat products	26	22	23	23	23	19	16	19	18	18	21
of which:											
bacon & ham	9	7	8	9	8	6	6	6	6	6	7
pork & dishes	2	3	4	4	4	2	2	3	3	3	3
chicken, turkey & dishes including coated	4	5	5	3	4	4	4	5	3	4	4
Fish & fish dishes	1	1	1	2	1	1	1	2	3	2	1
Vegetables (excluding potatoes)	6	18	14	15	15	16	23	15	14	17	15
Potatoes and savoury snacks	17	12	12	12	13	18	13	13	12	13	13
of which:											
potato chips	8	5	4	3	4	7	4	3	3	4	4
Fruit & nuts	1	2	2	3	2	2	2	3	4	3	3
Sugars, preserves & confectionery	1	1	1	0	0	1	1	1	0	1	1
Drinks*	3	3	2	2	2	3	2	3	2	2	2
Miscellaneous**	4	2	2	3	3	2	3	3	3	3	3
Average daily intake (mg)	1.60	2.08	2.04	2.07	2.00	1.45	1.55	1.52	1.60	1.54	1.77
Total number of respondents	108	219	253	253	833	104	210	318	259	891	1724

Note: * Includes soft drinks, alcoholic drinks, tea, coffee and water.

** Includes powdered beverages (except tea and coffee), soups, sauces, condiments and artificial sweeteners.

Table 2.15

Average daily intake of riboflavin (mg) by sex and age of respondent

Cumulative percentages

Riboflavin (mg)	Men aged (years):				All men	Women aged (years):				All women
	19–24	25–34	35–49	50–64		19–24	25–34	35–49	50–64	
	cum %	cum %	cum %	cum %	cum %	cum %	cum %	cum %	cum %	cum %
(a) Intakes from *all sources*										
Less than 0.80	7	1	2	2	2	13	10	5	5	7
Less than 1.00	12	5	4	6	6	33	20	12	11	16
Less than 1.10	33	10	9	9	12	43	36	21	18	26
Less than 1.30	40	17	17	14	19	52	48	32	28	37
Less than 1.60	52	30	28	23	30	64	60	46	39	49
Less than 1.80	62	41	35	30	39	73	73	56	46	59
Less than 2.00	71	49	46	41	49	76	82	67	57	69
Less than 2.20	79	57	52	51	57	83	88	75	65	76
Less than 2.40	82	65	62	61	65	86	91	81	70	81
Less than 2.60	88	74	70	67	73	86	94	85	78	85
Less than 2.80	90	76	75	72	76	88	95	86	83	88
Less than 3.00	90	81	81	77	81	93	97	89	85	90
All	100	100	100	100	100	100	100	100	100	100
Base	*108*	*219*	*253*	*253*	*833*	*104*	*210*	*318*	*259*	*891*
Mean (average value)	1.71	2.40	2.35	2.51	2.33	1.53	1.52	2.13	2.48	2.02
Median	1.56	2.03	2.11	2.16	2.02	1.31	1.41	1.69	1.85	1.62
Lower 2.5 percentile	0.47	0.90	0.88	0.85	0.80	0.51	0.56	0.65	0.70	0.60
Upper 2.5 percentile	3.81	5.13	4.56	4.82	4.77	3.56	3.34	3.95	4.22	3.91
Standard deviation	0.803	2.216	1.838	3.698	2.568	0.806	0.636	5.486	6.585	4.856
	cum %	cum %	cum %	cum %	cum %	cum %	cum %	cum %	cum %	cum %
(b) Intakes from *food sources*										
Less than 0.80	8	1	2	3	3	15	10	5	6	8
Less than 1.00	15	5	4	6	7	33	21	12	13	17
Less than 1.10	33	11	9	10	13	45	38	22	21	28
Less than 1.30	40	18	17	15	20	54	53	35	33	41
Less than 1.60	52	34	28	25	32	70	65	50	45	54
Less than 1.80	62	45	35	33	41	80	78	62	56	66
Less than 2.00	71	53	48	44	51	83	86	75	69	77
Less than 2.20	79	62	54	55	60	90	92	84	77	85
Less than 2.40	83	70	64	66	68	94	94	90	84	90
Less than 2.60	89	79	72	72	76	95	97	93	91	93
Less than 2.80	91	83	77	77	80	97	97	95	94	95
Less than 3.00	91	87	84	83	85	99	98	96	96	97
All	100	100	100	100	100	100	100	100	100	100
Base	*108*	*219*	*253*	*253*	*833*	*104*	*210*	*318*	*259*	*891*
Mean (average value)	1.68	2.12	2.19	2.20	2.11	1.39	1.44	1.66	1.75	1.60
Median	1.56	1.91	2.07	2.06	1.98	1.25	1.35	1.60	1.68	1.54
Lower 2.5 percentile	0.47	0.90	0.87	0.79	0.79	0.51	0.56	0.64	0.70	0.59
Upper 2.5 percentile	3.81	4.00	3.97	4.21	3.92	2.87	2.81	3.10	3.25	3.09
Standard deviation	0.780	1.097	0.894	0.847	0.939	0.636	0.546	0.614	0.688	0.638

Table 2.16

Average daily intake of riboflavin as a percentage of Reference Nutrient Intake (RNI) by sex and age of respondent

Percentages

Sex and age of respondent	Average daily intake as % of RNI*							
	(a) All sources			Base	(b) Food sources			Base
	Mean	Median	sd		Mean	Median	sd	
Men aged (years):								
19–24	132	120	61.8	108	129	120	60.0	108
25–34	185	156	170.5	219	163	147	84.4	219
35–49	181	163	141.4	253	168	159	68.8	253
50–64	193	166	284.4	253	169	159	65.2	253
All	179	156	197.5	833	162	152	72.2	833
Women aged (years):								
19–24	139	120	73.3	104	126	113	57.8	104
25–34	138	128	57.8	210	131	122	49.6	210
35–49	194	153	498.7	318	151	145	55.8	318
50–64	225	168	598.6	259	159	153	62.5	259
All	183	147	441.5	891	146	140	58.0	891

Note: * Intake as a percentage of RNI was calculated for each respondent. The values for all respondents in each age group were then pooled to give a mean, median and sd.

Table 2.17

Percentage contribution of food types to average daily intake of riboflavin by sex and age of respondent

Percentages

Type of food	Men aged (years):				All men	Women aged (years):				All women	All
	19–24	25–34	35–49	50–64		19–24	25–34	35–49	50–64		
	%	%	%	%	%	%	%	%	%	%	%
Cereals & cereal products	25	25	23	22	23	25	25	24	25	25	24
of which:											
whole grain and high fibre breakfast cereals	5	11	9	9	9	7	7	9	12	9	9
other breakfast cereals	8	5	5	5	5	8	8	6	6	6	6
Milk & milk products	24	30	32	31	30	34	34	36	36	36	33
of which:											
whole milk	3	6	6	6	6	8	7	6	4	6	6
semi-skimmed milk	15	14	17	15	15	13	16	17	17	16	16
skimmed milk	1	3	2	3	2	4	3	5	6	5	4
cheese	3	3	3	3	3	3	4	3	3	3	3
yogurt	1	2	2	2	2	2	3	3	3	3	2
Eggs & egg dishes	4	4	4	5	4	4	3	4	4	4	4
Fat spreads	0	0	0	0	0	0	0	0	0	0	0
Meat & meat products	18	15	17	16	16	14	12	13	13	13	15
of which:											
beef, veal & dishes	4	4	3	3	3	4	3	3	3	3	3
chicken, turkey & dishes including coated	5	4	4	3	4	4	4	4	3	4	4
liver, liver products & dishes	0	1	3	3	2	1	1	1	2	1	2
Fish & fish dishes	1	1	2	3	2	2	2	2	3	2	2
Vegetables (excluding potatoes)	3	3	4	4	4	5	6	4	4	5	4
Potatoes & savoury snacks	3	2	2	2	2	3	2	2	2	2	2
Fruit & nuts	1	1	2	2	2	2	2	2	3	2	2
Sugars, preserves & confectionery	3	2	2	1	2	3	2	2	1	2	2
Drinks*	12	13	11	12	12	7	6	7	6	6	10
of which:											
beer & lager	9	9	7	6	7	3	2	1	0	1	5
tea	2	2	3	4	3	2	3	4	4	3	3
Miscellaneous**	5	3	2	3	3	3	4	3	3	3	3
Average daily intake (mg)	1.68	2.12	2.19	2.20	2.11	1.39	1.44	1.66	1.75	1.60	1.85
Total number of respondents	108	219	253	253	833	104	210	318	259	891	1724

Note: * Includes soft drinks, alcoholic drinks, tea, coffee and water.

    ** Includes powdered beverages (except tea and coffee), soups, sauces, condiments and artificial sweeteners.

Table 2.18

Average daily intake of niacin equivalents (mg) by sex and age of respondent

Cumulative percentages

Niacin equivalents (mg)	Men aged (years):				All men	Women aged (years):				All women
	19–24	25–34	35–49	50–64		19–24	25–34	35–49	50–64	
	cum %	cum %	cum %	cum %	cum %	cum %	cum %	cum %	cum %	cum %
(a) Intakes from *all sources*										
Less than 12	-	-	0	0	0	4	-	1	1	1
Less than 13	-	-	0	0	0	4	1	2	1	2
Less than 16	2	-	1	1	1	7	8	4	3	5
Less than 17	2	-	2	1	1	7	9	4	4	6
Less than 21	4	-	3	2	2	15	18	10	7	12
Less than 28	17	12	8	8	10	40	49	33	25	35
Less than 35	35	21	21	24	24	65	76	59	56	63
Less than 42	59	41	37	41	42	85	90	81	78	83
Less than 49	80	64	60	63	64	95	96	91	91	93
Less than 56	91	77	75	78	79	99	100	96	96	97
Less than 63	98	86	88	89	89	100		98	98	99
All	100	100	100	100	100			100	100	100
Base	*108*	*219*	*253*	*253*	*833*	*104*	*210*	*318*	*259*	*891*
Mean (average value)	39.7	49.2	47.0	46.2	46.4	31.1	29.3	33.7	35.1	32.8
Median	39.8	45.0	46.5	44.7	44.5	32.1	28.8	32.8	33.9	32.1
Lower 2.5 percentile	17.1	23.6	19.5	19.9	21.4	10.5	13.6	14.2	13.8	13.6
Upper 2.5 percentile	62.1	83.9	83.8	79.5	81.8	55.7	51.4	60.9	60.4	57.2
Standard deviation	11.73	29.50	15.76	14.54	19.83	10.49	9.48	12.22	12.35	11.67
	cum %	cum %	cum %	cum %	cum %	cum %	cum %	cum %	cum %	cum %
(b) Intakes from *food sources*										
Less than 12	-	-	0	0	0	4	-	1	1	1
Less than 13	-	-	0	0	0	4	1	2	1	2
Less than 16	2	-	1	1	1	7	8	4	3	5
Less than 17	2	-	2	1	1	7	9	5	4	6
Less than 21	4	-	3	3	2	16	19	11	8	13
Less than 28	17	12	8	10	11	46	51	36	30	39
Less than 35	35	23	21	26	25	71	79	66	66	70
Less than 42	59	43	39	45	44	90	91	88	87	89
Less than 49	80	68	61	66	67	98	96	97	96	97
Less than 56	91	83	76	82	82	100	100	99	99	100
Less than 63	98	91	90	90	91			100	100	
All	100	100	100	100	100					
Base	*108*	*219*	*253*	*253*	*833*	*104*	*210*	*318*	*259*	*891*
Mean (average value)	39.4	46.2	45.9	44.6	44.7	29.5	28.8	31.5	32.3	30.9
Median	37.9	44.5	46.2	44.2	44.2	29.3	27.9	31.1	31.9	30.4
Lower 2.5 percentile	17.1	23.6	19.5	19.8	21.4	10.5	13.6	14.1	13.8	13.6
Upper 2.5 percentile	62.1	82.5	74.7	74.3	74.1	47.3	50.9	50.1	52.7	50.3
Standard deviation	11.46	18.17	13.40	13.43	14.73	9.61	9.16	9.09	8.85	9.20

Table 2.19

Average daily intake of niacin equivalents as a percentage of Reference Nutrient Intake (RNI) by sex and age of respondent

Percentages

Sex and age of respondent	Average daily intake as % of RNI*							
	(a) All sources			Base	(b) Food sources			Base
	Mean	Median	sd		Mean	Median	sd	
Men aged (years):								
19–24	233	234	69.0	108	232	223	67.4	108
25–34	289	265	173.5	219	272	262	106.9	219
35–49	277	273	92.7	253	270	271	78.8	253
50–64	289	280	90.9	253	279	276	83.9	253
All	278	266	118.1	833	268	263	88.3	833
Women aged (years):								
19–24	259	268	87.5	104	246	245	80.1	104
25–34	245	240	79.0	210	240	233	76.3	210
35–49	281	273	101.8	318	263	259	75.7	318
50–64	292	282	102.9	259	270	266	73.8	259
All	273	267	97.2	891	257	254	76.6	891

Note: * Intake as a percentage of RNI was calculated for each respondent. The values for all respondents in each age group were then pooled to give a mean, median and sd.

Table 2.20

Percentage contribution of food types to average daily intake of niacin equivalents by sex and age of respondent

Percentages

Type of food	Men aged (years):				All men	Women aged (years):				All women	All
	19–24	25–34	35–49	50–64		19–24	25–34	35–49	50–64		
	%	%	%	%	%	%	%	%	%	%	%
Cereals & cereal products	26	26	26	26	26	26	29	28	28	28	27
of which:											
white bread	8	7	7	7	7	7	7	6	5	6	7
wholemeal bread	1	2	3	3	2	1	3	3	3	3	2
soft grain bread and other bread	2	2	2	3	2	3	3	2	2	3	2
whole grain & high fibre breakfast cereals	3	6	5	6	5	4	4	7	8	6	6
other breakfast cereals	4	3	4	3	3	5	5	4	4	4	4
Milk & milk products	6	7	7	8	7	8	9	9	9	9	8
of which:											
milk	3	4	4	4	4	4	5	5	5	5	4
cheese	8	11	12	12	11	12	13	14	15	14	12
Eggs & egg dishes	2	2	2	2	2	2	2	2	2	2	2
Fat spreads	0	0	0	0	0	0	0	0	0	0	0
Meat & meat products	39	36	36	34	36	36	32	33	31	33	34
of which:											
bacon & ham	5	4	4	5	5	3	4	3	4	4	4
beef, veal & dishes	6	6	6	6	6	7	5	6	5	6	6
chicken, turkey & dishes including coated	16	16	15	12	15	17	17	16	14	15	15
Fish & fish dishes	3	4	6	7	5	6	6	8	10	8	6
of which:											
oily fish	1	3	4	4	3	5	4	5	7	5	4
Vegetables (excluding potatoes)	3	3	4	4	4	4	6	5	5	5	4
Potatoes and savoury snacks	7	5	4	4	5	8	6	5	4	5	5
Fruit & nuts	0	1	2	2	2	2	2	2	3	2	2
Sugars, preserves & confectionery	1	1	1	0	1	1	1	1	1	1	1
Drinks*	13	13	11	10	12	7	5	5	4	5	9
of which:											
beer & lager	10	10	8	7	9	4	3	2	1	2	6
coffee	1	2	2	2	2	1	2	3	3	2	2
Miscellaneous**	2	1	1	2	1	1	2	2	2	2	2
Average daily intake (mg)	39.4	46.2	45.9	44.6	44.7	29.5	28.8	31.5	32.3	30.9	37.6
Total number of respondents	108	219	253	253	833	104	210	318	259	891	1724

Note: * Includes soft drinks, alcoholic drinks, tea, coffee and water.

   ** Includes powdered beverages (except tea and coffee), soups, sauces, condiments and artificial sweeteners.

Table 2.21

Average daily intake of vitamin B₆ (mg) by sex and age of respondent

Cumulative percentages

Vitamim B₆ (mg)	Men aged (years):				All men	Women aged (years):				All women
	19–24	25–34	35–49	50–64		19–24	25–34	35–49	50–64	
	cum %	cum %	cum %	cum %	cum %	cum %	cum %	cum %	cum %	cum %
(a) Intakes from *all sources*										
Less than 0.8	-	-	0	-	0	5	1	2	2	2
Less than 1.0	-	0	1	1	1	8	5	4	3	5
Less than 1.2	2	0	3	1	1	12	14	9	7	10
Less than 1.4	12	4	5	6	6	16	24	14	12	16
Less than 1.7	24	8	8	11	11	32	38	29	27	31
Less than 2.0	24	16	16	17	17	51	56	46	37	46
Less than 2.5	49	36	36	34	37	74	82	70	63	71
Less than 3.0	62	56	57	56	57	88	90	83	79	84
Less than 3.5	75	69	74	73	73	94	95	90	87	91
Less than 4.0	88	81	83	85	84	96	96	94	92	94
Less than 4.5	97	87	91	89	90	99	98	96	94	96
All	100	100	100	100	100	100	100	100	100	100
Base	108	219	253	253	833	104	210	318	259	891
Mean (average value)	2.7	3.3	3.5	3.4	3.3	2.1	2.3	3.4	3.3	2.9
Median	2.7	2.8	2.8	2.8	2.8	2.0	1.9	2.1	2.2	2.1
Lower 2.5 percentile	1.2	1.4	1.2	1.2	1.2	0.7	0.8	0.9	1.0	0.8
Upper 2.5 percentile	4.5	6.8	6.4	6.4	6.4	4.2	4.2	8.4	12.6	5.2
Standard deviation	0.96	2.23	5.05	4.62	3.96	0.92	3.20	9.80	8.34	7.56
	cum %	cum %	cum %	cum %	cum %	cum %	cum %	cum %	cum %	cum %
(b) Intakes from *food sources*										
Less than 0.8	-	-	0	-	0	5	1	2	2	2
Less than 1.0	-	0	2	1	1	8	6	5	3	5
Less than 1.2	2	0	3	1	2	12	14	10	7	10
Less than 1.4	12	4	5	7	6	21	24	15	13	17
Less than 1.7	24	8	8	12	11	36	39	31	31	33
Less than 2.0	24	16	16	20	18	55	59	50	44	51
Less than 2.5	49	38	36	37	39	79	88	77	73	79
Less than 3.0	62	60	59	61	60	94	96	92	91	93
Less than 3.5	78	75	77	78	77	98	98	97	95	97
Less than 4.0	89	87	85	89	87	99	99	100	98	99
Less than 4.5	98	93	93	95	94	100	100		99	100
All		100	100	100	100	100				100
Base	108	219	253	253	833	104	210	318	259	891
Mean (average value)	2.6	3.0	2.9	2.8	2.9	2.0	1.9	2.0	2.1	2.0
Median	2.7	2.7	2.7	2.8	2.7	1.9	1.9	2.0	2.1	2.0
Lower 2.5 percentile	1.2	1.4	1.1	1.2	1.2	0.7	0.8	0.8	1.0	0.8
Upper 2.5 percentile	4.4	5.3	5.3	4.8	5.2	3.5	3.4	3.6	3.8	3.6
Standard deviation	0.94	1.16	1.00	0.95	1.03	0.73	0.64	0.66	0.73	0.69

Table 2.22

Average daily intake of vitamin B_6 as a percentage of Reference Nutrient Intake (RNI) by sex and age of respondent

Percentages

Sex and age of respondent	Average daily intake as % of RNI*							
	(a) All sources			Base	(b) Food sources			Base
	Mean	Median	sd		Mean	Median	sd	
Men aged (years):								
19–24	190	194	68.9	108	189	194	67.5	108
25–34	233	200	158.9	219	211	195	82.7	219
35–49	250	198	360.9	253	206	196	71.3	253
50–64	241	202	329.9	253	201	198	67.8	253
All	235	199	282.7	833	204	196	73.2	833
Women aged (years):								
19–24	178	166	76.9	104	165	161	60.9	104
25–34	188	160	267.0	210	158	156	53.0	210
35–49	284	173	816.4	318	170	167	55.0	318
50–64	273	183	695.1	259	177	174	60.9	259
All	246	172	629.7	891	169	165	57.4	891

Note: * Intake as a percentage of RNI was calculated for each respondent. The values for all respondents in each age group were then pooled to give a mean, median and sd.

Table 2.23

Percentage contribution of food types to average daily intake of vitamin B$_6$ by sex and age of respondent

Percentages

Type of food	Men aged (years):				All men	Women aged (years):				All women	All
	19–24	25–34	35–49	50–64		19–24	25–34	35–49	50–64		
	%	%	%	%	%	%	%	%	%	%	%
Cereals & cereal products	19	21	20	20	20	20	23	22	23	22	21
of which:											
white bread	3	2	2	2	2	3	2	2	2	2	2
wholemeal bread	0	1	1	1	1	0	1	1	1	1	1
soft grain bread and other bread	1	1	1	1	1	1	1	1	1	1	1
whole grain & high fibre breakfast cereals	3	8	6	6	6	4	5	7	9	7	7
other breakfast cereals	7	5	6	5	5	7	8	6	6	7	6
Milk & milk products	6	8	9	9	8	8	9	11	10	10	9
of which:											
whole milk	1	2	2	2	2	3	2	2	2	2	2
semi-skimmed milk	4	4	5	5	5	4	5	6	6	6	5
skimmed milk	0	1	1	1	1	1	1	2	2	1	1
Eggs & egg dishes	1	1	1	1	1	1	1	1	1	1	1
Fat spreads	0	0	0	0	0	0	0	0	0	0	0
Meat & meat products	24	22	22	21	22	21	19	20	18	19	21
of which:											
bacon & ham	4	3	4	4	4	2	3	3	3	3	3
beef, veal & dishes	5	5	5	5	5	6	4	5	4	4	5
chicken, turkey & dishes including coated	9	9	9	7	8	9	8	8	7	8	8
Fish & fish dishes	1	2	3	4	3	3	3	4	6	4	4
Vegetables (excluding potatoes)	4	5	6	6	5	5	8	8	7	7	6
Potatoes and savoury snacks	23	18	18	18	19	27	21	19	19	20	19
of which:											
potato chips	12	7	7	6	7	11	8	6	5	6	7
Fruit & nuts	2	3	5	6	5	4	6	7	10	7	6
Sugars, preserves & confectionery	0	0	0	0	0	0	0	0	0	0	0
Drinks*	18	18	14	12	15	10	7	5	3	6	11
of which:											
beer & lager	15	16	11	10	13	6	4	3	1	3	8
Miscellaneous**	1	2	1	2	2	1	2	2	2	2	2
Average daily intake (mg)	2.6	3.0	2.9	2.8	2.9	2.0	1.9	2.0	2.1	2.0	2.4
Total number of respondents	108	219	253	253	833	104	210	318	259	891	1724

Note: * Includes soft drinks, alcoholic drinks, tea, coffee and water.

* Includes powdered beverages (except tea and coffee), soups, sauces, condiments and artificial sweeteners.

Table 2.24

Average daily intake of vitamin B$_{12}$ (μg) by sex and age of respondent

Cumulative percentages

Vitamin B$_{12}$ (μg)	Men aged (years):				All men	Women aged (years):				All women
	19–24	25–34	35–49	50–64		19–24	25–34	35–49	50–64	
	cum %	cum %	cum %	cum %	cum %	cum %	cum %	cum %	cum %	cum %
(a) Intakes from all sources										
Less than 1.0	1	-	0	0	0	1	1	1	0	1
Less than 1.5	4	1	1	0	1	5	2	3	1	2
Less than 2.5	11	7	6	4	6	18	16	11	5	11
Less than 3.5	28	14	12	9	14	47	49	21	19	30
Less than 4.5	56	35	24	18	29	64	74	47	35	52
Less than 5.5	75	54	43	36	48	83	83	66	52	68
Less than 6.5	88	70	58	52	63	86	90	81	69	80
Less than 7.5	95	78	72	67	75	96	96	88	80	88
All	100	100	100	100	100	100	100	100	100	100
Base	108	219	253	253	833	104	210	318	259	891
Mean (average value)	4.5	6.2	7.4	7.6	6.8	4.1	4.0	5.5	6.1	5.1
Median	4.3	5.2	6.0	6.4	5.6	3.7	3.6	4.6	5.4	4.4
Lower 2.5 percentile	1.2	2.2	2.1	2.2	2.0	1.2	1.5	1.5	2.0	1.5
Upper 2.5 percentile	8.1	15.5	25.0	23.0	19.7	9.3	8.3	12.1	18.9	12.8
Standard deviation	1.67	4.26	7.25	6.55	5.93	2.09	2.17	6.43	3.66	4.57
	cum%	cum%	cum%	cum%	cum%	cum%	cum%	cum%	cum%	cum%
(b) Intakes from food sources										
Less than 1.0	1	-	0	0	0	1	1	1	0	1
Less than 1.5	4	1	1	0	1	5	2	3	1	3
Less than 2.5	11	7	6	4	6	20	17	12	6	12
Less than 3.5	28	16	12	9	14	47	50	22	22	32
Less than 4.5	56	38	25	20	31	66	76	52	40	56
Less than 5.5	75	56	44	39	50	85	84	69	57	71
Less than 6.5	88	70	60	55	65	88	90	83	73	82
Less than 7.5	97	80	73	70	77	97	96	90	84	91
All	100	100	100	100	100	100	100	100	100	100
Base	108	219	253	253	833	104	210	318	259	891
Mean (average value)	4.4	5.9	7.0	7.3	6.5	4.0	4.0	4.9	5.7	4.8
Median	4.3	5.1	5.9	6.2	5.5	3.7	3.4	4.5	5.1	4.3
Lower 2.5 percentile	1.2	2.2	2.1	2.2	2.0	1.2	1.5	1.4	2.0	1.5
Upper 2.5 percentile	7.5	15.5	20.4	23.0	19.6	9.3	8.3	10.6	14.4	10.7
Standard deviation	1.62	3.42	5.42	5.40	4.69	2.00	2.17	2.50	3.22	2.69

Table 2.25

Average daily intake of vitamin B$_{12}$ as a percentage of Reference Nutrient Intake (RNI) by sex and age of respondent

Percentages

Sex and age of respondent	Average daily intake as % of RNI*							
	(a) All sources			Base	(b) Food sources			Base
	Mean	Median	sd		Mean	Median	sd	
Men aged (years):								
19–24	298	287	111.3	108	296	287	108.0	108
25–34	410	347	283.9	219	395	341	227.8	219
35–49	491	399	483.6	253	465	397	361.1	253
50–64	508	427	436.4	253	485	412	359.7	253
All	450	377	395.1	833	431	369	312.5	833
Women aged (years):								
19–24	272	248	139.3	104	266	248	133.3	104
25–34	268	239	144.4	210	264	229	144.8	210
35–49	363	308	428.4	318	325	298	166.4	318
50–64	406	357	243.7	259	378	340	214.7	259
All	342	294	304.8	891	319	286	179.6	891

Note: * Intake as a percentage of RNI was calculated for each respondent. The values for all respondents in each age group were then pooled to give a mean, median and sd.

Table 2.26

Percentage contribution of food types to average daily intake of vitamin B$_{12}$ by sex and age of respondent

Percentages

Type of food	Men aged (years):				All men	Women aged (years):				All women	All
	19–24	25–34	35–49	50–64		19–24	25–34	35–49	50–64		
	%	%	%	%	%	%	%	%	%	%	%
Cereals & cereal products	11	9	6	6	7	8	8	7	7	7	7
Milk & milk products	30	37	34	31	33	38	41	41	36	39	36
of which:											
whole milk	*3*	*7*	*6*	*5*	*6*	*9*	*8*	*7*	*4*	*6*	*6*
semi-skimmed milk	*18*	*17*	*18*	*16*	*17*	*15*	*19*	*20*	*18*	*18*	*18*
skimmed milk	*1*	*4*	*2*	*3*	*3*	*5*	*4*	*6*	*7*	*6*	*4*
cheese	*6*	*6*	*5*	*5*	*5*	*5*	*7*	*5*	*5*	*5*	*5*
Eggs & egg dishes	8	7	6	6	6	6	5	5	5	5	6
Fat spreads	0	0	0	0	0	0	0	0	0	0	0
Meat & meat products	39	32	34	34	34	29	23	24	25	24	30
of which:											
beef, veal & dishes	*11*	*9*	*8*	*7*	*8*	*10*	*7*	*8*	*7*	*8*	*8*
liver, liver products & dishes	*1*	*5*	*12*	*13*	*10*	*2*	*3*	*4*	*8*	*5*	*8*
burgers & kebabs	*10*	*5*	*2*	*1*	*3*	*6*	*3*	*2*	*1*	*2*	*3*
sausages	*4*	*2*	*2*	*1*	*2*	*2*	*2*	*1*	*1*	*1*	*2*
Fish & fish dishes	8	12	18	19	16	16	19	21	26	22	18
of which:											
shellfish	*2*	*2*	*5*	*3*	*3*	*5*	*6*	*5*	*5*	*5*	*4*
oily fish	*2*	*7*	*10*	*12*	*9*	*9*	*10*	*13*	*16*	*13*	*11*
Vegetables (excluding potatoes)	1	1	0	0	0	1	1	1	0	1	1
Potatoes & savoury snacks	0	0	0	0	0	0	0	0	0	0	0
Fruit & nuts	0	0	0	0	0	0	0	0	0	0	0
Sugars, preserves & confectionery	1	0	0	0	0	1	1	0	0	0	0
Drinks*	1	1	1	2	1	0	0	0	0	0	1
Miscellaneous**	1	1	1	1	1	1	1	1	1	1	1
Average daily intake (µg)	4.4	5.9	7.0	7.3	6.5	4.0	4.0	4.9	5.7	4.8	5.6
Total number of respondents	108	219	253	253	833	104	210	318	259	891	1724

Note: * Includes soft drinks, alcoholic drinks, tea, coffee and water.

* * Includes powdered beverages (except tea and coffee), soups, sauces, condiments and artificial sweeteners.

Table 2.27

Average daily intake of folate (μg) by sex and age of respondent

Cumulative percentages

Folate (μg)	Men aged (years):				All men	Women aged (years):				All women
	19–24	25–34	35–49	50–64		19–24	25–34	35–49	50–64	
	cum %	cum %	cum %	cum %	cum %	cum %	cum %	cum %	cum %	cum %
(a) Intakes from *all sources*										
Less than 100	2	-	0	-	0	3	2	1	2	2
Less than 150	5	1	4	3	3	23	15	11	8	12
Less than 200	14	14	8	10	11	35	35	26	22	28
Less than 250	28	19	21	18	20	59	57	46	37	48
Less than 300	61	40	39	35	41	76	75	67	60	68
Less than 350	72	53	56	49	55	84	86	80	76	81
Less than 400	76	65	69	66	68	86	92	84	81	86
Less than 450	89	73	79	76	78	95	97	89	89	92
Less than 500	92	83	86	83	85	97	98	94	92	95
All	100	100	100	100	100	100	100	100	100	100
Base	*108*	*219*	*253*	*253*	*833*	*104*	*210*	*318*	*259*	*891*
Mean (average value)	305	376	355	373	359	248	249	280	359	292
Median	275	341	330	354	333	232	233	258	275	255
Lower 2.5 percentile	106	169	136	142	144	91	98	111	114	102
Upper 2.5 percentile	565	680	633	754	680	517	473	551	572	554
Standard deviation	113.7	223.6	171.2	150.8	176.2	109.2	113.2	123.4	916.9	505.2
	cum %	cum %	cum %	cum %	cum %	cum %	cum %	cum %	cum %	cum %
(b) Intakes from *food sources*										
Less than 100	2	-	0	-	0	3	2	2	2	2
Less than 150	5	1	4	4	3	24	15	12	10	13
Less than 200	14	14	9	10	11	40	36	28	25	30
Less than 250	32	20	22	18	21	65	60	50	43	52
Less than 300	61	43	39	36	42	82	79	72	67	74
Less than 350	72	57	58	50	57	93	90	87	84	87
Less than 400	76	70	72	68	71	95	97	93	89	93
Less than 450	89	78	82	79	81	99	100	97	96	97
Less than 500	94	89	89	86	89	99		100	98	99
All	100	100	100	100	100	100			100	100
Base	*108*	*219*	*253*	*253*	*833*	*104*	*210*	*318*	*259*	*891*
Mean (average value)	301	346	343	361	344	229	233	255	268	251
Median	275	326	327	349	327	225	229	251	267	245
Lower 2.5 percentile	106	169	133	141	141	91	98	111	114	101
Upper 2.5 percentile	535	617	605	637	612	444	403	463	465	451
Standard deviation	108.4	128.1	118.5	137.0	126.8	91.6	80.6	87.3	95.7	89.9

Table 2.28

Average daily intake of folate as a percentage of Reference Nutrient Intake (RNI) by sex and age of respondent

Percentages

Sex and age of respondent	Average daily intake as % of RNI*							
	(a) All sources			Base	(b) Food sources			Base
	Mean	Median	sd		Mean	Median	sd	
Men aged (years):								
19–24	153	138	57	108	151	138	54	108
25–34	188	170	112	219	173	163	64	219
35–49	177	165	86	253	171	164	59	253
50–64	186	177	75	253	181	174	68	253
All	180	166	88	833	172	163	63	833
Women aged (years):								
19–24	124	116	55	104	114	113	46	104
25–34	124	116	57	210	117	115	40	210
35–49	140	129	62	318	128	125	44	318
50–64	179	138	458	259	134	133	48	259
All	146	128	253	891	125	122	45	891

Note: * Intake as a percentage of RNI was calculated for each respondent. The values for all respondents in each age group were then pooled to give a mean, median and sd.

Table 2.29

Percentage contribution of food types to average daily intake of folate by sex and age of respondent

Percentages

Type of food	Men aged (years):				All men	Women aged (years):				All women	All
	19–24	25–34	35–49	50–64		19–24	25–34	35–49	50–64		
	%	%	%	%	%	%	%	%	%	%	%
Cereals & cereal products	34	34	33	32	33	34	35	32	34	33	33
of which:											
pizza	10	6	3	2	4	5	4	2	2	3	3
white bread	7	6	7	6	6	6	6	5	4	5	6
wholemeal and other bread	1	2	2	2	2	1	2	2	3	2	2
soft grain bread and other breads	2	3	3	4	3	4	4	3	3	3	3
whole grain & high fibre breakfast cereals	4	9	8	8	8	6	6	9	11	9	8
other breakfast cereals	7	5	6	6	6	10	9	7	7	7	7
Milk & milk products	5	7	8	7	7	7	8	9	9	9	8
Eggs & egg dishes	3	3	3	3	3	2	2	2	3	3	3
Fat spreads	0	0	0	0	0	0	0	0	0	0	0
Meat & meat products	8	7	8	7	7	7	6	7	6	6	7
Fish & fish dishes	1	1	2	2	2	1	1	2	2	2	2
Vegetables (excluding potatoes)	10	11	13	16	13	13	17	18	19	17	15
Potatoes & savoury snacks	15	12	12	10	12	18	13	12	10	12	12
of which:											
potato chips	8	5	5	4	5	8	5	4	3	4	5
Fruit & nuts	1	2	3	3	3	3	3	4	6	4	3
Sugars, preserves & confectionery	1	0	0	0	0	0	1	1	0	0	0
Drinks*	20	20	17	15	18	13	10	10	8	9	14
of which:											
fruit juice	3	2	3	3	2	4	3	3	3	3	3
beer & lager	14	15	11	8	11	6	4	3	1	3	8
tea	2	2	3	4	3	2	2	4	3	3	3
Miscellaneous**	3	2	2	4	3	2	3	3	4	3	3
Average daily intake (µg)	301	346	343	361	344	229	233	255	268	251	296
Total number of respondents	108	219	253	253	833	104	210	318	259	891	1724

Note: * Includes soft drinks, alcoholic drinks, tea, coffee and water.
   ** Includes powdered beverages (except tea and coffee), soups, sauces, condiments and artificial sweeteners.

Table 2.30

Average daily intake of biotin (µg) by sex and age of respondent

Cumulative percentages

Biotin (µg)	Men aged (years):				All men	Women aged (years):				All women
	19–24	25–34	35–49	50–64		19–24	25–34	35–49	50–64	
	cum %	cum %	cum %	cum %	cum %	cum %	cum %	cum %	cum %	cum %
(a) Intakes from all sources										
Less than 10	1	-	-	-	0	2	2	2	1	2
Less than 15	6	-	2	3	3	17	11	5	4	8
Less than 20	18	5	6	6	7	39	27	15	14	20
Less than 25	33	15	11	13	15	56	51	32	27	38
Less than 30	52	25	18	20	25	77	69	51	44	56
Less than 40	77	49	41	44	48	92	90	84	74	83
Less than 50	93	74	68	70	74	96	98	91	90	93
All	100	100	100	100	100	100	100	100	100	100
Base	*108*	*219*	*253*	*253*	*833*	*104*	*210*	*318*	*259*	*891*
Mean (average value)	31	45	47	46	44	27	28	34	37	33
Median	29	40	43	42	41	23	25	30	32	28
Lower 2.5 percentile	10	19	15	13	15	10	10	11	12	10
Upper 2.5 percentile	60	131	103	116	99	148	54	137	66	76
Standard deviation	12.3	27.4	38.5	24.8	29.6	22.7	22.1	25.5	41.3	30.3
	cum %	cum %	cum %	cum %	cum %	cum %	cum %	cum %	cum %	cum %
(b) Intakes from food sources										
Less than 10	1	-	-	-	0	2	2	2	1	2
Less than 15	6	-	3	3	3	17	11	5	4	8
Less than 20	18	5	7	6	8	42	27	15	14	21
Less than 25	33	16	12	13	16	59	51	33	28	39
Less than 30	56	26	19	21	26	80	70	53	46	58
Less than 40	81	51	41	45	50	95	93	86	78	86
Less than 50	93	77	69	72	75	99	100	94	93	96
All	100	100	100	100	100	100		100	100	100
Base	*108*	*219*	*253*	*253*	*833*	*104*	*210*	*318*	*259*	*891*
Mean (average value)	30	41	44	43	41	24	26	30	32	29
Median	28	39	43	42	40	23	25	29	31	28
Lower 2.5 percentile	10	19	15	13	15	10	10	11	12	10
Upper 2.5 percentile	58	83	83	91	83	47	47	59	60	55
Standard deviation	11.9	18.2	16.4	17.6	17.3	10.1	8.8	11.0	11.5	11.0

Table 2.31

Average daily intake of pantothenic acid (mg) by sex and age of respondent

Cumulative percentages

Pantothenic acid (mg)	Men aged (years):				All men	Women aged (years):				All women
	19–24	25–34	35–49	50–64		19–24	25–34	35–49	50–64	
	cum %	cum %	cum %	cum %	cum %	cum %	cum %	cum %	cum %	cum %
(a) Intakes from *all sources*										
Less than 2.5	2	0	1	1	1	9	4	2	3	3
Less than 3.0	6	1	2	2	2	13	11	6	5	8
Less than 3.5	8	4	3	2	4	18	18	13	8	13
Less than 4.5	28	11	12	6	12	45	43	25	20	30
Less than 5.5	46	30	21	19	26	70	66	46	40	52
Less than 6.5	66	45	35	31	40	83	85	68	59	71
Less than 7.0	72	54	47	37	49	89	86	76	66	77
Less than 7.5	78	61	54	48	57	89	89	80	71	81
Less than 8.5	86	74	69	65	71	92	93	85	81	87
All	100	100	100	100	100	100	100	100	100	100
Base	*108*	*219*	*253*	*253*	*833*	*104*	*210*	*318*	*259*	*891*
Mean (average value)	6.0	7.9	8.1	8.2	7.8	5.2	5.1	6.4	7.9	6.4
Median	5.6	6.7	7.2	7.6	7.1	4.7	4.9	5.7	6.0	5.4
Lower 2.5 percentile	2.6	3.3	3.3	3.3	3.2	2.1	2.1	2.7	2.5	2.3
Upper 2.5 percentile	12.2	13.8	14.8	16.2	14.5	12.7	10.0	13.2	16.0	13.2
Standard deviation	2.31	7.14	5.61	4.56	5.51	2.35	2.04	5.76	14.59	8.73
	cum %	cum %	cum %	cum %	cum %	cum %	cum %	cum %	cum %	cum %
(b) Intakes from *food sources*										
Less than 2.5	2	0	1	2	1	9	4	2	3	4
Less than 3.0	6	1	2	2	2	13	11	7	5	8
Less than 3.5	8	5	3	3	4	18	19	14	8	14
Less than 4.5	28	12	12	7	13	45	46	27	23	32
Less than 5.5	47	32	21	22	28	75	70	50	46	56
Less than 6.5	68	47	35	35	43	88	88	75	68	77
Less than 7.0	76	58	47	42	52	92	90	83	74	83
Less than 7.5	83	65	55	53	60	93	92	88	81	88
Less than 8.5	87	80	70	71	75	99	96	93	90	93
All	100	100	100	100	100	100	100	100	100	100
Base	*108*	*219*	*253*	*253*	*833*	*104*	*210*	*318*	*259*	*891*
Mean (average value)	5.9	7.1	7.5	7.5	7.2	4.8	4.9	5.6	5.9	5.4
Median	5.6	6.6	7.2	7.4	6.9	4.7	4.8	5.5	5.7	5.2
Lower 2.5 percentile	2.6	3.2	3.3	3.1	3.1	2.1	2.1	2.6	2.5	2.3
Upper 2.5 percentile	11.6	13.1	13.4	13.0	13.1	8.4	9.0	9.8	10.3	9.7
Standard deviation	2.14	3.45	2.59	2.57	2.83	1.78	1.71	1.83	2.00	1.89

Table 2.32

Average daily intake of vitamin C (mg) by sex and age of respondent

Cumulative percentages

Vitamin C (mg)	Men aged (years):				All men	Women aged (years):				All women
	19–24	25–34	35–49	50–64		19–24	25–34	35–49	50–64	
	cum %	cum %	cum %	cum %	cum %	cum %	cum %	cum %	cum %	cum %
(a) Intakes from *all sources*										
Less than 10	-	0	-	-	0	1	-	0	0	0
Less than 20	3	1	2	2	2	5	4	5	3	4
Less than 30	17	10	10	7	10	10	13	12	6	10
Less than 40	36	20	18	15	20	23	24	22	11	19
Less than 60	58	47	34	30	39	46	49	38	22	37
Less than 80	75	64	52	40	54	60	67	52	43	54
Less than 100	88	76	66	54	68	69	78	63	55	65
Less than 130	90	83	79	71	79	88	86	75	69	77
Less than 160	91	89	87	82	87	92	89	84	82	85
Less than 180	93	93	89	86	90	92	92	88	85	88
Less than 200	96	94	92	88	92	94	96	90	89	92
All	100	100	100	100	100	100	100	100	100	100
Base	*108*	*219*	*253*	*253*	*833*	*104*	*210*	*318*	*259*	*891*
Mean (average value)	67.2	83.7	107.7	125.0	101.4	96.1	85.1	123.1	126.7	112.0
Median	51.1	62.8	77.5	92.3	74.2	68.6	62.0	77.9	90.2	76.1
Lower 2.5 percentile	18.5	21.1	20.0	22.4	20.8	12.5	17.2	16.4	19.0	17.2
Upper 2.5 percentile	241.8	319.8	303.5	588.3	329.3	400.2	272.6	476.5	592.3	473.2
Standard deviation	55.09	65.97	208.27	142.30	145.60	133.71	85.49	299.37	161.22	208.58
	cum%	cum %	cum %	cum %	cum %	cum %	cum %	cum %	cum %	cum %
(b) Intakes from *food sources*										
Less than 10	-	0	-	-	0	1	-	0	0	0
Less than 20	3	1	2	2	2	5	4	6	3	4
Less than 30	17	10	10	7	10	14	14	14	7	12
Less than 40	39	22	19	16	21	25	25	24	12	21
Less than 60	59	51	35	33	42	52	51	44	26	41
Less than 80	75	67	54	44	57	76	71	58	51	61
Less than 100	89	79	69	59	71	83	83	70	62	72
Less than 130	90	87	82	78	83	91	90	83	77	84
Less than 160	93	94	89	88	90	96	92	92	89	92
Less than 180	97	97	92	92	94	96	95	96	93	95
Less than 200	97	97	95	95	96	98	98	98	96	97
All	100	100	100	100	100	100	100	100	100	100
Base	*108*	*219*	*253*	*253*	*833*	*104*	*210*	*318*	*259*	*891*
Mean (average value)	64.9	74.1	88.4	94.5	83.4	67.9	72.3	80.0	94.5	81.0
Median	51.1	58.5	75.9	85.5	70.7	59.0	59.4	66.6	79.0	68.7
Lower 2.5 percentile	15.3	21.0	20.0	22.4	20.8	12.5	17.2	16.1	19.0	17.2
Upper 2.5 percentile	228.8	208.9	221.7	226.4	216.8	180.8	198.0	199.5	217.7	205.1
Standard deviation	52.02	48.88	57.32	53.99	54.45	42.22	47.48	49.64	52.19	49.93

Table 2.33

Average daily intake of vitamin C as a percentage of Reference Nutrient Intake (RNI) by sex and age of respondent

Percentages

Sex and age of respondent	Average daily intake as % of RNI*							
	(a) All sources			Base	(b) Food sources			Base
	Mean	Median	sd		Mean	Median	sd	
Men aged (years):								
19–24	168	128	137.7	108	162	128	130.0	108
25–34	209	157	164.9	219	185	146	122.2	219
35–49	269	194	520.7	253	221	190	143.3	253
50–64	313	231	355.7	253	236	215	135.0	253
All	253	186	364.0	833	209	177	136.1	833
Women aged (years):								
19–24	240	169	334.3	104	170	148	105.6	104
25–34	213	155	213.7	210	181	148	118.7	210
35–49	308	195	748.4	318	200	167	124.1	318
50–64	317	226	403.0	259	236	198	130.5	259
All	280	190	521.5	891	202	172	124.8	891

Note: * Intake as a percentage of RNI was calculated for each respondent. The values for all respondents in each age group were then pooled to give a mean, median and sd.

Table 2.34

Percentage contribution of food types to average daily intake of vitamin C by sex and age of respondent

Percentages

Type of food	Men aged (years):				All men	Women aged (years):				All women	All
	19–24	25–34	35–49	50–64		19–24	25–34	35–49	50–64		
	%	%	%	%	%	%	%	%	%	%	%
Cereals & cereal products	6	8	5	4	6	5	5	5	6	5	5
Milk & milk products	4	6	5	5	5	4	4	5	4	5	5
Eggs & egg dishes	0	0	0	0	0	0	0	0	0	0	0
Fat spreads	0	0	0	0	0	0	0	0	0	0	0
Meat & meat products	6	6	6	5	5	4	4	4	3	4	4
Fish & fish dishes	0	0	0	0	0	0	0	1	1	0	0
Vegetables (excluding potatoes)	12	19	20	26	21	14	23	25	25	23	22
of which:											
salad and other raw vegetables	4	6	7	8	7	5	8	9	8	8	7
leafy green vegetables	2	3	5	8	5	3	5	6	8	6	6
Potatoes and savoury snacks	24	19	15	15	17	20	14	14	12	14	15
of which:											
potato chips	13	8	6	5	7	9	6	4	3	5	6
Fruit & nuts	6	12	17	19	16	13	17	21	28	22	19
Sugars, preserves & confectionery	0	0	0	1	0	0	0	0	0	0	0
Drinks*	40	28	30	24	28	40	32	24	21	26	27
of which:											
fruit juice	24	17	22	19	20	24	21	17	16	18	19
soft drinks including low calorie	16	11	8	4	8	16	11	6	4	8	8
Miscellaneous**	1	1	1	1	1	0	1	1	1	1	1
Average daily intake (mg)	64.9	74.1	88.4	94.5	83.4	67.9	72.3	80.0	94.5	81.0	82.2
Total number of respondents	108	219	253	253	833	104	210	318	259	891	1724

Note: * Includes soft drinks, alcoholic drinks, tea, coffee and water.

** Includes powdered beverages (except tea and coffee), soups, sauces, condiments and artificial sweeteners.

Table 2.35

Average daily intake of vitamin D (μg) by sex and age of respondent

Cumulative percentages

Vitamin D (μg)	Men aged (years):				All men	Women aged (years):				All women
	19–24	25–34	35–49	50–64		19–24	25–34	35–49	50–64	
	cum %	cum %	cum %	cum %	cum %	cum %	cum %	cum %	cum %	cum %
(a) Intakes from *all sources*										
Less than 0.5	1	0	1	-	1	5	4	3	0	3
Less than 1.0	9	1	4	1	3	13	12	7	3	8
Less than 1.5	16	5	9	4	7	30	29	21	12	21
Less than 2.0	32	20	19	13	19	44	42	32	21	33
Less than 2.5	43	35	32	24	32	56	59	48	30	46
Less than 3.0	57	48	42	36	43	62	69	57	39	55
Less than 3.5	65	57	52	42	52	73	76	64	48	63
Less than 5.0	83	72	74	63	71	86	89	80	63	78
Less than 7.0	98	89	87	80	87	94	96	89	75	87
Less than 7.5	98	90	89	83	88	94	97	91	78	89
Less than 9.0	100	93	93	90	93	97	99	94	85	93
All		100	100	100	100	100	100	100	100	100
Base	*108*	*219*	*253*	*253*	*833*	*104*	*210*	*318*	*259*	*891*
Mean (average value)	3.0	4.1	4.2	4.9	4.2	2.9	2.7	3.5	5.1	3.7
Median	2.8	3.1	3.5	4.1	3.4	2.1	2.2	2.6	3.8	2.7
Lower 2.5 percentile	0.8	1.1	0.6	1.1	0.8	0.2	0.5	0.5	1.0	0.5
Upper 2.5 percentile	6.5	11.7	12.6	13.4	11.8	9.2	8.2	10.2	17.1	13.7
Standard deviation	1.59	3.19	3.08	3.25	3.06	2.47	1.96	2.89	4.11	3.23
	cum %	cum %	cum %	cum %	cum %	cum %	cum %	cum %	cum %	cum %
(b) Intakes from *food sources*										
Less than 0.5	1	1	2	-	1	5	4	3	0	3
Less than 1.0	9	2	4	1	3	17	13	8	4	9
Less than 1.5	18	6	9	5	8	39	33	23	14	25
Less than 2.0	32	22	21	15	21	56	47	38	27	39
Less than 2.5	45	37	35	26	34	67	65	56	42	55
Less than 3.0	59	51	44	41	47	73	74	68	55	66
Less than 3.5	68	65	54	47	56	83	81	75	65	75
Less than 5.0	89	82	79	72	79	96	92	91	83	89
Less than 7.0	98	95	91	89	92	99	98	96	93	96
Less than 7.5	98	95	93	92	94	99	99	97	94	97
Less than 9.0	100	97	97	96	97	99	99	98	96	98
All		100	100	100	100	100	100	100	100	100
Base	*108*	*219*	*253*	*253*	*833*	*104*	*210*	*318*	*259*	*891*
Mean (average value)	2.9	3.5	3.7	4.2	3.7	2.3	2.4	2.8	3.5	2.8
Median	2.8	3.0	3.3	3.7	3.1	1.8	2.1	2.3	2.8	2.3
Lower 2.5 percentile	0.8	1.1	0.6	1.1	0.8	0.2	0.5	0.5	1.0	0.5
Upper 2.5 percentile	6.5	9.3	9.4	9.7	9.2	5.9	6.5	7.6	11.4	8.4
Standard deviation	1.54	2.18	2.31	2.40	2.25	1.55	1.64	2.11	2.41	2.09

Table 2.36

Percentage contribution of food types to average daily intake of vitamin D by sex and age of respondent

Percentages

Type of food	Men aged (years):				All men	Women aged (years):				All women	All
	19–24	25–34	35–49	50–64		19–24	25–34	35–49	50–64		
	%	%	%	%	%	%	%	%	%	%	%
Cereals & cereal products	22	22	20	17	20	21	25	22	22	22	21
of which:											
whole grain & high fibre breakfast cereals	5	9	6	5	6	6	6	6	8	6	6
other breakfast cereals	9	6	7	5	6	10	10	7	7	8	7
buns, cakes & pastries	4	4	4	5	4	1	5	4	4	4	4
Milk & milk products	2	4	3	3	3	3	3	3	3	3	3
of which:											
whole milk	0	0	0	0	0	0	0	0	0	0	0
Eggs & egg dishes	11	10	9	10	10	10	8	9	9	9	9
Fat spreads	24	20	17	18	19	16	17	16	13	15	17
of which:											
soft margarine, not polyunsaturated	5	3	3	2	3	3	2	2	2	2	3
low fat spreads	4	6	4	6	5	3	7	5	4	5	5
reduced fat spreads	13	10	9	9	10	10	7	7	6	7	8
Meat & meat products	33	26	25	20	24	24	20	19	15	18	22
of which:											
bacon & ham	4	3	3	3	3	2	3	2	2	2	3
beef, veal & dishes	5	4	4	3	4	5	3	4	3	3	4
chicken, turkey & dishes including coated	6	5	5	3	5	5	6	4	3	4	4
burgers & kebabs	5	3	2	0	2	3	1	1	0	1	2
sausages	6	4	4	3	3	3	3	2	1	2	3
Fish & fish dishes	3	15	23	28	21	21	22	28	37	30	25
of which:											
oily fish	3	15	23	27	20	21	22	28	36	29	24
Vegetables (excluding potatoes)	0	0	0	0	0	1	1	1	0	1	1
Potatoes & savoury snacks	1	1	1	1	1	1	1	1	0	0	1
Fruit & nuts	0	0	0	0	0	0	0	0	0	0	0
Sugar, preserves & confectionery	0	0	0	0	0	0	0	0	0	0	0
Drinks*	3	1	1	1	1	3	1	1	0	1	1
Miscellaneous**	0	1	1	1	1	1	1	1	1	1	1
Average daily intake (μg)	2.9	3.5	3.7	4.2	3.7	2.3	2.4	2.8	3.5	2.8	3.3
Total number of respondents	108	219	253	253	833	104	210	318	259	891	1724

Note: * Includes soft drinks, alcoholic drinks, tea, coffee and water.

** Includes powdered beverages (except tea and coffee), soups, sauces, condiments and artificial sweeteners.

Table 2.37

Average daily intake of vitamin E (α-tocopherol equivalents) (mg) by sex and age of respondent

Cumulative percentages

Vitamin E (α-tocopherol equivalents) (mg)	Men aged (years):				All men	Women aged (years):				All women
	19–24	25–34	35–49	50–64		19–24	25–34	35–49	50–64	
	cum %	cum %	cum %	cum %	cum %	cum %	cum %	cum %	cum %	cum %
(a) Intakes from *all sources*										
Less than 3	1	-	1	1	1	2	3	2	3	3
Less than 4	1	1	3	4	2	12	10	6	5	7
Less than 5	5	3	6	7	5	19	17	13	16	15
Less than 6	10	7	12	13	11	29	26	22	22	24
Less than 7	22	18	16	20	19	46	41	36	33	37
Less than 8	37	31	24	26	28	59	55	48	43	49
Less than 9	54	39	34	34	38	69	65	54	51	58
Less than 10	60	47	45	43	47	76	75	64	61	67
Less than 12	77	67	62	58	64	86	85	75	67	77
Less than 15	88	81	82	75	80	89	93	84	79	85
Less than 18	93	88	91	83	88	91	95	88	85	89
Less than 22	99	95	96	93	95	95	99	92	89	93
All	100	100	100	100	100	100	100	100	100	100
Base	*108*	*219*	*253*	*253*	*833*	*104*	*210*	*318*	*259*	*891*
Mean (average value)	10.1	11.9	14.4	15.2	13.4	9.4	8.6	14.3	23.2	15.0
Median	8.7	10.5	10.6	11.1	10.5	7.6	7.6	8.4	8.8	8.0
Lower 2.5 percentile	4.5	4.9	4.0	3.6	4.1	3.0	2.7	3.1	3.0	3.0
Upper 2.5 percentile	20.3	30.6	29.4	35.0	29.4	24.6	20.7	38.0	285.2	42.6
Standard deviation	4.31	7.17	27.35	27.73	21.87	9.24	4.70	40.14	60.53	41.01
	cum %	cum %	cum %	cum %	cum %	cum %	cum %	cum %	cum %	cum %
(b) Intakes from *food sources*										
Less than 3	1	-	1	1	1	3	3	3	3	3
Less than 4	1	1	3	4	3	12	10	7	7	8
Less than 5	5	6	7	7	6	20	18	15	17	17
Less than 6	10	9	13	14	12	32	27	25	25	26
Less than 7	22	20	17	25	21	50	43	41	38	42
Less than 8	37	33	26	30	30	66	58	55	53	57
Less than 9	54	41	35	38	40	74	70	65	66	68
Less than 10	64	50	46	49	50	81	80	75	77	77
Less than 12	79	72	65	65	69	90	91	87	87	88
Less than 15	90	89	87	84	87	93	97	97	98	97
Less than 18	96	97	94	91	94	97	98	99	100	99
Less than 22	99	98	98	97	98	99	100	100		100
All	100	100	100	100	100	100				
Base	*108*	*219*	*253*	*253*	*833*	*104*	*210*	*318*	*259*	*891*
Mean (average value)	9.8	10.5	10.8	11.0	10.6	7.9	7.9	8.2	8.2	8.1
Median	8.7	10.0	10.4	11.0	10.0	7.0	7.5	7.7	7.8	7.6
Lower 2.5 percentile	4.5	4.3	4.0	3.6	4.0	2.5	2.7	2.6	3.0	2.8
Upper 2.5 percentile	18.5	19.9	20.8	24.0	21.8	19.6	15.8	15.5	15.2	15.6
Standard deviation	4.04	4.45	4.33	5.45	4.70	4.53	3.37	3.33	3.12	3.44

Table 2.38

Percentage contribution of food types to average daily intake of vitamin E (α-tocopherol equivalents) by sex and age of respondent

Percentages

Type of food	Men aged (years):				All men	Women aged (years):				All women	All
	19–24	25–34	35–49	50–64		19–24	25–34	35–49	50–64		
	%	%	%	%	%	%	%	%	%	%	%
Cereals & cereal products	16	18	17	17	17	16	15	17	19	17	17
of which:											
pizza	4	3	1	1	2	2	2	1	1	1	2
white bread	2	2	2	2	2	5	1	1	1	2	2
breakfast cereals	1	5	4	5	4	2	4	5	7	5	5
biscuits	2	2	2	2	2	1	2	2	2	2	2
buns, cakes & pastries	2	2	3	3	3	1	3	3	3	3	3
Milk & milk products	2	3	4	4	3	3	4	4	4	4	4
Eggs & egg dishes	4	4	3	4	4	3	2	3	3	3	3
Fat spreads	21	17	19	23	20	10	15	15	16	15	18
of which:											
polyunsaturated low fat spread	3	4	3	5	4	2	3	2	2	3	3
polyunsaturated reduced fat spread	10	6	9	11	9	2	7	6	8	6	8
other reduced fat spread	3	4	3	2	3	4	2	2	2	2	3
Meat & meat products	15	13	12	9	12	12	10	10	7	9	11
of which:											
beef, veal & dishes	2	2	2	2	2	3	2	2	1	2	2
chicken, turkey & dishes including coated	6	5	5	4	5	6	5	5	3	5	5
Fish & fish dishes	2	3	4	5	4	4	4	5	8	6	5
Vegetables (excluding potatoes)	7	10	13	13	12	9	17	16	15	15	13
Potatoes & savoury snacks	20	14	12	10	13	21	14	12	8	12	13
of which:											
potato chips	9	6	6	4	6	10	6	5	4	5	6
savoury snacks	7	5	4	2	4	7	6	4	2	4	4
Fruit & nuts	1	4	4	5	4	7	5	6	9	7	5
Sugar, preserves & confectionery	4	3	2	1	2	3	2	3	2	2	2
Drinks*	2	1	1	1	1	2	1	1	1	1	1
Miscellaneous**	7	9	7	6	7	10	9	9	7	9	8
Average daily intake (mg)	**9.8**	**10.5**	**10.8**	**11.0**	**10.6**	**7.9**	**7.9**	**8.2**	**8.2**	**8.1**	**9.3**
Total number of respondents	**108**	**219**	**253**	**253**	**833**	**104**	**210**	**318**	**259**	**891**	**1724**

Note: *   Includes soft drinks, alcoholic drinks, tea, coffee and water.

   ** Includes powdered beverages (except tea and coffee), soups, sauces, condiments and artificial sweeteners.

Table 2.39

Average daily intake of vitamins by sex of respondent and region

Vitamin (unit of measurement)	Sex of respondent and region											
	Men											
	Scotland			Northern			Central, South West and Wales			London and the the South East		
	Mean	Median	sd	Mean	Median	sd	Mean	Median	sd	Mean	Median	sd
All Sources												
Vitamin A (retinol equivalents) (µg)	1104	700	1618	1000	671	1069	1000	721	1024	1031	714	1227
Total carotene (β-carotene equivalents) (µg)	2128	1596	2041	1980	1642	1360	2125	1794	1664	2050	1749	1326
Thiamin (mg)	2.32	1.87	1.940	2.20	1.81	2.516	2.25	1.92	3.085	2.18	1.80	2.229
Riboflavin (mg)	2.35	2.32	1.349	2.30	2.00	2.237	2.45	2.03	3.678	2.21	2.03	0.998
Vitamin B$_6$ (mg)	3.6	3.0	2.91	3.3	2.8	3.91	3.4	2.8	4.63	3.1	2.6	3.31
Vitamin B$_{12}$ (µg)	7.7	6.3	8.52	6.6	5.3	4.50	6.9	5.7	6.59	6.5	5.5	5.43
Folate (µg)	367	345	138.7	347	320	191.4	365	339	161.3	363	340	187.3
Vitamin C (mg)	92.9	74.7	62.07	86.2	70.0	77.70	105.3	67.2	196.71	113.7	83.5	138.17
Vitamin D (µg)	4.4	3.8	2.66	4.1	3.3	2.75	4.4	3.5	3.34	4.1	3.3	3.10
Vitamin E (α-tocopherol equivalents) (mg)	12.8	10.4	8.57	13.1	9.2	25.55	13.6	10.7	23.19	13.5	10.9	18.70
Base		65			234			294			240	
Food sources												
Vitamin A (retinol equivalents) (µg)	1028	666	1598	897	627	993	883	674	960	927	647	1141
Total carotene (β-carotene equivalents) (µg)	2091	1596	2044	1972	1637	1349	2082	1794	1424	2045	1749	1319
Thiamin (mg)	2.10	1.85	1.808	2.00	1.77	1.691	1.94	1.86	0.829	2.06	1.76	2.196
Riboflavin (mg)	2.22	2.09	1.107	2.07	1.95	0.841	2.14	1.98	1.055	2.08	1.98	0.824
Vitamin B$_6$ (mg)	3.1	3.0	1.06	2.8	2.8	1.00	2.9	2.8	1.10	2.8	2.6	0.94
Vitamin B$_{12}$ (µg)	7.1	6.1	6.56	6.5	5.3	4.29	6.5	5.7	4.88	6.3	5.4	4.20
Folate (µg)	358	340	128.0	332	318	116.0	350	333	136.9	344	333	123.3
Vitamin C (mg)	86.4	74.3	54.11	77.1	67.8	54.49	79.4	64.0	47.78	93.8	79.6	60.59
Vitamin D (µg)	3.9	3.6	2.09	3.6	3.0	2.19	3.8	3.2	2.43	3.5	3.1	2.12
Vitamin E (α-tocopherol equivalents) (mg)	11.4	9.9	7.04	10.1	9.2	4.37	10.8	10.2	4.62	10.7	10.5	4.30
Base		65			234			294			240	

	Scotland			Northern			Central, South West and Wales			London and the South East			Vitamin (unit of measurement)
	Mean	Median	sd	Mean	Median	sd	Mean	Median	sd	Mean	Median	sd	
Women													
All Sources													
	708	585	508	841	568	932	745	570	643	853	675	669	Vitamin A (retinol equivalents) (µg)
	1818	1525	1076	1778	1416	1334	1908	1521	1744	2229	1899	1673	Total carotene (β-carotene equivalents) (µg)
	1.51	1.34	0.760	1.71	1.47	1.225	2.20	1.48	6.921	1.94	1.47	4.667	Thiamin (mg)
	1.67	1.56	0.732	1.83	1.66	1.160	2.25	1.66	6.884	1.97	1.57	4.390	Riboflavin (mg)
	2.2	2.1	1.04	3.2	2.0	8.98	3.1	2.1	8.77	2.7	2.1	5.16	Vitamin B$_6$ (mg)
	4.8	4.1	2.32	5.2	4.5	3.51	5.1	4.3	6.24	5.3	4.7	3.18	Vitamin B$_{12}$ (µg)
	249	229	89.2	267	255	120.5	282	254	238.9	336	260	873.1	Folate (µg)
	104.1	82.5	85.94	101.5	69.0	162.65	125.4	75.2	300.07	106.5	80.4	100.94	Vitamin C (mg)
	3.1	2.4	2.28	3.6	2.6	2.98	3.3	2.5	2.57	4.4	3.1	4.12	Vitamin D (µg)
	16.0	7.4	44.51	15.6	7.7	50.62	13.8	7.9	35.62	15.5	9.1	37.12	Vitamin E (α-tocopherol equivalents) (mg)
		66			229			327			268		*Base*
Food sources													
	616	542	478	699	516	864	624	528	500	718	603	574	Vitamin A (retinol equivalents) (µg)
	1818	1525	1076	1741	1403	1240	1815	1478	1274	2206	1892	1657	Total carotene (β-carotene equivalents) (µg)
	1.41	1.24	0.651	1.51	1.42	0.730	1.58	1.40	1.233	1.56	1.41	0.976	Thiamin (mg)
	1.55	1.45	0.625	1.64	1.59	0.684	1.61	1.53	0.622	1.58	1.51	0.623	Riboflavin (mg)
	2.0	2.0	0.60	2.0	2.0	0.73	2.0	2.0	0.63	2.1	2.0	0.73	Vitamin B$_6$ (mg)
	4.7	4.0	2.24	4.9	4.3	3.22	4.5	4.1	2.15	5.0	4.5	2.88	Vitamin B$_{12}$ (µg)
	232	229	72.3	249	251	95.0	252	245	87.0	256	250	92.6	Folate (µg)
	87.8	79.7	49.12	77.5	65.6	50.53	77.6	65.6	46.15	86.3	73.0	53.56	Vitamin C (mg)
	2.4	2.1	1.34	2.8	2.3	1.95	2.6	2.2	1.47	3.3	2.6	2.81	Vitamin D (µg)
	7.7	7.0	3.22	7.7	7.4	3.31	7.9	7.5	3.45	8.7	8.0	3.53	Vitamin E (α-tocopherol equivalents) (mg)
		66			229			327			268		*Base*

Table 2.40

Average daily intake of vitamins as a percentage of the Reference Nutrient Intake (RNI) and proportion of respondents with intakes below the Lower Reference Nutrient Intake (LRNI) by sex of respondent and region

Vitamin (unit of measurement)	Sex of respondent and region							
	Men				Women			
	Scotland*	Northern	Central, South West and Wales	London and the South East	Scotland*	Northern	Central, South West and Wales	London and the South East
All sources								
Vitamin A (µg)								
mean daily intake as % RNI	158	143	143	147	118	140	124	142
% with intakes below LRNI	4	7	5	6	3	9	10	5
Thiamin (mg)**								
mean daily intake as % RNI					189	213	275	243
19 to 50 years	220	228	212	210				
over 50 years	[21]	218	286	262				
% with intakes below LRNI					-	2	1	0
19 to 50 years	-	1	-	1				
over 50 years	[-]	-	1	1				
Riboflavin (mg)								
mean daily intake as % RNI	181	177	189	170	152	167	205	180
% with intakes below LRNI	-	3	2	4	12	9	6	7
Niacin equivalents (mg)**								
mean daily intake as % RNI								
19 to 50 years	275	276	278	268	257	265	266	273
over 50 years	[21]	279	287	284	[16]	285	297	288
% with intakes below LRNI								
19 to 50 years	-	0	-	-	-	1	0	1
over 50 years	[-]	-	-	1	[-]	-	-	1
Vitamin B$_6$ (mg)								
mean daily intake as % RNI	259	235	243	219	181	270	258	225
% with intakes below LRNI	2	0	1	1	-	4	1	2
Vitamin B$_{12}$ (µg)								
mean daily intake as % RNI	510	438	460	434	317	344	340	350
% with intakes below LRNI	-	-	-	1	-	1	-	1
Folate (µg)								
mean daily intake as % RNI	184	173	182	181	124	133	141	168
% with intakes below LRNI	-	0	0	1	2	3	2	2
Vitamin C (mg)								
mean daily intake as % RNI	232	215	263	284	260	254	314	266
% with intakes below LRNI	-	-	0	-	1	1	-	0

Table 2.40 continued

Average daily intake of vitamins as a percentage of the Reference Nutrient Intake (RNI) and proportion of respondents with intakes below the Lower Reference Nutrient Intake (LRNI) by sex of respondent and region

Vitamin (unit of measurement)	Sex of respondent and region							
	Men				Women			
	Scotland*	Northern	Central, South West and Wales	London and the South East	Scotland*	Northern	Central, South West and Wales	London and the South East
Food sources								
Vitamin A (µg)								
mean daily intake as % RNI	147	128	126	132	103	117	104	120
% with intakes below LRNI	7	7	6	7	7	10	11	6
Thiamin (mg)**								
mean daily intake as % RNI					189	213	275	243
19 to 50 years	220	228	212	210				
over 50 years	[21]	218	286	262				
% with intakes below LRNI					-	2	1	0
19 to 50 years	-	1	-	1				
over 50 years	[-]	-	1	1				
Riboflavin (mg)								
mean daily intake as % RNI	170	159	165	160	141	149	147	143
% with intakes below LRNI	-	3	2	4	13	9	6	8
Niacin equivalents (mg)**								
mean daily intake as % RNI								
19 to 50 years	267	264	268	259	253	254	250	258
over 50 years	[21]	272	271	277	[16]	264	273	267
% with intakes below LRNI								
19 to 50 years	-	0	-	0	-	1	0	1
over 50 years	[-]	-	-	1	[-]	-	-	1
Vitamin B$_6$ (mg)								
mean daily intake as % RNI	220	203	205	198	165	168	168	171
% with intakes below LRNI	2	0	1	1	-	4	1	2
Vitamin B$_{12}$ (µg)								
mean daily intake as % RNI	476	430	432	418	311	328	303	333
% with intakes below LRNI	-	-	-	1	-	1	0	1
Folate (µg)								
mean daily intake as % RNI	179	166	175	172	116	125	126	128
% with intakes below LRNI	-	0	0	1	2	3	2	2
Vitamin C (mg)								
mean daily intake as % RNI	216	193	198	235	219	194	194	216
% with intakes below LRNI	-	-	0	-	1	1	-	0
Base – respondents aged 19 to 50 years	44	178	209	173	50	158	245	196
Base – respondents aged over 50 years	21	56	84	67	16	71	83	73

Note: * Square brackets enclosing numbers denote the actual number of cases, when the base is fewer than 30. The number of men and women aged over 50 years living in Scotland is less than 30 and mean values and percentages are not, therefore, presented for niacin equivalents or for men, thiamin.

** For niacin equivalents, and thiamin for men, RNI and LRNI values are different for 19 to 50 year olds and over 50 year olds, so data for these vitamins are presented separately by age.

Table 2.41

Average daily intake of vitamins by sex of respondent and whether someone in the respondent's household was receiving certain benefits

Vitamin (unit of measurement)	Whether receiving benefits											
	Men						Women					
	Receiving benefits			Not receiving benefits			Receiving benefits			Not receiving benefits		
	Mean	Median	sd	Mean	Median	sd	Mean	Median	sd	Mean	Median	sd
All sources												
Vitamin A (retinol equivalents) (μg)	829	558	994	1046	727	1171	585	435	469	843	636	764
Total carotene												
(β-carotene equivalents) (μg)	1770	1451	1345	2107	1774	1546	1417	1089	1348	2075	1768	1614
Thiamin (mg)	1.83	1.69	2.410	2.28	1.90	2.642	1.84	1.23	6.069	1.97	1.51	4.706
Riboflavin (mg)	1.95	1.62	2.462	2.39	2.05	2.580	1.88	1.31	5.980	2.05	1.67	4.600
Vitamin B_6 (mg)	3.1	2.2	5.76	3.3	2.9	3.61	2.7	1.7	7.17	3.0	2.1	7.64
Vitamin B_{12} (μg)	5.5	5.1	2.91	6.9	5.8	6.24	4.4	3.8	2.99	5.3	4.6	4.82
Folate (μg)	291	266	132.7	370	341	179.7	249	207	329.6	300	262	533.6
Vitamin C (mg)	64.9	49.2	46.35	106.9	76.8	154.48	66.6	48.4	53.12	121.2	79.9	226.39
Vitamin D (μg)	3.5	2.6	2.76	4.3	3.5	3.09	2.7	2.1	2.28	3.9	2.9	3.35
Vitamin E												
(α-tocopherol equivalents) (mg)	10.6	8.4	15.65	13.8	10.8	22.64	10.3	6.9	38.62	15.9	8.4	41.44
Base		*110*			*723*			*150*			*741*	
Food sources												
Vitamin A (retinol equivalents) (μg)	777	543	939	931	670	1102	506	404	409	704	567	664
Total carotene												
(β-carotene equivalents) (μg)	1755	1451	1320	2084	1774	1443	1406	1089	1342	2017	1743	1380
Thiamin (mg)	1.62	1.66	0.655	2.06	1.83	1.732	1.34	1.21	1.117	1.58	1.43	0.979
Riboflavin (mg)	1.73	1.62	0.758	2.17	2.02	0.951	1.40	1.30	0.650	1.64	1.58	0.629
Vitamin B_6 (mg)	2.4	2.2	1.03	2.9	2.8	1.01	1.8	1.7	0.70	2.1	2.1	0.67
Vitamin B_{12} (μg)	5.4	5.1	2.88	6.6	5.6	4.88	4.1	3.8	2.53	4.9	4.4	2.71
Folate (μg)	285	265	122.1	353	333	125.1	220	204	96.2	257	252	87.4
Vitamin C (mg)	62.7	48.7	44.27	86.6	73.5	55.18	60.4	44.9	43.83	85.1	73.3	50.09
Vitamin D (μg)	3.2	2.6	2.22	3.8	3.2	2.25	2.2	1.9	1.45	3.0	2.4	2.18
Vitamin E												
(α-tocopherol equivalents) (mg)	9.2	8.4	4.33	10.9	10.2	4.72	7.0	6.7	3.86	8.3	7.8	3.31
Base		*110*			*723*			*150*			*741*	

Table 2.42

Average daily intake of vitamins as a percentage of the Reference Nutrient Intake (RNI) and proportion of respondents with intakes below the Lower Reference Nutrient Intake (LRNI) by sex of respondent and whether someone in the respondent's household was receiving certain benefits

Vitamin (unit of measurement)	Whether receiving benefits			
	Men		Women	
	Receiving benefits*	Not receiving benefits	Receiving benefits*	Not receiving benefits
All sources				
Vitamin A (µg)				
mean daily intake as % RNI	118	149	97	141
% with intakes below LRNI	12	5	20	5
Thiamin (mg)**				
mean daily intake as % RNI			230	246
19 to 50 years	181	223		
over 50 years	[23]	268		
% with intakes below LRNI			6	1
19 to 50 years	1	1		
over 50 years	[1]	-		
Riboflavin (mg)				
mean daily intake as % RNI	150	184	171	186
% with intakes below LRNI	7	2	18	5
Niacin equivalents (mg)**				
mean daily intake as % RNI				
19 to 50 years	225	283	237	274
over 50 years	[23]	291	[25]	294
% with intakes below LRNI				
19 to 50 years	-	0	1	1
over 50 years	[1]	-	[-]	0
Vitamin B$_6$ (mg)				
mean daily intake as % RNI	224	237	221	250
% with intakes below LRNI	3	0	6	1
Vitamin B$_{12}$ (µg)				
mean daily intake as % RNI	363	463	292	353
% with intakes below LRNI	1	0	2	0
Folate (µg)				
mean daily intake as % RNI	146	185	125	150
% with intakes below LRNI	1	0	6	1
Vitamin C (mg)				
mean daily intake as % RNI	162	267	166	303
% with intakes below LRNI	1	-	1	0

Table 2.42 continued

Average daily intake of vitamins as a percentage of the Reference Nutrient Intake (RNI) and proportion of respondents with intakes below the Lower Reference Nutrient Intake (LRNI) by sex of respondent and whether someone in the respondent's household was receiving certain benefits

Vitamin (unit of measurement)	Whether receiving benefits			
	Men		Women	
	Receiving benefits*	Not receiving benefits	Receiving benefits*	Not receiving benefits
Food sources				
Vitamin A (µg)				
mean daily intake as % RNI	111	133	84	117
% with intakes below LRNI	13	6	22	6
Thiamin (mg)**				
mean daily intake as % RNI			230	246
19 to 50 years	181	223		
over 50 years	[23]	268		
% with intakes below LRNI			6	1
19 to 50 years	1	1		
over 50 years	[1]	-		
Riboflavin (mg)				
mean daily intake as % RNI	133	167	127	149
% with intakes below LRNI	8	2	19	5
Niacin equivalents (mg)**				
mean daily intake as % RNI				
19 to 50 years	222	272	227	260
over 50 years	[23]	281	[25]	272
% with intakes below LRNI				
19 to 50 years	0	0	1	1
over 50 years	[1]	-	[-]	0
Vitamin B$_6$ (mg)				
mean daily intake as % RNI	170	209	147	173
% with intakes below LRNI	2	0	6	1
Vitamin B$_{12}$ (µg)				
mean daily intake as % RNI	359	442	276	328
% with intakes below LRNI	1	0	3	1
Folate (µg)				
mean daily intake as % RNI	142	176	110	129
% with intakes below LRNI	1	0	6	1
Vitamin C (mg)				
mean daily intake as % RNI	157	216	151	213
% with intakes below LRNI	1	-	1	0
Base – respondents aged 19 to 50 years	*87*	*23*	*125*	*523*
Base – respondents aged over 50 years	*518*	*206*	*25*	*218*

Note: * Square brackets enclosing numbers denote the actual number of cases, when the base is fewer than 30. The number of men and women aged over 50 years living in benefit
        households is less than 30 and mean values and percentages are not, therefore, presented for niacin equivalents or for men, thiamin.

     ** For niacin equivalents, and thiamin for men, RNI and LRNI values are different for 19 to 50 year olds and over 50 year olds, so data for these vitamins are presented separately by age.

Table 2.43(a)

Comparison of average daily vitamin intakes from food sources by respondents in two surveys: 1986/87 Adults Survey; 2000/01 NDNS Adults aged 19 to 64 years (present survey): men

Vitamin (unit of measurement)	Men aged (years):									
	1986/87 Adults survey*				All men	2000/01 NDNS				All men
	16–24	25–34	35–49	50–64		19–24	25–34	35–49	50–64	
Vitamin A (retinol equivalents) (µg)										
mean	1164	1552	1759	1897	1628	560	724	989	1145	911
median	786	965	1084	1132	1012	489	585	670	789	660
se/sd**	86	127	99	119	56	351	525	1353	1269	1083
Pre-formed retinol (µg)										
mean	848	1184	1333	1425	1226	315	424	643	735	571
median	487	584	633	670	602	252	297	350	380	327
se/sd**	82	119	96	114	53	296	435	1327	1221	1034
Thiamin (mg)										
mean	1.72	1.66	1.71	1.70	1.70	1.60	2.08	2.04	2.07	2.00
median	1.68	1.57	1.65	1.69	1.65	1.67	1.69	1.89	1.89	1.78
se/sd**	0.04	0.03	0.03	0.03	0.02	0.555	2.263	1.620	1.263	1.638
Riboflavin (mg)										
mean	1.96	2.08	2.14	2.11	2.08	1.68	2.12	2.19	2.20	2.11
median	1.91	1.95	2.03	2.08	2.00	1.56	1.91	2.07	2.06	1.98
se/sd**	0.05	0.04	0.04	0.04	0.02	0.780	1.097	0.894	0.847	0.939
Niacin equivalents (mg)										
mean	39.0	40.2	40.5	39.5	39.9	39.4	46.2	45.9	44.6	44.7
median	38.3	39.8	39.7	38.9	39.2	37.9	44.5	46.2	44.2	44.2
se/sd**	0.77	0.67	0.58	0.62	0.33	11.46	18.17	13.40	13.43	14.73
Vitamin B$_6$ (mg)										
mean	2.6	2.5	2.5	2.3	2.5	2.6	3.0	2.9	2.8	2.9
median	2.5	2.5	2.4	2.2	2.4	2.7	2.7	2.7	2.8	2.7
se/sd**	0.07	0.05	0.05	0.05	0.03	0.94	1.16	1.00	0.95	1.03
Vitamin B$_{12}$ (µg)										
mean	6.2	7.1	7.6	7.8	7.2	4.4	5.9	7.0	7.3	6.5
median	5.1	5.7	5.9	5.9	5.7	4.3	5.1	5.9	6.2	5.5
se/sd**	0.29	0.34	0.31	0.35	0.17	1.62	3.42	5.42	5.40	4.69
Folate (µg)										
mean	302	317	321	300	311	301	346	343	361	344
median	285	303	308	289	300	275	326	327	349	327
se/sd**	7.6	6.4	5.6	5.7	3.1	108.4	128.1	118.5	137.0	126.8
Pantothenic acid (mg)										
mean	6.3	6.4	6.4	6.1	6.3	5.9	7.1	7.5	7.5	7.2
median	6.0	6.1	6.2	5.8	6.1	5.6	6.6	7.2	7.4	6.9
se/sd**	0.17	0.15	0.10	0.10	0.06	2.14	3.45	2.59	2.57	2.83
Biotin (µg)										
mean	35	40	41	39	39	30	41	44	43	41
median	34	39	39	37	38	28	39	43	42	40
se/sd**	1.0	1.1	0.8	0.8	0.4	11.9	18.2	16.4	17.6	17.3
Vitamin C (mg)										
mean	64.9	69.7	65.0	66.5	66.5	64.9	74.1	88.4	94.5	83.4
median	52.6	59.3	58.3	60.2	57.6	51.1	58.5	75.9	85.5	70.7
se/sd**	3.26	2.64	1.97	2.04	1.20	52.02	48.88	57.32	53.99	54.45
Vitamin D (µg)										
mean	2.8	3.2	3.7	3.8	3.4	2.9	3.5	3.7	4.2	3.7
median	2.4	2.6	3.2	3.2	2.9	2.8	3.0	3.3	3.7	3.1
se/sd**	0.14	0.15	0.14	0.17	0.08	1.54	2.18	2.31	2.40	2.25
Vitamin E (α–tocopherol equivalents) (mg)										
mean	9.7	10.2	10.4	9.2	9.9	9.8	10.5	10.8	11.0	10.6
median	9.2	9.6	9.4	8.8	9.3	8.7	10.0	10.4	11.0	10.0
se/sd**	0.26	0.26	0.31	0.25	0.14	4.04	4.45	4.33	5.45	4.70
Base – number of respondents	*214*	*254*	*346*	*273*	*1087*	*108*	*219*	*253*	*253*	*833*

Note: * Gregory J, Foster K, Tyler H, Wiseman M. The Dietary and Nutritional Survey of British Adults. HMSO (London, 1990).

  ** 1986/87 survey reported standard errors; present survey reports standard deviations.

Table 2.43(b)

Comparison of average daily vitamin intakes from food sources by respondents in two surveys: 1986/87 Adults Survey; 2000/01 NDNS Adults aged 19 to 64 years (present survey): women

Vitamin (unit of measurement)	Women aged (years):									
	1986/87 Adults survey*				All women	2000/01 NDNS				All women
	16–24	25–34	35–49	50–64		19–24	25–34	35–49	50–64	
Vitamin A (retinol equivalents) (µg)										
mean	1051	1234	1531	1655	1413	467	587	675	816	671
median	633	719	884	951	810	393	510	571	635	549
se/sd**	99	102	86	101	49	347	692	507	766	633
Pre–formed retinol (µg)										
mean	788	906	1140	1263	1058	251	302	339	449	352
median	389	438	481	516	463	187	230	248	267	241
se/sd**	98	98	83	99	48	323	654	445	726	584
Thiamin (mg)										
mean	1.26	1.21	1.25	1.25	1.24	1.45	1.55	1.52	1.60	1.54
median	1.23	1.18	1.24	1.23	1.22	1.25	1.32	1.47	1.44	1.40
se/sd**	0.03	0.03	0.02	0.02	0.01	0.781	1.288	0.970	0.864	1.007
Riboflavin (mg)										
mean	1.45	1.50	1.64	1.63	1.57	1.39	1.44	1.66	1.75	1.60
median	1.33	1.41	1.54	1.59	1.50	1.25	1.35	1.60	1.68	1.54
se/sd**	0.04	0.04	0.03	0.03	0.02	0.636	0.546	0.614	0.688	0.638
Niacin equivalents (mg)										
mean	27.3	27.7	29.5	28.7	28.5	29.5	28.8	31.5	32.3	30.9
median	27.1	27.3	28.9	28.3	28.1	29.3	27.9	31.1	31.9	30.4
se/sd**	0.54	0.49	0.42	0.48	0.24	9.61	9.16	9.09	8.85	9.20
Vitamin B_6 (mg)										
mean	1.6	1.5	1.6	1.5	1.6	2.0	1.9	2.0	2.1	2.0
median	1.6	1.5	1.6	1.5	1.5	1.9	1.9	2.0	2.1	2.0
se/sd**	0.04	0.03	0.03	0.03	0.02	0.73	0.64	0.66	0.73	0.69
Vitamin B_{12} (µg)										
mean	4.4	4.5	5.6	5.8	5.2	4.0	4.0	4.9	5.7	4.8
median	3.4	3.5	4.1	4.3	3.9	3.7	3.4	4.5	5.1	4.3
se/sd**	0.28	0.25	0.24	0.28	0.13	2.00	2.17	2.50	3.22	2.69
Folate (µg)										
mean	198	206	220	218	213	229	233	255	268	251
median	194	198	212	214	208	225	229	251	267	245
se/sd**	4.7	4.4	3.7	3.9	2.1	91.6	80.6	87.3	95.7	89.9
Pantothenic acid (mg)										
mean	4.4	4.5	4.7	4.4	4.5	4.8	4.9	5.6	5.9	5.4
median	4.3	4.5	4.5	4.3	4.4	4.7	4.8	5.5	5.7	5.2
se/sd**	0.10	0.09	0.08	0.08	0.04	1.78	1.71	1.83	2.00	1.89
Biotin (µg)										
mean	24	27	31	29	28	24	26	30	32	29
median	24	25	29	27	26	23	25	29	31	28
se/sd**	0.7	0.7	0.9	0.7	0.4	10.1	8.8	11.0	11.5	11.0
Vitamin C (mg)										
mean	60.4	55.9	62.7	67.6	62.0	67.9	72.3	80.0	94.4	81.0
median	48.8	48.5	54.8	58.8	52.6	59.0	59.4	66.6	79.0	68.7
se/sd**	3.27	2.08	1.96	2.42	1.18	42.22	47.48	49.64	52.19	49.93
Vitamin D (µg)										
mean	2.1	2.3	2.6	2.8	2.5	2.3	2.4	2.8	3.5	2.8
median	1.9	2.1	2.2	2.3	2.2	1.8	2.1	2.3	2.8	2.3
se/sd**	0.09	0.10	0.09	0.12	0.05	1.55	1.64	2.11	2.41	2.09
Vitamin E (α–tocopherol equivalents) (mg)										
mean	6.8	7.3	7.6	7.0	7.2	7.9	7.9	8.2	8.2	8.1
median	6.1	7.0	7.0	6.6	6.7	7.0	7.5	7.7	7.8	7.6
se/sd**	0.22	0.22	0.17	0.18	0.10	4.53	3.37	3.33	3.12	3.44
Base – number of respondents	189	253	385	283	1110	104	210	318	259	891

Note: * Gregory J, Foster K, Tyler H, Wiseman M. The Dietary and Nutritional Survey of British Adults. HMSO (London, 1990).

** 1986/87 survey reported standard errors; present survey reports standard deviations.

Table 2.44(a)

Comparison of average daily vitamin intakes from all sources by respondents in two surveys: 1986/87 Adults Survey; 2000/01 NDNS Adults aged 19 to 64 years (present survey): men

Vitamin (unit of measurement)	Men aged (years):									
	1986/87 Adults survey*				All men	2000/01 NDNS				All men
	16–24	25–34	35–49	50–64		19–24	25–34	35–49	50–64	
Vitamin A (retinol equivalents) (µg)										
mean	1192	1585	1834	1953	1679	579	852	1069	1296	1017
median	805	995	1118	1144	1033	489	643	715	865	697
se/sd**	86	127	102	122	57	361	711	1380	1339	1151
Pre–formed retinol (µg)										
mean	877	1216	1408	1481	1277	334	551	721	877	673
median	494	600	647	683	618	280	332	367	444	363
se/sd**	82	120	99	117	54	305	647	1350	1278	1095
Total carotene (µg)										
mean	1893	2211	2555	2833	2414	1470	1806	2088	2514	2063
median	1229	1676	1999	2360	1895	1392	1474	1853	1936	1716
se/sd**	118	122	102	132	60	970	1258	1276	1965	1524
Thiamin (mg)										
mean	1.93	2.28	1.95	1.87	2.01	1.62	2.32	2.26	2.35	2.22
median	1.72	1.62	1.65	1.69	1.67	1.67	1.78	1.92	1.96	1.86
se/sd**	0.13	0.57	0.18	0.15	0.15	0.570	2.624	2.551	3.132	2.615
Riboflavin (mg)										
mean	2.18	2.43	2.24	2.33	2.29	1.71	2.40	2.35	2.51	2.33
median	1.93	2.00	2.05	2.08	2.03	1.56	2.03	2.11	2.16	2.02
se/sd**	0.14	0.29	0.05	0.19	0.09	0.803	2.216	1.838	3.698	2.568
Niacin equivalents (mg)										
mean	40.0	41.0	42.0	39.9	40.9	39.7	49.2	47.0	46.2	46.4
median	38.7	40.1	40.0	38.9	39.6	39.8	45.0	46.5	44.7	44.5
se/sd**	0.93	0.76	0.99	0.68	0.44	11.73	29.50	15.76	14.54	19.83
Vitamin B_6 (mg)										
mean	2.8	2.9	2.6	2.5	2.7	2.7	3.3	3.5	3.4	3.3
median	2.5	2.5	2.4	2.2	2.4	2.7	2.8	2.8	2.8	2.8
se/sd**	0.14	0.30	0.06	0.16	0.09	0.96	2.23	5.05	4.62	3.96
Vitamin B_{12} (µg)										
mean	6.3	7.1	7.7	8.0	7.3	4.5	6.2	7.4	7.6	6.8
median	5.1	5.7	6.0	5.9	5.7	4.3	5.2	6.0	6.4	5.6
se/sd**	0.29	0.34	0.31	0.41	0.17	1.67	4.26	7.25	6.55	5.93
Folate (µg)										
mean	302	319	322	301	312	305	376	355	373	359
median	285	303	310	289	300	275	341	330	354	333
se/sd**	7.6	6.7	5.7	5.9	3.2	113.7	223.6	171.2	150.8	176.2
Pantothenic acid (mg)										
mean	6.5	6.9	6.6	6.3	6.6	6.0	7.9	8.1	8.2	7.8
median	6.1	6.1	6.2	5.8	6.1	5.6	6.7	7.2	7.6	7.1
se/sd**	0.25	0.45	0.13	0.22	0.14	2.31	7.14	5.61	4.56	5.51
Biotin (µg)										
mean	35	40	41	39	39	31	45	47	46	44
median	34	39	40	37	38	29	40	43	42	41
se/sd**	1.1	1.1	0.8	0.8	0.5	12.3	27.4	38.5	24.8	29.6
Vitamin C (mg)										
mean	70.9	79.8	77.9	68.5	74.6	67.2	83.7	107.7	125.0	101.4
median	53.1	60.5	59.0	60.2	58.5	51.1	62.8	77.5	92.3	74.2
se/sd**	4.45	5.94	5.38	2.42	2.45	55.09	65.97	208.27	142.30	145.60
Vitamin D (µg)										
mean	3.0	3.4	4.2	4.2	3.8	3.0	4.1	4.2	4.9	4.2
median	2.5	2.7	3.4	3.3	3.0	2.8	3.1	3.5	4.1	3.4
se/sd**	0.17	0.16	0.20	0.23	0.10	1.59	3.19	3.08	3.25	3.06
Vitamin E (α–tocopherol equivalents) (mg)										
mean	10.7	13.0	12.2	10.6	11.7	10.1	11.9	14.4	15.2	13.4
median	9.2	9.6	9.4	8.9	9.3	8.7	10.5	10.6	11.1	10.5
se/sd**	0.91	2.42	1.17	0.90	0.74	4.31	7.17	27.35	27.73	21.87
Base – number of respondents	*214*	*254*	*346*	*273*	*1087*	*108*	*219*	*253*	*253*	*833*

Note: * Gregory J, Foster K, Tyler H, Wiseman M. The Dietary and Nutritional Survey of British Adults. HMSO (London, 1990).

   ** 1986/87 survey reported standard errors; present survey reports standard deviations.

Table 2.44(b)

Comparison of average daily vitamin intakes from all sources by respondents in two surveys: 1986/87 Adults Survey; 2000/01 NDNS Adults aged 19 to 64 years (present survey): women

Vitamin (unit of measurement)	Women aged (years):									
	1986/87 Adults survey*				All women	2000/01 NDNS				All women
	16–24	25–34	35–49	50–64		19–24	25–34	35–49	50–64	
Vitamin A (retinol equivalents) (µg)										
mean	1091	1273	1606	1784	1488	590	634	803	1015	800
median	658	738	926	1024	849	418	534	624	754	606
se/sd**	99	102	88	104	50	595	718	629	838	729
Pre–formed retinol (µg)										
mean	829	945	1215	1391	1133	341	341	462	645	472
median	401	456	519	562	491	201	257	285	331	277
se/sd**	98	98	85	102	48	402	668	541	800	654
Total carotene (µg)										
mean	1576	1965	2344	2353	2129	1498	1754	2047	2222	1964
median	1179	1567	1934	1848	1696	1054	1428	1753	2019	1608
se/sd**	102	105	98	119	55	1936	1357	1710	1395	1591
Thiamin (mg)										
mean	1.46	1.32	1.56	2.05	1.61	1.58	1.62	1.97	2.33	1.94
median	1.26	1.21	1.29	1.27	1.26	1.29	1.36	1.52	1.62	1.46
se/sd**	0.16	0.04	0.12	0.54	0.15	0.961	1.344	5.688	6.560	4.958
Riboflavin (mg)										
mean	1.53	1.67	1.98	2.00	1.84	1.53	1.52	2.13	2.48	2.02
median	1.37	1.47	1.61	1.63	1.56	1.31	1.41	1.69	1.85	1.62
se/sd**	0.05	0.10	0.14	0.11	0.06	0.806	0.636	5.486	6.585	4.856
Niacin equivalents (mg)										
mean	28.4	28.5	30.9	32.2	30.3	31.1	29.3	33.7	35.1	32.8
median	27.3	27.7	29.8	28.8	28.6	32.1	28.8	32.8	33.9	32.1
se/sd**	0.85	0.54	0.53	2.24	0.63	10.49	9.48	12.22	12.35	11.67
Vitamin B$_6$ (mg)										
mean	1.7	2.9	3.5	2.7	2.8	2.1	2.3	3.4	3.3	2.9
median	1.6	1.6	1.6	1.5	1.6	2.0	1.9	2.1	2.2	2.1
se/sd**	0.05	0.60	0.62	0.42	0.28	0.92	3.20	9.80	8.34	7.56
Vitamin B$_{12}$ (µg)										
mean	4.4	4.6	5.9	5.9	5.4	4.1	4.0	5.5	6.1	5.1
median	3.4	3.5	4.1	4.4	3.9	3.7	3.6	4.6	5.4	4.4
se/sd**	0.28	0.25	0.27	0.28	0.14	2.09	2.17	6.43	3.66	4.57
Folate (µg)										
mean	217	208	224	222	219	248	249	280	359	292
median	198	198	213	214	209	232	233	258	275	255
se/sd**	17.0	4.6	4.1	4.2	3.6	109.2	113.2	123.4	916.9	505.2
Pantothenic acid (mg)										
mean	4.4	4.7	5.3	5.6	5.1	5.2	5.1	6.4	7.9	6.4
median	4.3	4.6	4.6	4.4	4.5	4.7	4.9	5.7	6.0	5.4
se/sd**	0.10	0.15	0.25	0.69	0.20	2.35	2.04	5.76	14.59	8.73
Biotin (µg)										
mean	24	27	32	29	29	27	28	34	37	33
median	24	25	29	27	26	23	25	30	32	28
se/sd**	0.7	0.7	1.0	0.8	0.4	22.7	22.1	25.5	41.3	30.3
Vitamin C (mg)										
mean	61.5	66.0	81.8	75.5	73.1	96.1	85.1	123.1	126.7	112.0
median	49.2	50.0	56.8	62.0	54.1	68.6	62.0	77.9	90.2	76.1
se/sd**	3.34	6.71	6.42	3.59	2.91	133.71	85.49	299.37	161.22	208.58
Vitamin D (µg)										
mean	2.4	2.6	3.2	3.8	3.1	2.9	2.7	3.5	5.1	3.7
median	1.9	2.1	2.3	2.6	2.3	2.1	2.2	2.6	3.8	2.7
se/sd**	0.16	0.14	0.16	0.22	0.09	2.47	1.96	2.89	4.11	3.23
Vitamin E (α–tocopherol equivalents) (mg)										
mean	7.0	8.1	8.5	10.2	8.6	9.4	8.6	14.3	23.2	15.0
median	6.1	7.0	7.1	6.8	6.8	7.6	7.6	8.4	8.8	8.0
se/sd**	0.24	0.51	0.48	1.16	0.36	9.24	4.70	40.14	60.53	41.01
Base – number of respondents	189	253	385	283	1110	104	210	318	259	891

Note: * Gregory J, Foster K, Tyler H, Wiseman M. The Dietary and Nutritional Survey of British Adults. HMSO (London, 1990).

** 1986/87 survey reported standard errors; present survey reports standard deviations.

3 Minerals

3.1 Introduction

Minerals are inorganic elements. Some minerals are required for the body's normal function and these essential minerals are derived from the diet; they include iron, calcium, phosphorus, potassium, magnesium, sodium and chloride. Trace elements are required in minute amounts, and include zinc, copper, iodine and manganese.

Data are presented in this chapter for average daily intakes of the above minerals, which were derived from the records of the 1,724 respondents in the survey who completed a full seven-day dietary record. No attempt has been made to adjust the intakes to take account of under-reporting.

For all minerals other than haem iron, dietary supplements made some contribution to intake and thus data are presented from *all sources*, including dietary supplements, and from *food sources* alone. For haem iron, intakes are presented from food sources only.

For those minerals where UK Reference Nutrient Intake values (RNIs) and Lower Reference Nutrient Intake values (LRNIs) have been published for adults in the appropriate sex and age groups, the proportion of respondents with intakes below the LRNIs are shown, and mean daily intakes are compared with current RNIs. Current RNIs and LRNIs are shown in Table 3.1[1]. Table 3.2 shows the proportion of respondents with intakes below the LRNIs for those vitamins where LRNIs have been published. A further explanation of RNIs and LRNIs can be found in Chapter 2, section 2.1.1.

(Tables 3.1 and 3.2)

3.2 Total iron, haem and non-haem iron

Dietary iron occurs in two forms. About 90% of iron in the average British diet is in the form of iron salts and is referred to as *non-haem iron*[2]. The extent to which this type of iron is absorbed is highly variable and depends both on the individual's iron status and on other components of the diet. The other 10% of dietary iron is in the form of *haem iron* and comes mainly from the haemoglobin and myoglobin of meat. Haem iron is well absorbed, and its absorption is less strongly influenced by the individual's iron stores or other constituents of the diet.

Meat, poultry and fish, and ascorbic acid (vitamin C) are major enhancers of non-haem iron absorption. Meat, poultry and fish contain haem iron, which itself is relatively well absorbed but also enhances non-haem iron absorption from other foods consumed at the same time. Similarly, ascorbic acid (vitamin C) enhances non-haem iron absorption when consumed as part of a meal. The strongest inhibitors of non-haem iron are phytates, present in cereal grains, vegetables, seeds and nuts, and also polyphenols which are found particularly in tea and coffee. Current research, focusing on measuring absorption of non-haem iron from the diet as a whole, suggests that there may be interactions between the various enhancers and inhibitors and an adaptive response over time[3].

Table 3.3 shows the mean daily intake of total iron and Tables 3.4 and 3.5 mean daily intake of haem and non-haem iron respectively. The mean daily intake of total iron from food sources was 13.2mg for men and, significantly lower, 10.0mg for women (p<0.01). Haem iron contributed a mean of 0.8mg and 0.5mg towards total iron intake for men and women respectively, while non-haem iron contributed a mean of 12.3mg and 9.5mg respectively.

Women had a significantly lower mean daily intake of haem and non-haem iron than men (p<0.01). For women, intakes of total iron, haem iron and non-haem iron were significantly lower than for men in each age group (19 to 24 years for total iron and non-haem iron: p<0.05; all others: p<0.01).

The youngest group of men and women had significantly lower mean daily intakes of total and non-haem iron from food sources than those aged 35 to 64 years (women aged 19 to 24 compared with 50 to 64: p<0.01; all other women and men: p<0.05). For example, for men and women aged 19 to 24 years mean daily intake of total iron from food sources was 11.4mg and 8.8mg respectively compared with 13.6mg and 10.9mg for those aged 50 to 64 years. In addition, women aged 25 to 34 years had significantly lower mean daily intakes of total and non-haem iron than women aged 35 to 64 years (35 to 49 years: p<0.05; 50 to 64 years: p<0.01). Women aged 25 to 34 years had significantly lower mean daily intakes of haem iron, 0.4mg, than those aged 50 to 64 years, 0.6mg (p<0.05). There were no significant differences in mean daily intake of haem iron by age for men.

Dietary supplements providing iron increased the mean intake of total iron from food sources, overall, by 6% for men, from 13.2mg to 14.0mg, and by 16% for women, from 10.0mg to 11.6mg. The effect of dietary supplements on mean intakes was most marked for the oldest group of men and for women aged 35 to 49 years. Mean intakes for men aged 50 to 64 years increased by 12%, from 13.6mg to 15.2mg, and for women aged 35 to 49 years by 26%, from 10.2mg to 12.9mg.

Table 3.6 shows mean daily intake of total iron as a percentage of the RNI for men and women by age. For men, mean daily intake of total iron from food sources was 151% of the RNI and was above the RNI in each age group[4]. For women aged 19 to 50 years the RNI is set higher than for older women, 14.8mg/day compared with 8.7mg/day for women aged over 50 years, to take account of menstrual losses. As the table shows, for women, mean daily intake from food sources was 82% of the RNI overall, and was below the RNI for all age groups except the oldest group of women. Dietary supplements increased mean daily intakes of total iron as a percentage of the RNI for all sex/age groups, but mean intakes including supplements for women aged 19 to 49 years were still well below the RNI.

Table 3.2 shows that overall 1% of men and, a significantly higher proportion of women, 25%, had a mean daily intake of total iron from food sources

below the LRNI (p<0.01). No more than 3% of men in any age group had a mean daily intake of total iron from food sources below the LRNI. The proportion of women aged 19 to 49 years with intakes below the LRNI was significantly higher than for those aged 50 to 64 years, 42% of those aged 19 to 24 years, 41% of those aged 25 to 34 years, and 27% of those aged 35 to 49 years compared with 4% of those aged 50 to 64 years (p<0.01). In addition, a significantly higher proportion of women aged 25 to 34 years had intakes of iron below the LRNI than those aged 35 to 49 years (p<0.05). The inclusion of dietary supplements providing iron had little effect on the proportions with mean daily intakes below the LRNI.

(Tables 3.3 to 3.6 and 3.2)

Food sources of total iron, haem and non haem iron

Some foods are fortified with iron, for example flour and many breakfast cereals. All wheat flour, other than wholemeal flour, is fortified with iron by law; other foods are not subject to compulsory fortification but are fortified voluntarily by manufacturers. Thus cereals & cereal products were found to be the major source of iron for respondents in this survey. Indeed as Table 3.7 shows, respondents obtained over two-fifths, 44%, of mean daily intake of total iron from cereals & cereal products. Within this group the major sources were breakfast cereals, providing 20% of mean total iron intake overall, and white bread, contributing 9% overall.

The two other main sources of iron in the diets of respondents were meat & meat products and vegetables (excluding potatoes). Meat & meat products contributed 17% to total iron intake overall, including 5% which came from beef, veal & dishes and 4% from chicken, turkey & dishes, including coated chicken. On average, liver, liver products & dishes contributed less than 1% to total iron intake. Vegetables (excluding potatoes) provided 10% of intake overall.

Tables 3.8 and 3.9 show the food sources of haem and non-haem iron in the diets of respondents in the survey. Haem iron is found mainly in the haemoglobin and myoglobin of meat, and overall 85% of haem iron in the diets of the respondents came from meat & meat products. Men obtained a significantly higher proportion of their haem iron intake from meat & meat products, 87%, than women, 82% (p<0.05). Within this group the major sources were beef, veal & dishes, 24%, followed by chicken, turkey & dishes, including coated chicken, 14%. Compared with men aged 50 to 64 years, men aged 19 to 34 years obtained a significantly lower proportion of their haem iron intake from liver, liver products & dishes, and men aged 19 to 49 years a significantly higher proportion from burgers & kebabs (all: p<0.05). Other meat & meat products, including game, haggis and corned beef, provided a significantly lower proportion of haem iron intake for women aged 19 to 49 years than for women aged 50 to 64 years (p<0.01).

Fish & fish products provided a further 9% of haem iron intake for men and 15% for women (p<0.05). For men the contribution to haem iron intake from fish & fish dishes was significantly lower for those aged 19 to 24 years, 3%, than for men aged 35 to 49 years, 12% (p<0.05).

In contrast, meat & meat products contributed only 13% to mean daily intake of non-haem iron. Nearly half, 47%, of mean daily intake of non-haem iron came from cereals & cereal products, including 20% from breakfast cereals and 10% from white bread. A further 11% overall came from vegetables (excluding potatoes).

(Tables 3.7 to 3.9)

3.3 Calcium

Calcium is the most abundant mineral in the body. Of the 1000g or so in the human adult body, about 99% is in the bones and teeth where its primary role is structural.

Table 3.10 shows average daily intake of calcium. Men in the survey had a significantly higher mean daily intake of calcium from food sources, 1007mg, than women, 777mg (p<0.01). Intakes were significantly lower for the youngest group of men and women than for the two oldest age groups (men aged 19 to 24 compared with 35 to 49: p<0.01; all others: p<0.05). For example, men and women aged 19 to 24 years had mean daily calcium intakes of 860mg and 694mg respectively, compared with 1027mg for men and 823mg for women aged 50 to 64 years. In addition, women aged 25 to 34 years had a significantly lower mean daily intake of calcium than women aged 35 to 64 years (35 to 49 years: p<0.05; 50 to 64 years: p<0.01).

The contribution of dietary supplements to calcium intakes was very small, except for the oldest group of women, where supplements providing calcium increased mean intake from food sources alone by about 10% from 823mg to 903mg.

Overall, mean daily intake of calcium from food sources was 144% and 111% of the RNI for men

and women respectively[4]. Mean intakes were above the RNI for all age and sex groups apart from the youngest group of women, where mean intake was 99% of the RNI. Dietary supplements increased mean daily calcium intake to above the RNI for women aged 19 to 24 years.

Table 3.2 shows that 2% of men and, a significantly higher proportion of women, 5%, had a mean daily intake of calcium from food sources which was below the LRNI (p<0.05). Dietary supplements providing calcium had a negligible effect on these proportions.

(Tables 3.10, 3.11 and 3.2)

Food sources of calcium[5]

Table 3.12 shows that the main source of calcium for the respondents in the survey was milk & milk products, contributing 43% to mean intake overall. Within this group, semi-skimmed milk and cheese were the main contributors, providing 17% and 11% respectively.

White flour is fortified with calcium, and cereals & cereal products were therefore another main source of calcium in the diets of the respondents, contributing 30% to mean intake overall. Over a third of the contribution from cereals & cereal products came from white bread, 13%.

There were no significant differences by sex or age in the proportion of mean daily calcium intake accounted for by the different food groups.

(Table 3.12)

3.4 Phosphorus

Phosphorus is the second most abundant mineral in the body and has a variety of functions. About 80% of the phosphorus in the human body is present in bones as a calcium salt that gives rigidity to the skeleton.

Table 3.13 shows that the mean daily intake of phosphorus from food sources for men, 1493mg, was significantly higher than for women, 1112mg (p<0.01). For women, intakes were significantly lower than for men in each age group (p<0.01). The youngest group of men had a significantly lower mean daily intake of phosphorus than men in any other age group (35 to 49 years: p<0.01; all others: p<0.05). For example, men aged 19 to 24 years had a mean daily phosphorus intake of 1335mg compared with 1527mg for men aged 25 to 34 years. Women aged 19 to 24 years had a significantly lower mean daily intake than those aged 50 to 64 years, 1046mg and 1176mg respectively (p<0.05). In addition, women aged 25 to 34 years had a significantly lower mean daily phosphorus intake than those aged 35 to 64 years (35 to 49 years: p<0.05; 50 to 64: p<0.01).

Dietary supplements made a negligible contribution to mean daily phosphorus intakes.

Table 3.14 shows mean daily intakes of phosphorus as a percentage of the RNI. Mean daily intakes from food sources were 272% and 202% of the RNI for men and women respectively, and were above the RNI for each age group[4]. Overall, no men and less than 0.5% of women had an intake of phosphorus below the appropriate LRNI (*see* Table 3.2).

(Tables 3.13, 3.14 and 3.2)

Food sources of phosphorus

Table 3.15 shows the contribution made by the different food groups to intakes of phosphorus. The three main sources of phosphorus in the diets of respondents in the survey were cereals & cereal products, milk & milk products and meat & meat products. There were no significant differences by age in the contribution of food groups to mean daily intake of phosphorus.

Cereals & cereal products contributed 23% to the intake of phosphorus for both men and women, including 9% which came from bread and 5% from breakfast cereals.

Overall, milk & milk products contributed 24% to the mean daily intake of phosphorus. Within this group the main contributor was semi-skimmed milk which provided 9% of the phosphorus intake overall. Cheese contributed a further 5%.

Overall, respondents derived 21% of their mean daily intake of phosphorus from meat & meat products, a third of which, 7%, came from chicken, turkey & dishes, including coated chicken.

For men a further 10%, and for women 6%, of intake came from drinks (p<0.05). For men, half of the contribution made by drinks came from beer & lager, 5% compared with 1% for women (p<0.01).

(Table 3.15)

3.5 Magnesium

As shown in Table 3.16, the mean daily intake of magnesium from food sources for men, 308mg, was over one third higher than that for women, 229mg (p<0.01). As with phosphorus, the youngest group of men had a significantly lower mean daily magnesium intake than men in any other age group (p<0.01). For example, mean daily

intake of magnesium for men aged 19 to 24 years was 258mg compared with 318mg for men aged 50 to 64 years. Women aged 19 to 34 years had significantly lower mean daily magnesium intakes than those aged 35 to 64 years (19 to 24 compared with 35 to 49: p<0.05; all others: p<0.01).

Dietary supplements providing magnesium increased mean intakes from food sources alone by no more than about 2.5%.

Table 3.17 shows that overall, mean daily intakes of magnesium from food sources for men and women in the survey were, respectively, 103% and 85% of the RNI and were below the RNI for women in all age groups and men in the youngest age group[4]. For men aged 19 to 24 years mean intake was 86% of the RNI. For women intakes ranged from 76% of the RNI for those aged 19 to 24 years to 91% for those aged 50 to 64 years. Dietary supplements providing magnesium had little effect on mean daily intake as a percentage of the RNI.

Overall, about one in ten men and one in seven women had mean daily intakes of magnesium from food sources below the LRNI (*see* Table 3.2). A significantly higher proportion of women in the two youngest age groups, 22% and 20%, had intakes of magnesium below the LRNI than those aged 50 to 64 years, 7% (19 to 24: p<0.05; 25 to 34: p<0.01). In addition, women aged 25 to 34 years were significantly more likely than those aged 35 to 49 years to have a mean daily intake of magnesium below the LRNI, 20% compared with 10% (p<0.05). Dietary supplements providing magnesium made a negligible difference to the proportions with intakes below the LRNI.

(Tables 3.16, 3.17 and 3.2)

Food sources of magnesium

Table 3.18 shows that cereals & cereal products were the main source of magnesium, providing just over one quarter, 27%, of mean intake overall, about half of which, 13%, came from bread, mainly as white bread, 6%. A further 7% came from breakfast cereals.

The other main source of magnesium in the diets of respondents was drinks, contributing 20% to mean intake of magnesium for men and, significantly lower, 13% for women (p<0.01). For men, half of the contribution made by drinks came from beer & lager, 10% compared with 2% for women (p<0.01). Coffee contributed 4% to magnesium intake for men and women.

Meat & meat products contributed 12% overall to mean daily magnesium intake, with about half of this, 5%, coming from the consumption of chicken, turkey & dishes, including coated chicken.

Overall milk & milk products contributed 11% to the mean daily intake of magnesium, about half of which, 5%, came from semi-skimmed milk. Potatoes & savoury snacks contributed a further 10% to the intake for both sexes.

There were no significant differences by age in the contribution of food groups to mean daily intake of magnesium.

(Table 3.18)

3.6 Sodium and chloride

Sodium and chloride are the principal cation and anion respectively in extracellular fluid in the body. Both sodium and chloride are required in small amounts in the diet and their concentrations are maintained by a variety of regulatory mechanisms.

Sodium and chloride are not generally found in high concentrations in unprocessed foods, but tend to be added to many foods, in the form of salt, during processing as well as in the home during cooking or at the table. About 75% of salt intake is estimated to come from processed food. Although the average intake of sodium and chloride from foods was assessed, it was not possible to measure the amount of salt added to the respondent's food during cooking or at the table. Thus intakes of both sodium and chloride are based on average values attributed to foods eaten and do not allow for additions in cooking and at the table. The results are therefore underestimates of total sodium and chloride intake. Sodium intake can, however, be estimated from urinary sodium excretion and this is discussed in Chapter 4, section 4.3.

Questions on the habitual use of salt in cooking the respondent's food and on the addition of salt at the table were asked in the dietary interview. These questions asked about frequency of use, and did not ask how much salt was used.

Table 3.19 presents data on the use of salt in cooking and at the table. In the dietary interview, 73% of respondents, overall, reported that salt was usually added to their food during cooking[6], and 61% of men and 51% of women said that salt was added to food at the table, either usually or occasionally (men compared with women: p<0.01). There was no significant difference between men and women in the likelihood of salt being used in cooking. However, a significantly higher proportion

of men than women said they usually added salt to their food at the table, 37% compared with 28% (p<0.01); while women were more likely to say that they never added salt at the table, 30% compared with 24% (p<0.05). There were no clear age patterns in the use of salt in cooking or at the table. However, the youngest group of men were less likely than those aged 35 to 64 years to report using a salt alternative in cooking (p<0.01). The oldest group of women were more likely to report using a salt alternative in cooking than those aged 25 to 34 years, and less likely to report not adding salt in cooking than those aged 25 to 49 years (p<0.05).

The use of salt in cooking and the addition of salt to food at the table are to some extent related. Table 3.20 shows that for 41% of men and 30% of women who reported adding salt in cooking, salt was also usually added to their food at the table, and 54% and 57% of men and women who did not add salt in cooking, rarely or never added salt at the table.

(Tables 3.19 and 3.20)

Table 3.21 shows mean daily intake of sodium from all and food sources, excluding additions in cooking or at the table. Mean daily intake from food sources for men in the survey was 3313mg and for women, significantly lower, 2302mg (p<0.01). There were no significant differences by age for men or women.

Dietary supplements made a negligible contribution to mean sodium intakes.

Mean daily intake of sodium from food sources, excluding additions in cooking or at the table, was well above the RNI for each sex and age group, and overall was over twice the RNI for men, 207%, and 144% of the RNI for women[4]. Less than 0.5% of men or women had an intake below the LRNI (see Table 3.2). Mean daily intakes at the upper 2.5 percentile for men were about 3½ times the RNI and for women about 2½ times the RNI.

(Tables 3.21, 3.22 and 3.2)

The average daily intake of chloride was, like the intake of sodium, several grams per day. Mean daily intake for men was 4995mg and significantly lower for women, 3481mg (p<0.01), representing 200% and 139% of the RNI.

As with sodium, dietary supplements made a negligible contribution to mean chloride intakes.

(Tables 3.23 and 3.24)

Food sources of sodium and chloride[7]

The main food sources of sodium and chloride in the diets of adults are very similar, since these two minerals are generally found together in foods in the form of salt. Only the food sources of sodium are discussed here, but Table 3.26 shows the percentage contribution made by food types to mean daily intake of chloride.

Over one third, 35%, of the mean intake of sodium came from cereals & cereal products, with white bread alone providing 14% of mean daily intake. Breakfast cereals contributed 5% to the mean daily intake of sodium overall, and biscuits, buns, cakes & pastries 4%.

Meat & meat products contributed 26% to the mean intake of sodium overall. Within this group the main source was bacon & ham, contributing 8%, with chicken, turkey & dishes, including coated chicken, providing 5%.

Milk & milk products contributed a further 8% to mean intake of sodium, and vegetables (excluding potatoes) an additional 7%.

There were no significant sex or age differences in the contribution of food groups to mean daily intake of sodium or chloride.

(Tables 3.25 and 3.26)

3.7 Potassium

Table 3.27 shows that the mean daily intake of potassium from food sources for men in the survey was 3367mg and for women, significantly lower, 2653mg (p<0.01). The youngest group of men had a significantly lower mean daily potassium intake than men in any other age group (25 to 34 years: p<0.05; all others: p<0.01). For example, men aged 19 to 24 years had a mean daily intake of potassium of 2841mg compared with 3552mg for men aged 50 to 64 years. For women, mean intakes were significantly lower for the two youngest age groups than for the two oldest age groups (p<0.01). For example, women aged 19 to 24 years had a mean daily potassium intake of 2362mg compared with 2884mg for women aged 50 to 64 years.

Dietary supplements made a negligible contribution to mean potassium intakes.

Table 3.28 shows mean daily intake of potassium as a percentage of the RNI[4]. Mean daily potassium intake from food sources for men in the survey provided 96% of the RNI, and 76% for women. Only for the oldest group of men was mean intake

above the RNI. Mean daily intake as a percentage of the RNI ranged from 81% and 67% for men and women aged 19 to 24 years respectively, to 101% and 82% for men and women aged 50 to 64 years. When intakes from food sources are compared with LRNIs (*see* Table 3.2) the data show that 6% of men and, a significantly higher proportion of women, 19% had intakes below the LRNI (p<0.01). Compared with men aged 25 to 34 years, a significantly higher proportion of men aged 19 to 24 years had an mean daily intake of potassium lower than the LRNI, 18% compared with 3% (p<0.05). The two youngest groups of women were significantly more likely than the oldest group of women to have a potassium intake below the LRNI, 30% of women aged 19 to 24 years and 25 to 34 years compared with 10% of women aged 50 to 64 years (19 to 24: p<0.05; 25 to 34: p<0.01). In addition, women aged 25 to 34 years were significantly more likely than those aged 35 to 49 years to have a mean daily intake of potassium below the LRNI, 30% compared with 16% (p<0.05).

(Tables 3.27, 3.28 and 3.2)

Food sources of potassium

Table 3.29 shows the percentage contribution of food types to mean daily intake of potassium. The main contributor to potassium intake was potatoes & savoury snacks, with respondents, overall, obtaining 18% of their mean intake of potassium from this source, about a third of which, 7%, came from potato chips.

Overall, drinks contributed 15% to mean intake of potassium, including 5% for men and 1% for women from beer & lager (beer & lager: p<0.01). Meat & meat products contributed 15% to mean potassium intake, a third of which, 5%, came from chicken, turkey & dishes, including coated chicken, and a fifth of which, 3%, came from beef, veal & dishes.

Milk & milk products contributed a further 13% to mean intake of potassium overall, about half of which, 6%, came from semi-skimmed milk. Cereals & cereal products contributed 13% to mean intake of potassium. This was principally in the form of white bread and breakfast cereals, each contributing 3%. A further 10% of potassium intake came from vegetables (excluding potatoes).

There were no significant differences by age in the proportion of mean daily potassium intake accounted for by the different food groups.

(Table 3.29)

3.8 Trace elements

3.8.1 Zinc

Table 3.30 shows that the mean daily intake of zinc from food sources for men in the survey was 10.2mg and for women, significantly lower, 7.4mg (p<0.01). Men aged 19 to 24 years had significantly lower mean daily intakes of zinc than men in any other age group (25 to 34 years: p<0.05; all others: p<0.01). For example, mean daily intake of zinc was 9.0mg for the youngest group of men compared with 10.6mg for men aged 35 to 49 years. For women, mean intakes were significantly lower for the youngest age group, 6.8mg, than for the oldest age group, 7.8mg (p<0.05). In addition, women aged 25 to 34 years had significantly lower mean zinc intakes than the two oldest age groups (p<0.01).

Dietary supplements providing zinc increased mean intakes from food sources alone by 5% for men, from 10.2mg to 10.7mg, and 7% for women, from 7.4mg to 7.9mg. For men the effect of supplements on mean intake was most marked for those aged 35 to 49 years, where intake of zinc from all sources was 8% higher than from food sources alone, 11.4mg and 10.6mg respectively; for the youngest group of men supplements increased mean intake by 2%, from 9.0mg to 9.2mg. Among women the effect was most marked for the oldest group, where intake from all sources was 10% higher than from food sources alone, 8.6mg and 7.8mg respectively; for the youngest group of women supplements increased mean intake by 4%, from 6.8mg to 7.1mg.

Mean daily intake of zinc from food sources was 107% of the RNI for men and 105% for women, and fell below the RNI for the youngest age group of men (at 95% of the RNI) and for women aged 19 to 24 years and 25 to 34 years (98% and 96% of the RNI respectively)[4]. Dietary supplements providing zinc increased mean daily intake for women aged 19 to 24 years and 25 to 34 years to above the RNI. The data in Table 3.2 show that 4% of both men and women had an intake of zinc from food sources which was below the LRNI. Dietary supplements made a negligible difference to the proportions with intakes below the LRNI.

(Tables 3.30, 3.31 and 3.2)

Food sources of zinc

Table 3.32 shows that the main source of zinc in the diets of respondents was meat & meat products. About a third, 34%, of the mean daily intake of zinc came from this source, with beef,

veal & dishes contributing 11% overall, and chicken, turkey & dishes, including coated chicken, 5%.

One quarter of zinc intake, 25%, came from cereals & cereal products. This was chiefly in the form of white bread, 6%, and breakfast cereals, 5%. Milk & milk products contributed a further 17% to mean daily intake of zinc, about a third of which, 6%, came from cheese and a further third, 6%, from semi-skimmed milk.

There were no significant sex or age differences in the contribution of food groups to mean daily intake of zinc.

(Table 3.32)

3.8.2 Copper

The mean daily intake of copper from food sources was 1.43mg for men and for women, significantly lower, 1.03mg (p<0.01). Mean daily intake was significantly lower for the youngest group of men than for men in any other age group (p<0.01). For example, men aged 19 to 24 years had a mean daily copper intake of 1.14mg compared with 1.53mg for men aged 35 to 49 years. For women, mean daily intake was significantly lower for those aged 19 to 24 years, 0.91mg, than for those aged 35 to 49 years, 1.05mg, and those aged 50 to 64 years, 1.07mg (p<0.05).

Supplements providing copper increased mean intakes from food sources alone by 3% for men, from 1.43mg to 1.48mg, and by 4% for women, from 1.03mg to 1.07mg.

Table 3.34 shows mean daily intake of copper as a percentage of the RNI. For men, overall, mean daily intake of copper from food sources exceeded the RNI, providing 119% of the reference value[4]. Mean intakes were above the RNI for all age groups apart from the youngest, where intakes from food sources and all sources provided 95% and 97% of the RNI respectively. Mean daily intake for women, overall, was 86% of the RNI, and mean intakes for all age groups, from both food and all sources, were below the RNI.

There are no LRNIs for copper.

(Tables 3.33 and 3.34)

Food sources of copper

Table 3.35 shows that the main contributor to mean daily copper intake was cereals & cereal products, 31% came from this source, about a quarter of which, 8%, came from white bread.

75

Meat & meat products contributed 17% to mean copper intake for men and 12% for women (p<0.05). Potatoes & savoury snacks, drinks and fruit & nuts each contributed about 10% to mean copper intake.

There were no significant differences by age in the contribution of food groups to mean daily copper intake.

(Table 3.35)

3.8.3 Iodine

The mean daily intake of iodine from food sources for men in the survey was 215µg; mean intake for women was significantly lower, 159µg (p<0.01). As with zinc and copper, the youngest group of men had significantly lower mean daily iodine intakes than men in any other age group (25 to 34 years: p<0.05; all others: p<0.01). For example, men aged 19 to 24 years had a mean daily intake of iodine of 166µg compared with 230µg for those aged 50 to 64 years. For women, mean daily intake was significantly lower for the two youngest age groups than for the two oldest age groups (25 to 34 compared with 35 to 49: p<0.05; all others: p<0.01). For example, mean daily intake was 130µg for women aged 19 to 24 years compared with 178µg for those aged 50 to 64 years.

Dietary supplements providing iodine taken by respondents in the survey increased mean intake from food sources alone by 2% for men, from 215µg to 220µg, and by 5% for women, from 159µg to 167µg.

As Table 3.37 shows, mean daily intakes of iodine from food sources were in excess of the RNI for both men and women, providing 154% and 114% of the reference value respectively[4]. However, mean daily intakes for women in the youngest age group were below the reference value, providing 93% of the RNI. Dietary supplements increased mean daily intake as a percentage of the RNI for all sex/age groups except for the youngest men. The mean intake of iodine for the youngest group of women from all sources was still below the RNI, 97%, when supplements were included.

Table 3.2 shows that overall 2% of men and a significantly higher proportion of women, 4%, had an intake of iodine from food sources below the LRNI (p<0.05). A significantly higher proportion of the youngest group of women, 12%, had a mean daily intake of iodine below the LRNI than the oldest group of women, 1% (p<0.05). Dietary supplements made no difference to the proportion with intakes below the LRNI.

(Tables 3.36, 3.37 and 3.2)

Food sources of iodine

Milk & milk products were clearly the most important source of iodine in the diets of respondents in the survey; providing 35% of the mean daily intake of iodine for men, and 42% for women (p<0.05). For both sexes about half of the contribution made by milk & milk products came from semi-skimmed milk, 18%.

The other major source of iodine for men was from drinks, which contributed 19% to iodine intake, including 15% from beer & lager. Drinks overall and beer & lager accounted for a significantly lower proportion of iodine intake for women, 9% and 3% respectively, compared with men (p<0.01).

Other food groups contributing more than 10% to iodine intake were cereals & cereal products contributing 12% overall, and fish & fish dishes. Fish & fish dishes, which are a rich source of iodine, contributed 11% to intake overall.

(Table 3.38)

3.8.4 Manganese

The mean daily intake of manganese from food sources was 3.32mg for men, and significantly lower for women, 2.69mg (p<0.01). The youngest group of men had significantly lower mean intakes of manganese than men in any other age group. In addition those aged 25 to 34 years had significantly lower intakes than men aged 50 to 64 years (25 to 34 compared with 50 to 64: p<0.05; all others: p<0.01). For example, men aged 19 to 24 years had a mean daily manganese intake of 2.45mg compared with 3.70mg for men aged 50 to 64 years. As with iodine, mean intakes were significantly lower for women aged 19 to 34 years than for those aged 35 to 64 years (25 to 34 compared with 35 to 49: p<0.05: all others: p<0.01). For example, mean daily intake of manganese was 2.12mg for women aged 19 to 24 years compared with 3.01mg for women aged 50 to 64 years.

Dietary supplements providing manganese had little effect on mean intakes, increasing intakes from food sources alone by 3% for both men and women.

There are no RNIs for manganese but safe intakes are believed to lie above 1.4mg/day for adults[1]. Mean daily intakes were above the safe level for each age and sex group. However, 4% of men and, a significantly higher proportion of women, 9%, had intakes from food sources below this level (p<0.05). A significantly higher proportion of women aged 19 to 24 years, 22%, had a mean daily intake of manganese below 1.4mg/day than women aged 50 to 64 years, 6% (p<0.05). Dietary supplements had little effect on the proportions with intakes below 1.4mg/day.

(Table 3.39)

Food sources of manganese

The principal source of manganese in the diets of respondents in this survey was cereals & cereal products, contributing 50% overall to mean daily intake. About half the contribution from cereals & cereal products, 26%, came from bread, mainly white. Breakfast cereals contributed 11% to intake overall, and biscuits, buns, cakes & pastries an additional 5%.

The other main sources of manganese in the diets of respondents were vegetables (excluding potatoes) and drinks. Vegetables (excluding potatoes) contributed 10% to intake overall and drinks 17%. Tea, which is a rich source of manganese, contributed 12%.

There were no significant sex or age differences in the proportion of mean daily manganese intake accounted for by the different food groups.

(Table 3.40)

3.9   Variations in mineral intake

In this section, variation in the average daily intake of minerals from *food sources* and *all sources* in relation to the region in which the respondent lives and household receipt of benefits is considered. (see caveat to section 2.7). Variation in average daily intake as a percentage of the RNI, and in the proportion of respondents with intakes below the LRNI, by these characteristics, is also considered for *food sources* and *all sources*.

3.9.1   Region

Table 3.41 shows the average daily intake of minerals from food sources and all sources for men and women in the sample living in different regions[8]. There were no significant regional differences in mean daily intake of minerals from food sources for men or women. The same is true when dietary supplements are included.

For those minerals where mean daily intakes were below the RNI for the group as a whole, the same was true for all regions (*see* Table 3.42). Including dietary supplements had little effect on mean daily intakes as a proportion of the RNI of any mineral except for iron. Including supplements increased mean daily intakes of iron for women aged 19 to 50 years, but these remained below the RNI in all regions.

Table 3.42 also shows the proportion of men and women in the four regions with intakes of minerals from food sources below the LRNI. For men there were no significant regional differences in the proportion with intakes of minerals below the LRNI. A significantly higher proportion of women in the Northern region, 6%, than women in Scotland, 1%, had intakes of zinc that were below the LRNI (p<0.05). In addition, women in the Northern region, Central and South West regions of England and in Wales and women in London and the South East were significantly more likely to have an iodine intake which was below the LRNI than women in Scotland (p<0.05).

Within each region, dietary supplements made a negligible difference to the proportions of men or women with intakes below the LRNI.

(Tables 3.41 and 3.42)

3.9.2   Household receipt of benefits

Table 3.43 shows average daily intakes of minerals from food sources and all sources for men and women according to whether or not they were living in a household where someone was receiving state benefits[9].

Mean daily intakes from food sources of all minerals, apart from haem iron and sodium, were significantly lower for men living in benefit households than for those in households not receiving benefits (chloride and zinc: p<0.05; all others: p<0.01). For example, mean daily intake of calcium was 883mg for men in benefit households compared with 1025mg for those in non-benefit households. Among women, mean daily intakes from food sources of all minerals, apart from haem iron, were significantly lower for those living in benefit households than for those in households not receiving benefits (sodium and chloride: p<0.05; all others: p<0.01). For example, mean daily total iron intake was 8.8mg for women in households in receipt of benefits compared with 10.3mg for women in non-benefit households.

When dietary supplements are included, there is no longer a significant difference in mean daily intakes of non-haem iron for women by household benefit status. All other differences remain significant when dietary supplements are included[10].

Table 3.44 shows mean daily intake of minerals from food sources and all sources as a percentage of the RNI. For all minerals, mean daily intakes from food sources as a percentage of the RNI were lower for men and women living in benefit households than for those in non-benefit households.

For both men and women, mean daily intakes of potassium, and additionally for women mean daily intakes of iron, magnesium and copper were below the RNI for both those in benefit and those in non-benefit households. For example, mean daily intakes of potassium were 84% of the RNI for men and 65% of the RNI for women in benefit households and 98% of the RNI for men and 78% of the RNI for women in non-benefit households. Mean daily iron intake was 58% of the RNI for women aged 19 to 50 years living in benefit households and 67% for those in non-benefit households. Mean daily intakes of zinc and magnesium for men and calcium, zinc and iodine for women were below the RNI for those in benefit households but above the RNI for those in non-benefit households. For example, mean intake of zinc was 98% of the RNI for men and 93% of the RNI for women in benefit households compared with 109% for men and 108% for women in non-benefit households.

Irrespective of household benefit status, including dietary supplements made no difference to mean daily intakes of potassium for men and women as a percentage of the RNI, and no difference to intakes of magnesium for men. However, including dietary supplements did increase mean daily intakes of zinc for men, and calcium and iodine for women, in benefit households to at or above the RNI. Mean daily intakes of zinc increased for women in benefit households when dietary supplements were included, but remained below the RNI, 95%. Dietary supplements increased mean daily intakes of copper and magnesium for women in benefit and non-benefit households, but intakes remained below the RNI. Mean daily intake of iron for women aged 19 to 50 years increased to 66% of the RNI for women in benefit households, and to 80% of the RNI for women in non-benefit households, when supplements were included.

Table 3.44 also shows the proportions of men and women with intakes of minerals from food sources below the LRNI. A significantly higher proportion of men in benefit households than those in non-benefit households had an intake, from food sources, of magnesium and potassium below the LRNI (potassium: p<0.05; magnesium: p<0.01). For example, 27% of men in benefit households had an intake of magnesium, and 16% an intake of potassium, below the appropriate LRNI, compared with 7% and 5% respectively of men in non-benefit households.

For all minerals, except sodium, chloride and phosphorus, a significantly higher proportion of women living in benefit households than in non-benefit households had intakes from food sources that were below the LRNI (calcium, zinc and iodine: p<0.05; all others: p<0.01). For example, 34% of women in benefit households had an intake of potassium below the LRNI compared with 16% of women in non-benefit households. More than half, 53%, of women aged 19 to 50 years living in benefit households had an iron intake below the LRNI, compared with about a third, 29%, of those in non-benefit households.

Dietary supplements made a negligible difference to the proportions of men or women in either benefit or non-benefit households with intakes below the LRNI for any mineral except iron. The proportion of women aged 19 to 50 years with an average daily intake of iron below the LRNI decreased to 50% of those in benefit households and 28% of those in non-benefit households when dietary supplements were included.

(Tables 3.43 and 3.44)

3.10 Comparison of mineral intakes between the 1986/87 Adults Survey and present NDNS

Tables 3.45 and 3.46(a) and (b) compare data from this present survey of adults with data on average daily intakes of minerals from the Dietary and Nutritional Survey of British Adults aged 16 to 64 years carried out in 1986/87 (1986/87 Adults Survey)[11]. Data are presented for men and women by age. Comparisons are made between comparable age groups in the two surveys; no attempt is made to use the data to undertake cohort analysis[12]. It should be noted that in the 1986/87 Adults Survey the youngest age group was adults aged 16 to 24 years, while in the current NDNS the youngest age group is adults aged 19 to 24 years. This should be borne in mind where there are differences between these groups. A summary of the methodology and findings from the 1986/87 Adults Survey is given in Appendix S of the Technical Report[13]. Table 3.45 presents data on absolute intakes from food sources and Tables 3.46(a) and (b) present data on absolute intakes from all sources for men and women respectively. Comparisons do not take into account differences in energy intake.

Data from the 1986/87 Adults Survey on intakes from food sources is only available for total iron, calcium, copper and iodine, and the following discussion focuses firstly on differences between the two surveys in intakes of these minerals from food sources alone. The effect of dietary supplements on intakes between the two surveys is then commented on.

For both sexes and all age groups there were no significant differences between the two sets of survey data for mean daily intakes from food sources of total iron. Overall, men and women had significantly higher mean daily intakes of calcium in the present survey than in the 1986/87 Adults Survey (p<0.01). Men aged 35 to 64 years and women aged 50 to 64 years had significantly higher intakes of calcium in the present survey than the equivalent age groups in the 1986/87 Adults Survey (women 50 to 64: p<0.01; all others: p<0.01).

Overall men and women in the present survey had significantly lower mean daily intakes from food sources of the trace elements, copper and iodine than those in the 1986/87 Adults Survey (p<0.01). Men aged 19 to 34 years and women in all age groups had significantly lower mean copper intakes in the present survey than the equivalent age groups in the 1986/87 Adults Survey (women 16/19 to 24, men 19 to 24 and 25 to 34: p<0.05; all others: p<0.01). Mean daily intakes of iodine were significantly lower in the present survey for men aged 19 to 24 years and 35 to 49 years and for women aged 19 to 49 years than the equivalent age groups in the 1986/87 Adults Survey (men 16/19 to 24: p<0.05; all others: p<0.01).

Many of the differences in mean daily intakes from food sources between the two sets of survey data are still evident when dietary supplements are included (see Table 3.46)[10]. When dietary supplements are included significant differences between the two sets of survey data remain, overall, for both men and women for intakes of calcium, for men for intakes of iodine and for women for intakes of copper. There are no consistent patterns by age for men or women in the significant differences that remain when dietary supplements are included.

Tables 3.46(a) and (b) also present data on intakes of sodium, chloride, potassium, magnesium, phosphorus and zinc from all sources for men and women by age for the two sets of survey data.

For both sexes and all age groups there were no significant differences between the two sets of survey data for mean daily intakes of sodium and chloride from all sources.

For two minerals, potassium and phosphorus, mean daily intakes from all sources were higher in the present survey compared with the 1986/87 Adults Survey. Potassium intake was significantly higher for both men and women overall, and phosphorus significantly higher for women in the present survey than in the 1986/87 Adults Survey (women, phosphorus: p<0.05; all others: p<0.01). For example, mean daily intakes of potassium were 3371mg for men and 2655mg for women in the present survey compared with 3187mg for men and 2434mg for women in the earlier survey. Mean daily intake of phosphorus was 1116mg for women in the present survey compared with 1072mg for women in the earlier survey. There were few significant differences by age. In the present survey, men and women aged 35 to 49 years and 50 to 64 years had significantly higher mean intakes of potassium, and women aged 50 to 64 years significantly higher phosphorus intakes than equivalent age groups in the 1986/87 Adults Survey (potassium for men and women 35 to 49: p<0.01; all others: p<0.01).

In the present survey, for two minerals, magnesium and zinc, mean daily intakes from all sources for some age and sex groups were significantly lower in the present survey compared with the 1986/87 Adults Survey. Mean daily intakes of zinc were significantly lower for both men and women, 10.7mg and 7.9mg, respectively, in the present survey compared with 11.4mg for men and 8.4mg for women in the earlier survey (p<0.05). In the present survey, men aged 19 to 24 years and women aged 25 to 34 years had significantly lower intakes of magnesium and zinc than the equivalent age groups in the 1986/87 Adults Survey (zinc, women aged 25 to 34: p<0.01; all others: p<0.05).

As noted in Chapter 2, section 2.8, the extent to which these differences reflect changes in the diets of adults over the period is not clear. Many factors contribute to any differences, including changes in nutrient composition and, as noted previously, new analytical methods, changes in fortification practices, as well as in food consumption patterns and increased use of dietary supplements.

(Tables 3.45, 3.46(a) and 3.46(b))

References and endnotes

1   Department of Health. Report on Health and Social Subjects: 41. *Dietary Reference Values for Food Energy and Nutrients for the United Kingdom.* HMSO (London, 1991).

2   Bull NI, Buss DH. Haem and Non-haem Iron in British Diets. *J Hum Nutr* 1980; **34:** 141-145.

3   Cook JD, Reddy MB. Effect of ascorbic acid intake on non-haem iron absorption from a complete diet. *Am J Clin Nutr* 2001; **73:** 93-98.

4   Intakes as a percentage of the RNI were calculated for each respondent, taking the appropriate RNI for each sex/age group. The values for all respondents in each age group were then pooled to give a mean, median and standard deviation.

5   Hard water typically provides 200mg calcium daily, while in soft water areas it provides none. Due to regional differences it was not possible to ascertain the contribution of water to calcium intake. In addition, it was not possible to distinguish whether tap water consumed had been filtered, which would reduce, for example, the levels of calcium, chloride and heavy metals found in tap water.

6   Includes the use of a salt alternative in cooking.

7   Excludes the use of salt added in cooking or at the table.

8   The areas included in each of the four analysis 'regions' are given in the response chapter, Chapter 2 of the Technical Report, online at http://www.food.gov.uk/science. Definitions of 'regions' are given in the glossary (*see* Appendix C).

9   Households receiving benefits are those where someone in the respondent's household was currently receiving Working Families Tax Credit or had, in the previous 14 days, drawn Income Support or (Income-related) Job Seeker's Allowance. Definitions of 'household' and 'benefits (receiving)' are given in the glossary (*see* Appendix C).

10 Where there are no longer significant differences once dietary supplements are included this does not necessarily mean that dietary supplements reduce differences between sub-groups, as the inclusion of dietary supplements is likely to increase the variance and skew the distribution.

11 Gregory J, Foster K, Tyler H, Wiseman M. *The Dietary and Nutritional Survey of British Adults.* HMSO (London, 1990).

12 Due to the number of years between the two surveys it would only be possible to undertake cohort analysis for those who were aged 16 to 40 years in the 1986/87 Adults Survey. The numbers available to undertake this form of analysis are therefore limited.

13 The Technical Report is available online at http://www.food.gov.uk/science.

Table 3.1

Reference Nutrient Intakes (RNIs) and Lower Reference Nutrient Intakes (LRNIs) for minerals*

RNI and LRNI by age (years)** and sex		Minerals									
		Iron	Calcium	Phosphorus***	Magnesium	Sodium	Chloride****	Potassium	Zinc	Copper	Iodine
Men		mg/d	mg/d	mg/d	mg/d	mg/d	mg/d	mg/d	mg/d	mg/d	µg/d
19 to 50	RNI	8.7	700	550	300	1600	2500	3500	9.5	1.2	140
	LRNI	4.7	400	310	190	575	890	2000	5.5	n/a	70
51 to 64	RNI	8.7	700	550	300	1600	2500	3500	9.5	1.2	140
	LRNI	4.7	400	310	190	575	890	2000	5.5	n/a	70
Women											
19 to 50	RNI	14.8	700	550	270	1600	2500	3500	7.0	1.2	140
	LRNI	8.0	400	310	150	575	890	2000	4.0	n/a	70
51 to 64	RNI	8.7	700	550	270	1600	2500	3500	7.0	1.2	140
	LRNI	4.7	400	310	150	575	890	2000	4.0	n/a	70

Note: * Source: Department of Health. Report on Health and Social Subjects: 41. Dietary Reference Values for Food Energy and Nutrients for the United Kingdom. HMSO (London, 1991).

** The age groups presented represent those for which different RNI and LRNI values are calculated.

*** RNIs and LRNIs for phosphorus are set equal to the RNI and LRNI for calcium in molar terms.

**** RNIs and LRNIs for chloride correspond to those for sodium in molar terms.

n/a no reference value set.

Table 3.2

Proportion of respondents with average daily intakes of minerals below the Lower Reference Nutrient Intake (LRNI) by sex and age of respondent

Percentages

Mineral	% with average daily intake below LRNI									
	Men aged (years):				All men	Women aged (years):				All women
	19–24	25–34	35–49	50–64		19–24	25–34	35–49	50–64	
	%	%	%	%	%	%	%	%	%	%
All sources										
Total iron	3	0	1	1	1	40	40	25	4	24
Calcium	5	2	2	2	2	8	6	6	3	5
Phosphorus	-	-	-	-	-	-	-	0	0	0
Magnesium	17	9	7	8	9	22	20	10	7	13
Sodium*	-	-	-	0	0	-	-	0	0	0
Chloride*	-	-	-	0	0	-	-	0	0	0
Potassium	18	3	4	5	6	30	30	16	10	19
Zinc	7	2	4	3	4	5	5	3	3	4
Iodine	2	1	2	1	2	12	5	4	1	4
Base	*108*	*219*	*253*	*253*	*833*	*104*	*210*	*318*	*259*	*891*
Food sources										
Total iron	3	0	1	1	1	42	41	27	4	25
Calcium	5	2	2	2	2	8	6	6	3	5
Phosphorus	-	-	-	-	-	-	-	0	0	0
Magnesium	17	9	7	9	9	22	20	10	7	13
Sodium*	-	-	0	0	0	-	-	0	0	0
Chloride*	-	-	0	0	0	-	-	0	0	0
Potassium	18	3	5	5	6	30	30	16	10	19
Zinc	7	2	4	3	4	5	5	4	3	4
Iodine	2	1	2	1	2	12	5	4	1	4
Base	*108*	*219*	*253*	*253*	*833*	*104*	*210*	*318*	*259*	*891*

Note: * Data in this table are for intakes from food and dietary supplements only and do not include further additions of salt in cooking or at the table.

Table 3.3

Average daily intake of total iron (mg) by sex and age of respondent

Cumulative percentages

Total iron (mg)	Men aged (years):				All men	Women aged (years):				All women
	19–24	25–34	35–49	50–64		19–24	25–34	35–49	50–64	
	cum %	cum %	cum %	cum %	cum %	cum %	cum %	cum %	cum %	cum %
(a) Intakes from all sources										
Less than 4.7	3	0	1	1	1	8	4	4	3	4
Less than 6.0	11	0	4	2	3	16	17	9	8	11
Less than 8.0	18	11	11	10	12	40	40	25	20	29
Less than 8.7	25	15	14	12	15	44	46	32	26	35
Less than 10.0	38	26	20	20	24	63	64	44	39	50
Less than 12.0	63	45	34	37	42	78	81	67	63	71
Less than 14.0	78	63	58	54	61	86	90	80	74	81
Less than 14.8	84	71	63	61	67	87	91	83	79	84
Less than 16.0	87	78	71	68	74	89	93	88	85	88
Less than 18.0	92	84	80	79	82	91	96	90	90	92
Less than 20.0	92	87	86	86	87	93	97	93	91	93
Less than 22.0	93	93	93	92	93	96	98	95	92	95
All	100	100	100	100	100	100	100	100	100	100
Base	*108*	*219*	*253*	*253*	*833*	*104*	*210*	*318*	*259*	*891*
Mean (average value)	11.5	13.9	14.1	15.2	14.0	10.0	9.8	12.9	12.3	11.6
Median	11.3	12.8	13.2	13.6	12.9	9.3	9.0	10.5	11.0	10.0
Lower 2.5 percentile	4.5	6.9	5.4	6.1	5.4	4.2	4.0	4.1	4.5	4.2
Upper 2.5 percentile	23.5	27.7	28.1	29.1	27.5	23.5	20.1	28.8	28.7	26.7
Standard deviation	4.60	7.50	5.63	13.21	9.00	4.88	5.98	23.30	8.00	14.99
	cum %	cum %	cum %	cum %	cum %	cum %	cum %	cum %	cum %	cum %
(b) Intakes from food sources										
Less than 4.7	3	0	1	1	1	9	4	4	3	4
Less than 6.0	11	0	4	2	3	16	17	10	8	12
Less than 8.0	18	11	11	11	12	42	41	27	21	30
Less than 8.7	25	15	15	14	16	48	47	35	28	38
Less than 10.0	42	28	21	21	26	73	65	49	43	54
Less than 12.0	63	49	35	39	44	87	83	73	67	75
Less than 14.0	78	66	59	58	63	95	92	87	81	88
Less than 14.8	84	75	65	65	70	96	93	90	88	91
Less than 16.0	87	81	73	72	77	97	96	95	93	95
Less than 18.0	92	89	83	83	86	99	97	98	96	97
Less than 20.0	94	92	89	90	91	99	99	99	97	98
Less than 22.0	96	95	95	96	96	99	99	99	98	99
All	100	100	100	100	100	100	100	100	100	100
Base	*108*	*219*	*253*	*253*	*833*	*104*	*210*	*318*	*259*	*891*
Mean (average value)	11.4	13.0	13.7	13.6	13.2	8.8	9.2	10.2	10.9	10.0
Median	11.2	12.5	13.1	13.3	12.6	9.1	9.0	10.1	10.6	9.6
Lower 2.5 percentile	4.5	6.9	5.4	5.9	5.4	4.2	4.0	3.8	4.5	4.1
Upper 2.5 percentile	22.8	24.5	23.7	23.2	23.4	16.5	18.5	17.4	20.9	18.1
Standard deviation	4.40	5.13	4.75	4.58	4.81	3.12	3.37	3.58	3.91	3.65

Table 3.4

Average daily intake of haem iron (mg) from food sources by sex and age of respondent

Cumulative percentages

Haem iron (mg)	Men aged (years):				All men	Women aged (years):				All women
	19–24	25–34	35–49	50–64		19–24	25–34	35–49	50–64	
	cum %	cum %	cum %	cum %	cum %	cum %	cum %	cum %	cum %	cum %
Intakes from *food sources**										
Zero	2	–	1	0	1	7	3	2	2	3
Less than 0.1	2	1	4	2	2	10	15	9	5	10
Less than 0.2	2	3	6	6	5	23	25	17	11	18
Less than 0.3	11	9	11	10	10	37	37	32	25	32
Less than 0.4	21	16	18	19	18	50	55	44	41	46
Less than 0.5	37	28	27	28	29	60	74	58	55	61
Less than 0.6	45	42	37	41	41	78	86	74	71	76
Less than 0.8	60	54	50	54	54	84	94	82	78	84
Less than 1.0	83	73	68	70	72	89	96	91	88	91
Less than 1.2	92	84	81	80	83	95	98	96	92	95
Less than 1.5	95	96	89	89	91	100	99	99	95	98
All	100	100	100	100	100		100	100	100	100
Base	*108*	*219*	*253*	*253*	*833*	*104*	*210*	*318*	*259*	*891*
Mean (average value)	0.7	0.8	0.9	0.9	0.8	0.5	0.4	0.5	0.6	0.5
Median	0.7	0.7	0.8	0.7	0.7	0.5	0.4	0.5	0.5	0.5
Lower 2.5 percentile	0.2	0.2	0.1	0.1	0.1	0.0	0.0	0.0	0.0	0.0
Upper 2.5 percentile	1.6	1.6	2.5	2.4	2.3	1.3	1.1	1.3	1.8	1.4
Standard deviation	0.37	0.40	0.58	0.58	0.52	0.32	0.44	0.33	0.51	0.42

*Note: * None of the dietary supplements taken by respondents in this survey provided any haem iron.*

Table 3.5

Average daily intake of non-haem iron (mg) by sex and age of respondent

Cumulative percentages

Non-haem iron (mg)	Men aged (years):				All men	Women aged (years):				All women
	19–24	25–34	35–49	50–64		19–24	25–34	35–49	50–64	
	cum %	cum %	cum %	cum %	cum %	cum %	cum %	cum %	cum %	cum %
(a) Intakes from *all sources*										
Less than 4.0	2	-	0	1	1	5	3	3	2	3
Less than 6.0	14	1	6	5	5	20	19	12	9	14
Less than 8.0	26	17	13	12	16	44	44	32	27	35
Less than 10.0	43	34	26	25	30	66	68	50	47	55
Less than 12.0	70	51	45	44	50	80	83	70	69	74
Less than 14.0	84	72	63	61	68	87	91	81	78	83
Less than 16.0	90	81	76	74	79	89	95	89	87	90
Less than 18.0	92	84	83	84	85	93	97	91	90	92
Less than 20.0	92	90	91	91	91	93	98	94	91	94
Less than 22.0	96	94	95	94	95	97	99	95	95	96
All	100	100	100	100	100	100	100	100	100	100
Base	*108*	*219*	*253*	*253*	*833*	*104*	*210*	*318*	*259*	*891*
Mean (average value)	10.8	13.1	13.3	14.3	13.2	9.5	9.4	12.4	11.7	11.1
Median	10.4	12.0	12.3	12.6	12.0	8.8	8.5	10.0	10.4	9.5
Lower 2.5 percentile	4.2	6.2	4.7	5.8	5.1	3.5	3.6	3.9	4.3	3.8
Upper 2.5 percentile	23.1	26.4	27.4	28.7	26.4	22.9	19.4	27.9	27.8	25.8
Standard deviation	4.60	7.41	5.53	13.15	8.93	4.85	5.93	23.31	7.92	14.97
	cum %	cum %	cum %	cum %	cum %	cum %	cum %	cum %	cum %	cum %
(b) Intakes from *food sources*										
Less than 4.0	2	-	0	1	1	5	3	4	2	3
Less than 6.0	14	1	6	5	5	22	20	13	9	15
Less than 8.0	26	18	14	13	16	50	45	34	28	37
Less than 10.0	46	37	27	27	32	75	69	55	51	59
Less than 12.0	70	54	46	47	52	89	84	76	74	79
Less than 14.0	84	76	66	65	71	96	93	89	87	90
Less than 16.0	90	84	78	78	81	97	98	96	94	96
Less than 18.0	92	90	85	88	88	99	98	98	97	98
Less than 20.0	94	94	93	95	94	99	99	99	97	99
Less than 22.0	98	97	97	98	97	99	100	99	99	99
All	100	100	100	100	100	100		100	100	100
Base	*108*	*219*	*253*	*253*	*833*	*104*	*210*	*318*	*259*	*891*
Mean (average value)	10.7	12.2	12.8	12.7	12.3	8.3	8.8	9.7	10.3	9.5
Median	10.2	11.7	12.3	12.3	11.8	8.2	8.4	9.5	10.0	9.2
Lower 2.5 percentile	4.2	6.2	4.7	5.8	5.1	3.5	3.6	3.6	4.3	3.7
Upper 2.5 percentile	22.2	23.1	22.2	23.1	22.2	16.3	15.7	16.9	20.4	17.0
Standard deviation	4.39	5.01	4.65	4.41	4.69	3.10	3.22	3.54	3.72	3.54

Table 3.6

Average daily intake of total iron as a percentage of Reference Nutrient Intake (RNI) by sex and age of respondent

Percentages

Sex and age of respondent	Average daily intake as % of RNI*							
	(a) All sources			Base	(b) Food sources			Base
	Mean	Median	sd		Mean	Median	sd	
Men aged (years):								
19–24	133	130	52.8	108	131	128	50.6	108
25–34	160	146	86.2	219	150	143	58.9	219
35–49	163	152	64.7	253	157	151	54.7	253
50–64	174	156	151.8	253	156	152	52.6	253
All	161	148	103.5	833	151	145	55.3	833
Women aged (years):								
19–24	68	63	32.9	104	60	61	21.1	104
25–34	66	61	40.4	210	62	61	22.8	210
35–49	87	71	157.4	318	69	68	24.2	318
50–64	137	123	92.5	259	122	119	45.0	259
All	94	75	112.4	891	82	72	40.4	891

Note: * Intake as a percentage of RNI was calculated for each respondent. The values for all respondents in each age group were then pooled to give a mean, median and sd.

Table 3.7

Percentage contribution of food types to average daily intake of total iron by sex and age of respondent

Percentages

Type of food	Men aged (years):				All men	Women aged (years):				All women	All
	19–24	25–34	35–49	50–64		19–24	25–34	35–49	50–64		
	%	%	%	%	%	%	%	%	%	%	%
Cereals & cereal products	42	46	43	44	44	44	45	45	44	45	44
of which:											
white bread	11	10	10	9	10	11	9	8	7	8	9
wholemeal bread	2	3	3	4	3	1	3	3	4	3	3
soft grain and other bread	2	3	3	3	3	4	4	3	3	3	3
whole grain and high fibre breakfast cereals	6	14	12	13	12	10	10	14	16	13	13
other breakfast cereals	9	5	6	6	6	9	9	7	7	7	7
biscuits, buns, cakes & pastries	3	4	4	5	4	3	5	5	5	5	5
Milk & milk products	1	2	1	1	1	2	1	1	2	2	1
Eggs & egg dishes	3	3	3	3	3	3	2	3	3	3	3
Fat spreads	0	0	0	0	0	0	0	0	0	0	0
Meat & meat products	22	20	19	18	19	17	14	15	14	15	17
of which:											
beef, veal & dishes	6	5	5	4	5	5	4	4	4	4	5
chicken, turkey & dishes, including coated	5	4	5	3	4	4	4	4	3	4	4
liver, liver products & dishes	0	1	1	2	1	0	1	1	1	1	1
burgers & kebabs	4	2	1	0	2	3	1	1	0	1	1
Fish & fish dishes	2	2	3	3	2	2	3	3	4	3	3
Vegetables (excluding potatoes)	8	9	10	10	9	10	13	11	10	11	10
Potatoes & savoury snacks	10	7	7	7	7	10	8	7	7	8	7
Fruit & nuts	1	2	2	3	2	2	2	3	5	3	3
Sugars, preserves & confectionery	4	2	2	1	2	2	2	2	2	2	2
Drinks*	5	6	8	7	7	6	6	7	7	6	7
Miscellaneous**	3	3	3	3	3	2	3	3	3	3	3
Average daily intake (mg)	11.4	13.0	13.7	13.6	13.2	8.8	9.2	10.2	10.9	10.0	11.5
Total number of respondents	108	219	253	253	833	104	210	318	259	891	1724

Note: * Includes soft drinks, alcoholic drinks, tea, coffee and water.

   ** Includes powdered beverages (except tea and coffee), soups, sauces, condiments and artificial sweeteners.

Table 3.8

Percentage contribution of food types to average daily intake of haem iron by sex and age of respondent

Percentages

Type of food	Men aged (years):				All men	Women aged (years):				All women	All
	19–24	25–34	35–49	50–64		19–24	25–34	35–49	50–64		
	%	%	%	%	%	%	%	%	%	%	%
Meat & meat products	92	90	85	86	87	87	81	82	80	82	85
of which:											
bacon & ham	7	7	6	7	7	5	7	6	6	6	6
beef, veal & dishes	26	26	22	23	24	31	22	28	22	25	24
lamb & lamb dishes	6	5	5	6	6	4	6	6	8	6	6
pork & pork dishes	2	4	5	5	4	3	4	4	4	4	4
chicken, turkey & dishes including coated	16	16	14	11	14	18	18	16	12	16	14
liver, liver products & dishes	2	4	9	11	8	2	5	5	8	6	7
burgers & kebabs	16	12	7	1	7	14	8	5	2	5	7
sausages	6	4	4	3	4	4	4	3	2	3	3
meat pies & pastries	5	4	4	4	4	3	3	4	3	3	4
other meat & meat products	5	9	9	14	10	3	4	5	14	7	9
Fish and fish products	3	6	12	10	9	10	15	14	17	15	11
of which:											
shellfish	1	1	5	2	3	3	7	3	5	5	3
oily fish	1	4	6	7	6	7	7	9	10	9	7
Average daily intake (mg)	0.7	0.8	0.9	0.9	0.8	0.5	0.4	0.5	0.6	0.5	0.7
Total number of respondents	108	219	253	253	833	104	210	318	259	891	1724

Table 3.9

Percentage contribution of food types to average daily intake of non-haem iron by sex and age of respondent

Percentages

Type of food	Men aged (years):				All men	Women aged (years):				All women	All
	19–24	25–34	35–49	50–64		19–24	25–34	35–49	50–64		
	%	%	%	%	%	%	%	%	%	%	%
Cereals & cereal products	44	49	46	46	47	46	47	47	47	47	47
of which:											
white bread	12	10	11	10	11	11	9	8	7	8	10
wholemeal bread	2	4	4	4	4	1	3	4	4	3	3
soft grain and other bread	3	4	3	4	3	4	4	3	3	4	4
whole grain & high fibre breakfast cereals	7	15	13	13	13	10	10	15	17	14	13
other breakfast cereals	10	6	6	6	6	9	9	7	7	8	7
biscuits, buns, cakes & pastries	4	4	5	6	5	3	5	5	6	5	5
Milk & milk products	1	2	1	1	1	2	2	2	2	2	1
Eggs & egg dishes	3	3	3	4	3	3	2	3	3	3	3
Fat spreads	0	0	0	0	0	0	0	0	0	0	0
Meat & meat products	18	16	15	13	15	13	11	12	10	11	13
of which:											
beef, veal & dishes	4	4	3	3	4	4	3	3	3	3	3
chicken, turkey & dishes including coated	4	4	4	3	4	4	3	3	2	3	3
burgers & kebabs	3	2	1	0	1	2	1	1	0	1	1
Fish & fish dishes	1	1	2	2	2	2	2	2	3	2	2
Vegetables (excluding potatoes)	9	9	10	10	10	11	13	12	11	12	11
Potatoes & savoury snacks	10	8	7	8	8	11	8	7	8	8	8
Fruit & nuts	1	2	2	3	2	2	3	3	5	4	3
Sugars, preserves & confectionery	4	2	2	1	2	2	2	2	2	2	2
Drinks*	5	6	8	8	7	6	7	7	7	7	7
Miscellaneous**	3	3	3	3	3	2	3	3	3	3	3
Average daily intake (mg)	10.7	12.2	12.8	12.7	12.3	8.3	8.8	9.7	10.3	9.5	10.9
Total number of respondents	108	219	253	253	833	104	210	318	259	891	1724

Note: * Includes soft drinks, alcoholic drinks, tea, coffee and water.

 ** Includes powdered beverages (except tea and coffee), soups, sauces, condiments and artificial sweeteners.

Table 3.10

Average daily intake of calcuim (mg) by sex and age of respondent

Cumulative percentages

Calcuim (mg)	Men aged (years):				All men	Women aged (years):				All women
	19–24	25–34	35–49	50–64		19–24	25–34	35–49	50–64	
	cum %	cum %	cum %	cum %	cum %	cum %	cum %	cum %	cum %	cum %
(a) Intakes from *all sources*										
Less than 300	4	-	0	0	1	4	2	2	1	2
Less than 400	5	2	2	2	2	8	6	6	3	5
Less than 500	12	4	4	4	5	21	14	12	11	13
Less than 600	22	11	9	7	11	36	29	24	20	26
Less than 700	34	20	14	14	18	55	47	37	32	40
Less than 800	46	31	23	21	28	69	67	52	45	56
Less than 900	58	42	35	36	40	79	79	65	57	67
Less than 1000	61	56	48	49	52	89	86	75	69	77
Less than 1250	88	82	77	79	80	96	96	93	86	92
Less than 1500	96	91	90	92	92	98	100	98	93	97
All	100	100	100	100	100	100		100	100	100
Base	*108*	*219*	*253*	*253*	*833*	*104*	*210*	*318*	*259*	*891*
Mean (average value)	867	1030	1049	1035	1016	706	736	814	903	809
Median	825	951	1017	1002	987	669	718	789	850	763
Lower 2.5 percentile	261	401	429	459	410	248	337	316	373	324
Upper 2.5 percentile	1516	2017	1783	1762	1794	1304	1279	1444	1833	1550
Standard deviation	324.6	606.3	358.7	331.0	430.7	263.9	232.6	292.8	381.7	314.0
	cum %	cum %	cum %	cum %	cum %	cum %	cum %	cum %	cum %	cum %
(b) Intakes from *food sources*										
Less than 300	4	-	0	0	1	4	2	2	2	2
Less than 400	5	2	2	2	2	8	6	6	3	5
Less than 500	12	4	4	4	5	21	14	12	12	14
Less than 600	23	12	9	7	11	37	30	24	25	27
Less than 700	34	20	14	14	18	56	47	38	36	42
Less than 800	46	31	23	23	28	69	68	54	50	58
Less than 900	58	43	35	37	41	84	79	68	63	71
Less than 1000	61	58	49	49	53	92	87	77	77	81
Less than 1250	90	83	78	79	81	96	97	95	92	95
Less than 1500	99	92	91	93	93	98	100	99	97	99
All	100	100	100	100	100	100		100	100	100
Base	*108*	*219*	*253*	*253*	*833*	*104*	*210*	*318*	*259*	*891*
Mean (average value)	860	1017	1040	1027	1007	694	731	796	823	777
Median	825	934	1014	1002	979	661	709	777	810	752
Lower 2.5 percentile	261	401	418	459	409	248	337	300	372	320
Upper 2.5 percentile	1418	2017	1775	1671	1783	1304	1272	1384	1509	1372
Standard deviation	316.4	564.8	351.9	323.9	411.2	256.8	228.9	271.9	287.2	268.7

Table 3.11

Average daily intake of calcuim as a percentage of Reference Nutrient Intake (RNI) by sex and age of respondent

Percentages

Sex and age of respondent	Average daily intake as % of RNI*							
	(a) All sources			Base	(b) Food sources			Base
	Mean	Median	sd		Mean	Median	sd	
Men aged (years):								
19–24	124	119	46.4	*108*	123	119	45.2	*108*
25–34	147	136	86.6	*219*	145	133	80.7	*219*
35–49	150	145	51.2	*253*	149	145	50.3	*253*
50–64	148	143	47.3	*253*	147	143	46.3	*253*
All	145	141	61.5	*833*	144	140	58.7	*833*
Women aged (years):								
19–24	101	96	37.7	*104*	99	95	36.7	*104*
25–34	105	103	33.2	*210*	104	101	32.7	*210*
35–49	116	113	41.8	*318*	114	111	38.8	*318*
50–64	129	121	54.5	*259*	118	117	41.0	*259*
All	116	109	44.9	*891*	111	107	38.4	*891*

Note: * Intake as a percentage of RNI was calculated for each respondent. The values for all respondents in each age group were then pooled to give a mean, median and sd.

Table 3.12

Percentage contribution of food types to average daily intake of calcium by sex and age of respondent

Percentages

Type of food	Men aged (years):				All men	Women aged (years):				All women	All
	19–24	25–34	35–49	50–64		19–24	25–34	35–49	50–64		
	%	%	%	%	%	%	%	%	%	%	%
Cereals & cereal products	35	33	31	30	32	31	30	27	27	28	30
of which:											
pizza	7	3	2	1	3	4	3	2	1	2	2
white bread	16	13	14	14	14	13	12	11	10	11	13
wholemeal bread	1	2	2	2	2	1	2	2	2	2	2
soft grain and other bread	3	4	3	4	4	4	4	3	3	4	4
breakfast cereals	2	5	3	3	4	4	3	3	4	4	4
Milk & milk products	33	41	42	43	41	42	43	47	48	46	43
of which:											
whole milk	3	7	7	6	6	8	7	7	5	6	6
semi-skimmed milk	15	15	18	17	17	13	16	18	19	17	17
skimmed milk	1	4	2	3	3	5	3	6	7	6	4
cheese	11	11	11	11	11	10	11	9	10	10	11
yogurt	2	2	3	3	3	3	4	4	5	4	3
Eggs & egg dishes	2	2	2	2	2	2	2	2	2	2	2
Fat spreads	0	0	0	0	0	0	0	0	0	0	0
Meat & meat products	9	7	7	6	7	7	6	5	4	5	6
Fish & fish dishes	2	2	2	3	2	2	2	3	3	3	2
Vegetables (excluding potatoes)	4	4	4	5	4	4	6	5	5	5	5
Potatoes & savoury snacks	2	2	1	1	1	2	2	1	1	2	1
Fruit & nuts	0	1	1	2	1	1	1	2	3	2	1
Sugars, preserves & confectionery	3	2	2	1	2	3	2	2	2	2	2
Drinks*	7	6	5	5	6	6	4	3	3	4	5
Miscellaneous**	2	1	1	2	2	1	2	2	2	2	2
Average daily intake (mg)	860	1017	1040	1027	1007	694	731	796	823	777	888
Total number of respondents	108	219	253	253	833	104	210	318	259	891	1724

Note: * Includes soft drinks, alcoholic drinks, tea, coffee and water.

    ** Includes powdered beverages (except tea and coffee), soups, sauces, condiments and artificial sweeteners.

Table 3.13

Average daily intake of phosphorus (mg) by sex and age of respondent

Cumulative percentages

Phosphorus (mg)	Men aged (years):				All men	Women aged (years):				All women
	19–24	25–34	35–49	50–64		19–24	25–34	35–49	50–64	
	cum %	cum %	cum %	cum %	cum %	cum %	cum %	cum %	cum %	cum %
(a) Intakes from all sources										
Less than 550	-	-	1	1	0	4	2	4	3	3
Less than 750	4	-	1	3	2	20	14	8	6	10
Less than 1000	18	13	8	10	11	42	47	30	29	35
Less than 1250	38	29	24	27	28	76	79	68	60	69
Less than 1500	67	52	50	51	53	94	96	90	86	91
Less than 1750	90	81	75	73	78	99	98	97	96	97
Less than 2000	99	90	88	89	90	100	99	100	99	99
All	100	100	100	100	100		100		100	100
Base	*108*	*219*	*253*	*253*	*833*	*104*	*210*	*318*	*259*	*891*
Mean (average value)	1341	1550	1524	1508	1502	1050	1045	1134	1180	1116
Median	1287	1485	1500	1499	1474	1057	1017	1124	1174	1107
Lower 2.5 percentile	582	839	770	654	770	440	577	488	524	522
Upper 2.5 percentile	1948	2856	2418	2373	2406	1657	1579	1776	1820	1764
Standard deviation	318.9	727.4	429.1	402.8	510.7	298.8	278.9	296.4	309.0	301.0
	cum %	cum %	cum %	cum %	cum %	cum %	cum %	cum %	cum %	cum %
(b) Intakes from food sources										
Less than 550	1	-	1	1	1	4	2	4	3	3
Less than 750	4	-	2	3	2	20	14	8	6	10
Less than 1000	18	13	8	10	11	42	47	31	29	35
Less than 1250	38	29	24	27	28	80	79	69	61	70
Less than 1500	67	54	50	51	53	94	96	90	86	91
Less than 1750	92	82	75	73	78	99	98	97	96	97
Less than 2000	99	90	88	90	90	100	99	100	99	99
All	100	100	100	100	100		100		100	100
Base	*108*	*219*	*253*	*253*	*833*	*104*	*210*	*318*	*259*	*891*
Mean (average value)	1335	1527	1520	1505	1493	1046	1041	1130	1176	1112
Median	1287	1461	1500	1499	1466	1057	1016	1119	1170	1097
Lower 2.5 percentile	559	839	767	654	766	440	577	488	524	522
Upper 2.5 percentile	1948	2856	2415	2365	2381	1657	1562	1774	1820	1763
Standard deviation	313.4	574.7	428.5	402.8	455.8	296.7	275.6	295.1	309.2	299.6

Table 3.14

Average daily intake of phosphorus as a percentage of Reference Nutrient Intake (RNI) by sex and age of respondent

Percentages

Sex and age of respondent	Average daily intake as % of RNI*							
	(a) All sources			Base	(b) Food sources			Base
	Mean	Median	sd		Mean	Median	sd	
Men aged (years):								
19–24	244	234	58.0	*108*	243	234	57.0	*108*
25–34	282	270	132.3	*219*	278	266	104.5	*219*
35–49	277	273	78.0	*253*	276	273	77.9	*253*
50–64	274	272	73.2	*253*	274	272	73.2	*253*
All	273	268	92.9	*833*	272	267	82.9	*833*
Women aged (years):								
19–24	191	193	54.3	*104*	190	193	54.0	*104*
25–34	190	185	50.7	*210*	189	185	50.1	*210*
35–49	206	204	53.9	*318*	205	203	53.7	*318*
50–64	215	213	56.2	*259*	214	213	56.2	*259*
All	203	201	54.7	*891*	202	200	54.5	*891*

*Note : * Intake as a percentage of RNI was calculated for each respondent. The values for all respondents in each age group were then pooled to give a mean, median and sd.*

Table 3.15

Percentage contribution of food types to average daily intake of phosphorus by sex and age of respondent

Percentages

Type of food	Men aged (years):				All men	Women aged (years):				All women	All
	19–24	25–34	35–49	50–64		19–24	25–34	35–49	50–64		
	%	%	%	%	%	%	%	%	%	%	%
Cereals & cereal products	22	23	23	23	23	21	24	23	24	23	23
of which:											
white bread	6	5	6	5	5	6	5	4	4	4	5
wholemeal bread	1	2	3	3	2	1	2	3	3	2	2
soft grain and other bread	2	2	2	2	2	3	3	2	2	3	2
breakfast cereals	2	5	5	5	4	3	4	5	7	5	5
biscuits, buns, cakes & pastries	2	3	3	4	3	2	3	3	4	3	3
Milk & milk products	17	22	23	23	22	23	25	27	27	26	24
of which:											
whole milk	1	4	4	3	3	4	4	4	3	4	3
semi-skimmed milk	8	8	10	9	9	7	9	10	10	10	9
skimmed milk	1	2	1	2	2	3	2	3	4	3	2
cheese	5	6	5	6	6	5	6	5	5	5	5
yogurt	1	1	2	2	2	2	2	3	3	3	2
Eggs & egg dishes	3	3	3	3	3	3	2	3	3	3	3
Fat spreads	0	0	0	0	0	0	0	0	0	0	0
Meat & meat products	26	23	23	21	23	22	19	19	17	19	21
of which:											
bacon & ham	3	3	3	3	3	2	2	2	3	2	3
beef, veal & dishes	4	4	4	4	4	4	3	4	3	3	4
chicken, turkey & dishes including coated	9	8	8	6	7	9	8	7	6	7	7
burgers & kebabs	4	2	1	0	1	3	1	1	0	1	1
Fish & fish dishes	3	3	4	6	4	4	4	5	7	5	5
Vegetables (excluding potatoes)	5	5	5	6	5	5	7	6	6	6	6
Potatoes & savoury snacks	7	5	5	5	5	8	6	5	5	6	5
Fruit & nuts	0	1	2	2	2	2	2	2	3	2	2
Sugars, preserves & confectionery	2	2	1	1	1	2	2	2	1	2	1
Drinks*	13	11	9	8	10	10	7	5	4	6	8
of which:											
carbonated soft drinks	5	3	1	1	2	6	4	1	1	2	2
beer & lager	6	6	5	4	5	2	1	1	0	1	3
Miscellaneous**	2	1	1	2	2	1	2	2	2	2	2
Average daily intake (mg)	1335	1527	1520	1505	1493	1046	1041	1130	1176	1112	1297
Total number of respondents	108	219	253	253	833	104	210	318	259	891	1724

Note: *   Includes soft drinks, alcoholic drinks, tea, coffee and water.

   ** Includes powdered beverages (except tea and coffee), soups, sauces, condiments and artificial sweeteners.

Table 3.16

Average daily intake of magnesium (mg) by sex and age of respondent

Cumulative percentages

Magnesium (mg)	Men aged (years):				All men	Women aged (years):				All women
	19–24	25–34	35–49	50–64		19–24	25–34	35–49	50–64	
	cum %	cum %	cum %	cum %	cum %	cum %	cum %	cum %	cum %	cum %
(a) Intakes from *all sources*										
Less than 120	3	-	1	0	1	8	4	5	3	4
Less than 150	5	1	2	2	2	22	20	10	7	13
Less than 190	17	9	7	8	9	42	41	24	21	29
Less than 210	23	15	11	15	15	55	56	38	29	42
Less than 240	42	26	21	22	25	73	71	53	49	59
Less than 270	58	36	31	33	36	85	82	68	65	72
Less than 300	74	50	45	44	50	92	90	81	76	83
Less than 350	86	69	65	64	68	97	96	92	90	93
Less than 400	97	85	79	79	83	99	99	97	96	98
All	100	100	100	100	100	100	100	100	100	100
Base	*108*	*219*	*253*	*253*	*833*	*104*	*210*	*318*	*259*	*891*
Mean (average value)	260	311	322	320	311	208	211	241	252	233
Median	251	300	310	314	300	206	203	234	241	223
Lower 2.5 percentile	115	169	158	139	151	96	107	98	112	102
Upper 2.5 percentile	413	503	562	529	528	373	371	408	427	399
Standard deviation	72.8	104.8	106.3	102.8	102.9	69.9	64.9	79.3	82.4	77.9
	cum %	cum %	cum %	cum %	cum %	cum %	cum %	cum %	cum %	cum %
(b) Intakes from *food sources*										
Less than 120	3	-	1	0	1	8	4	5	3	4
Less than 150	5	1	2	2	2	22	20	10	7	13
Less than 190	17	9	7	9	9	43	41	24	22	30
Less than 210	23	15	12	16	15	56	57	38	30	42
Less than 240	46	27	22	23	27	73	72	55	50	60
Less than 270	58	37	31	34	37	85	84	71	66	74
Less than 300	76	50	45	44	50	95	92	83	78	85
Less than 350	88	71	66	64	70	99	98	94	91	94
Less than 400	97	86	79	80	84	99	100	98	97	99
All	100	100	100	100	100	100		100	100	100
Base	*108*	*219*	*253*	*253*	*833*	*104*	*210*	*318*	*259*	*891*
Mean (average value)	258	308	318	318	308	205	209	235	246	229
Median	249	298	310	314	300	205	203	230	240	222
Lower 2.5 percentile	115	169	157	139	151	96	107	98	112	102
Upper 2.5 percentile	413	503	545	529	527	321	359	386	403	377
Standard deviation	71.0	101.8	97.5	102.1	99.0	65.5	61.4	69.2	72.7	69.8

Table 3.17

Average daily intake of magnesium as a percentage of Reference Nutrient Intake (RNI) by sex and age of respondent

Percentages

Sex and age of respondent	Average daily intake as % of RNI*							
	(a) All sources			Base	(b) Food sources			Base
	Mean	Median	sd		Mean	Median	sd	
Men aged (years):								
19–24	87	84	24.3	108	86	83	23.7	108
25–34	104	100	34.9	219	103	100	33.9	219
35–49	107	103	35.4	253	106	103	32.5	253
50–64	107	105	34.3	253	106	105	34.0	253
All	104	100	34.3	833	103	100	33.0	833
Women aged (years):								
19–24	77	76	25.9	104	76	76	24.3	104
25–34	78	75	24.0	210	77	75	22.7	210
35–49	89	87	29.4	318	87	85	25.6	318
50–64	93	89	30.5	259	91	89	26.9	259
All	86	83	28.8	891	85	82	25.9	891

Note: * Intake as a percentage of RNI was calculated for each respondent. The values for all respondents in each age group were then pooled to give a mean, median and sd.

Table 3.18

Percentage contribution of food types to average daily intake of magnesium by sex and age of respondent

Percentages

Type of food	Men aged (years):				All men	Women aged (years):				All women	All
	19–24	25–34	35–49	50–64		19–24	25–34	35–49	50–64		
	%	%	%	%	%	%	%	%	%	%	%
Cereals & cereal products	25	27	27	27	27	24	27	27	28	27	27
of which:											
white bread	7	6	6	6	6	7	6	5	4	5	6
wholemeal bread	2	4	4	4	4	1	4	4	4	4	4
soft grain and other bread	2	3	2	3	3	3	3	3	3	3	3
breakfast cereals	4	7	7	7	7	5	6	8	10	8	7
Milk & milk products	8	10	11	11	10	12	12	13	13	13	11
of which:											
whole milk	1	2	2	2	2	2	2	2	1	2	2
semi-skimmed milk	4	4	5	5	5	4	5	5	5	5	5
skimmed milk	0	1	1	1	1	2	1	2	2	2	1
Eggs & egg dishes	1	1	1	1	1	1	1	1	1	1	1
Fat spreads	0	0	0	0	0	0	0	0	0	0	0
Meat & meat products	16	14	13	12	13	14	11	11	10	11	12
of which:											
beef, veal & dishes	3	3	3	2	3	3	2	2	2	2	3
chicken, turkey & dishes including coated	6	5	5	4	5	5	5	5	4	5	5
Fish & fish dishes	2	2	3	3	3	3	3	3	4	3	3
Vegetables (excluding potatoes)	7	6	7	7	7	8	10	9	8	9	8
Potatoes & savoury snacks	13	10	9	9	10	15	11	10	9	10	10
Fruit & nuts	2	5	6	7	5	5	7	8	10	8	7
Sugars, preserves & confectionery	3	2	2	1	2	3	2	2	2	2	2
Drinks*	20	21	20	20	20	15	13	13	12	13	17
of which:											
beer & lager	12	12	9	9	10	4	3	2	1	2	7
coffee	2	3	4	4	4	2	3	4	4	4	4
tea	1	1	2	2	2	1	2	2	3	2	2
Miscellaneous**	2	2	2	2	2	2	3	3	2	2	2
Average daily intake (mg)	258	308	318	318	308	205	209	235	246	229	267
Total number of respondents	108	219	253	253	833	104	210	318	259	891	1724

Note: *   Includes soft drinks, alcoholic drinks, tea, coffee and water.
       ** Includes powdered beverages (except tea and coffee), soups, sauces, condiments and artificial sweeteners.

Table 3.19

Use of salt in cooking and at the table by sex and age of respondent*

Responding sample   Percentages

Use of salt in cooking and at the table**	Men aged (years):				All men	Women aged (years):				All women	All
	19–24	25–34	35–49	50–64		19–24	25–34	35–49	50–64		
	%	%	%	%	%	%	%	%	%	%	%
Salt added to cooking:											
usually added	73	68	70	73	71	67	67	64	73	68	68
uses salt alternative	–	4	4	6	4	5	3	6	10	6	5
not usually added	27	29	26	21	26	30	31	30	19	27	27
Salt added at table:											
usually	39	32	35	41	37	34	24	31	26	28	33
occasionally	30	23	23	22	24	24	24	20	26	23	23
rarely	14	17	18	12	15	16	20	21	16	19	17
never	17	28	24	24	24	26	32	28	32	30	27
Base	*142*	*287*	*330*	*330*	*1088*	*136*	*275*	*415*	*337*	*1163*	*2251*

Note: * As reported in the dietary interview.
      ** Includes cases where salt alternative used.

Table 3.20

Use of salt in cooking and at the table by sex and age of respondent*

Responding sample   Percentages

Sex of respondent and use of salt at the table	Use of salt in cooking** and age of respondent (years)														
	Salt added					No salt added					All				
	19–24	25–34	35–49	50–64	All	19–24	25–34	35–49	50–64	All	19–24	25–34	35–49	50–64	All
	%	%	%	%	%	%	%	%	%	%	%	%	%	%	%
Men															
Use salt at the table:															
Usually	47	36	37	45	41	19	21	28	29	25	39	32	35	41	37
Occasionally	26	24	25	25	25	41	23	18	13	21	30	23	23	22	24
Rarely or never	27	41	38	31	35	40	57	54	58	54	31	45	42	36	39
Base	*103*	*204*	*241*	*260*	*808*	*39*	*83*	*87*	*70*	*278*	*142*	*287*	*327*	*330*	*1086*
Women															
Use salt at the table:															
Usually	40	29	32	25	30	20	11	30	27	23	34	24	31	26	28
Occasionally	27	22	22	28	24	17	29	16	16	20	24	24	20	26	23
Rarely or never	34	49	46	46	46	63	60	55	56	57	43	52	49	48	49
Base	*95*	*191*	*289*	*272*	*848*	*40*	*85*	*123*	*64*	*311*	*135*	*275*	*412*	*336*	*1159*

Note: * As reported in the dietary interview.
      ** Includes cases where salt alternative used.

Table 3.21

Average daily intake of sodium (mg) by sex and age of respondent*

Cumulative percentages

Sodium (mg)	Men aged (years):				All men	Women aged (years):				All women
	19–24	25–34	35–49	50–64		19–24	25–34	35–49	50–64	
	cum %	cum %	cum %	cum %	cum %	cum %	cum %	cum %	cum %	cum %
(a) Intakes from *all sources*										
Less than 575	-	-	0	0	0	-	-	0	0	0
Less than 1200	1	-	1	1	1	6	4	4	3	4
Less than 1600	8	2	3	3	3	13	16	13	15	14
Less than 2000	9	6	6	8	7	32	30	33	35	33
Less than 2500	24	18	21	18	20	69	61	68	67	66
Less than 3000	36	37	38	45	40	86	86	84	88	86
Less than 3500	56	64	60	65	62	93	96	95	95	95
Less than 4000	71	81	77	77	77	98	99	98	99	98
Less than 4500	88	89	88	89	89	100	100	99	100	100
All	100	100	100	100	100			100		
Base	*108*	*219*	*253*	*253*	*833*	*104*	*210*	*318*	*259*	*891*
Mean (average value)	3342	3366	3340	3249	3320	2304	2325	2317	2267	2303
Median	3356	3187	3312	3077	3255	2247	2283	2241	2243	2247
Lower 2.5 percentile	1385	1678	1517	1576	1517	997	953	982	1060	1013
Upper 2.5 percentile	5505	5984	5830	5397	5795	3974	3648	3943	3701	3767
Standard deviation	1090.3	1077.5	1007.6	943.6	1018.2	721.3	666.4	707.5	652.3	683.1
	cum %	cum %	cum %	cum %	cum %	cum %	cum %	cum %	cum %	cum %
(b) Intakes from *food sources*										
Less than 575	-	-	0	0	0	-	-	0	0	0
Less than 1200	1	-	1	1	1	6	4	4	3	4
Less than 1600	8	2	3	3	3	13	16	13	15	14
Less than 2000	9	6	6	8	7	32	30	33	35	33
Less than 2500	24	18	21	18	20	69	61	68	67	66
Less than 3000	36	38	38	45	40	86	86	84	88	86
Less than 3500	56	65	60	65	62	93	96	95	95	95
Less than 4000	71	81	77	77	77	98	99	98	99	98
Less than 4500	88	90	88	89	89	100	100	99	100	100
All	100	100	100	100	100			100		
Base	*108*	*219*	*253*	*253*	*833*	*104*	*210*	*318*	*259*	*891*
Mean (average value)	3342	3347	3337	3248	3313	2303	2324	2316	2266	2302
Median	3356	3179	3312	3077	3234	2247	2283	2241	2243	2247
Lower 2.5 percentile	1385	1678	1511	1576	1513	997	953	982	1060	1013
Upper 2.5 percentile	5505	5984	5830	5397	5623	3974	3648	3943	3701	3767
Standard deviation	1091.2	1059.7	1012.1	943.8	1014.6	722.3	666.3	706.3	653.5	683.1

*Note: * Data in this table are for intakes from food and dietary supplements only and do not include further additions of salt in cooking or at the table.*

Table 3.22

Average daily intake of sodium as a percentage of Reference Nutrient Intake (RNI) by sex and age of respondent*

Percentages

Sex and age of respondent	Average daily intake as % of RNI**							
	(a) All sources			Base	(b) Food sources			Base
	Mean	Median	sd		Mean	Median	sd	
Men aged (years):								
19–24	209	210	68.1	108	209	210	68.2	108
25–34	210	199	67.3	219	209	199	66.2	219
35–49	209	207	63.0	253	209	207	63.3	253
50–64	203	192	59.0	253	203	192	59.0	253
All	207	203	63.6	833	207	202	63.4	833
Women aged (years):								
19–24	144	140	45.1	104	144	140	45.1	104
25–34	145	143	41.6	210	145	143	41.6	210
35–49	145	140	44.2	318	145	140	44.1	318
50–64	142	140	40.8	259	142	140	40.8	259
All	144	140	42.7	891	144	140	42.7	891

Note: *   Data in this table are for intakes from food and dietary supplements only and do not include further additions of salt in cooking or at the table.

   **   Intake as a percentage of RNI was calculated for each respondent. The values for all respondents in each age group were then pooled to give a mean, median and sd.

Table 3.23

Average daily intake of chloride (mg) by sex and age of respondent*

Cumulative percentages

Chloride (mg)	Men aged (years):				All men	Women aged (years):				All women
	19–24	25–34	35–49	50–64		19–24	25–34	35–49	50–64	
	cum %	cum %	cum %	cum %	cum %	cum %	cum %	cum %	cum %	cum %
(a) Intakes from all sources										
Less than 890	-	-	-	0	0	-	-	0	0	0
Less than 1500	-	-	0	1	0	-	3	2	1	2
Less than 2000	2	-	2	1	1	8	5	6	6	6
Less than 2500	8	4	3	3	4	13	17	14	15	15
Less than 3000	12	5	7	7	7	37	29	31	30	31
Less than 3500	20	11	15	12	14	59	55	53	52	54
Less than 4000	31	27	27	25	27	75	71	73	75	73
Less than 4500	41	38	35	44	39	84	86	85	85	85
Less than 5000	45	53	50	55	52	93	93	93	92	93
Less than 5500	63	68	67	67	67	95	99	95	96	96
Less than 6000	72	81	77	75	77	99	99	98	99	99
Less than 6500	87	85	86	85	86	100	100	99	100	99
Less than 7000	89	90	90	95	91			99		100
All	100	100	100	100	100			100		
Base	108	219	253	253	833	104	210	318	259	891
Mean (average value)	4921	5135	5052	4923	5018	3412	3479	3514	3474	3482
Median	5157	4870	5011	4739	4965	3342	3433	3451	3443	3425
Lower 2.5 percentile	2036	2352	2243	2492	2261	1532	1404	1492	1601	1515
Upper 2.5 percentile	7879	9084	8587	7710	8306	5813	5337	5977	5692	5695
Standard deviation	1554.9	1879.6	1498.5	1385.8	1583.3	1013.8	985.1	1051.6	991.9	1013.3
	cum %	cum %	cum %	cum %	cum %	cum %	cum %	cum %	cum %	cum %
(b) Intakes from food sources										
Less than 890	-	-	0	0	0	-	-	0	0	0
Less than 1500	-	-	0	1	0	-	3	2	1	2
Less than 2000	2	-	2	1	1	8	5	6	6	6
Less than 2500	8	4	3	3	4	13	17	15	15	15
Less than 3000	12	5	7	7	7	37	29	31	30	31
Less than 3500	20	11	15	12	14	59	55	53	53	54
Less than 4000	31	27	27	25	27	75	71	73	75	73
Less than 4500	41	38	35	44	39	84	86	85	85	85
Less than 5000	45	54	50	56	52	93	93	93	92	93
Less than 5500	63	68	67	67	67	95	99	95	96	96
Less than 6000	72	81	77	75	77	99	99	98	99	99
Less than 6500	87	86	86	85	86	100	100	99	100	99
Less than 7000	89	90	90	95	92			99		100
All	100	100	100	100	100			100		
Base	108	219	253	253	833	104	210	318	259	891
Mean (average value)	4921	5056	5047	4922	4995	3409	3478	3512	3474	3481
Median	5157	4845	5011	4739	4940	3342	3433	3451	3443	3423
Lower 2.5 percentile	2036	2352	2243	2492	2261	1532	1404	1492	1601	1515
Upper 2.5 percentile	7879	8909	8587	7710	8261	5813	5337	5903	5692	5695
Standard deviation	1556.1	1621.5	1501.9	1385.8	1506.5	1014.1	984.6	1051.4	991.9	1013.2

Note: * Data in this table are for intakes from food and dietary supplements only and do not include further additions of salt in cooking or at the table.

Table 3.24

Average daily intake of chloride as a percentage of Reference Nutrient Intake (RNI) by sex and age of respondent*

Percentages

Sex and age of respondent	Average daily intake as % of RNI**							
	(a) All sources			Base	(b) Food sources			Base
	Mean	Median	sd		Mean	Median	sd	
Men aged (years):								
19–24	197	206	62.2	108	197	206	62.2	108
25–34	205	195	75.2	219	202	194	64.9	219
35–49	202	200	59.9	253	202	200	60.1	253
50–64	197	189	55.4	253	197	189	55.4	253
All	201	199	63.3	833	200	198	60.3	833
Women aged (years):								
19–24	136	134	40.6	104	136	134	40.6	104
25–34	139	137	39.4	210	139	137	39.4	210
35–49	141	138	42.1	318	140	138	42.1	318
50–64	139	138	39.7	259	139	138	39.7	259
All	139	137	40.5	891	139	137	40.5	891

Note: * Data in this table are for intakes from food and dietary supplements only and do not include further additions of salt in cooking or at the table.

** Intake as a percentage of RNI was calculated for each respondent. The values for all respondents in each age group were then pooled to give a mean, median and sd.

Table 3.25

Percentage contribution of food types to average daily intake of sodium by age and sex of respondent*

Percentages

Type of food	Men aged (years):				All men	Women aged (years):				All women	All
	19–24	25–34	35–49	50–64		19–24	25–34	35–49	50–64		
	%	%	%	%	%	%	%	%	%	%	%
Cereals & cereal products	34	35	35	37	35	33	36	35	37	36	35
of which:											
pizza	5	3	2	1	2	3	3	1	1	2	2
white bread	15	15	16	15	15	14	13	13	13	13	14
wholemeal bread	1	3	3	4	3	1	3	3	4	3	3
soft grain and other bread	3	4	4	4	4	5	5	4	4	4	4
breakfast cereals	3	4	4	6	4	4	4	5	7	6	5
biscuits, buns, cakes & pastries	2	3	3	4	3	2	3	4	5	4	4
Milk & milk products	5	7	7	8	7	7	8	9	9	9	8
of which:											
milk	2	3	3	3	3	3	3	4	4	4	3
cheese	3	4	4	4	4	4	4	4	4	4	4
Eggs & egg dishes	2	2	2	2	2	2	2	2	3	2	2
Fat spreads	4	3	3	4	3	3	3	3	3	3	3
Meat & meat products	31	29	28	27	28	27	22	23	22	23	26
of which:											
bacon & ham	8	8	9	10	9	6	6	6	8	7	8
beef, veal & dishes	3	3	3	3	3	4	3	3	3	3	3
chicken, turkey & dishes including coated	6	5	6	4	5	6	5	6	4	5	5
burgers & kebabs	4	3	1	0	2	4	2	1	0	1	2
sausages	5	4	4	3	4	3	3	2	2	3	3
meat pies & pastries	3	3	3	3	3	2	2	2	2	2	2
Fish & fish dishes	2	2	4	4	3	4	4	5	6	5	4
Vegetables (excluding potatoes)	7	6	7	5	6	7	9	7	6	7	7
Potatoes & savoury snacks	5	4	3	2	3	7	5	4	2	4	4
of which:											
savoury snacks	4	3	2	1	2	5	4	2	1	3	2
Fruit & nuts	0	0	1	0	0	1	0	1	1	1	0
Sugars, preserves & confectionery	1	1	1	0	1	1	1	1	1	1	1
Drinks**	2	2	2	2	2	2	2	2	1	2	2
Miscellaneous***	7	8	8	8	8	8	10	10	10	10	9
Average daily intake (mg)	3342	3347	3337	3248	3313	2303	2324	2316	2266	2302	2791
Total number of respondents	108	219	253	253	833	104	210	318	259	891	1724

Note: *   Data in this table are for intakes from food only and do not include further additions of salt in cooking or at the table.

  **   Includes soft drinks, alcoholic drinks, tea, coffee and water.

  ***   Includes powdered beverages (except tea and coffee), soups, sauces, condiments and artificial sweeteners.

Table 3.26

Percentage contribution of food types to average daily intake of chloride by age and sex of respondent*

Percentages

Type of food	Men aged (years):				All men	Women aged (years):				All women	All
	19–24	25–34	35–49	50–64		19–24	25–34	35–49	50–64		
	%	%	%	%	%	%	%	%	%	%	%
Cereals & cereal products	34	35	34	36	35	33	35	35	36	35	35
of which:											
pizza	6	3	2	1	3	4	3	2	1	2	2
white bread	15	14	15	15	15	14	13	13	12	13	14
wholemeal bread	1	3	3	4	3	1	3	4	4	3	3
soft grain and other bread	3	4	3	4	4	4	5	4	4	4	4
breakfast cereals	3	4	5	6	5	5	5	6	8	6	5
biscuits, buns, cakes & pastries	2	2	3	3	3	2	3	3	4	3	3
Milk & milk products	6	8	9	9	8	9	9	11	11	10	9
of which:											
milk	2	4	4	4	4	4	4	5	5	5	4
cheese	3	3	3	4	3	3	4	3	4	4	4
Eggs & egg dishes	2	2	1	2	2	1	1	2	2	2	2
Fat spreads	3	3	3	4	3	3	2	3	3	3	3
Meat & meat products	29	27	26	25	26	25	20	21	20	21	24
of which:											
bacon & ham	8	8	8	9	8	6	6	6	7	6	7
beef, veal & dishes	3	3	3	2	3	3	2	2	2	2	3
chicken, turkey & dishes including coated	5	4	5	3	4	6	5	5	3	5	4
burgers & kebabs	4	2	1	0	2	3	1	1	0	1	1
sausages	5	4	4	3	4	3	3	2	2	2	3
meat pies & pastries	3	3	3	3	3	2	2	2	2	2	2
Fish & fish dishes	2	2	4	4	3	4	4	5	6	5	4
Vegetables (excluding potatoes)	8	6	7	6	6	8	10	8	6	8	7
Potatoes & savoury snacks	7	5	5	3	5	9	7	5	4	5	5
of which:											
savoury snacks	4	3	2	1	2	5	4	2	1	3	3
Fruit & nuts	0	1	1	1	1	1	1	1	1	1	1
Sugars, preserves & confectionery	1	1	1	0	1	1	1	1	1	1	1
Drinks**	2	3	3	3	3	1	1	1	1	1	2
Miscellaneous***	7	7	7	7	7	7	9	9	9	9	8
Average daily intake (mg)	4921	5056	5047	4922	4995	3409	3478	3512	3474	3481	4212
Total number of respondents	108	219	253	253	833	104	210	318	259	891	1724

Note: *   Data in this table are for intakes from food only and do not include further additions of salt in cooking or at the table.
      ** Includes soft drinks, alcoholic drinks, tea, coffee and water.
      *** Includes powdered beverages (except tea and coffee), soups, sauces, condiments and artificial sweeteners.

Table 3.27

Average daily intake of potassium (mg) by sex and age of respondent

Cumulative percentages

Potassium (mg)	Men aged (years):				All men	Women aged (years):				All women
	19–24	25–34	35–49	50–64		19–24	25–34	35–49	50–64	
	cum %	cum %	cum %	cum %	cum %	cum %	cum %	cum %	cum %	cum %
(a) Intakes from *all sources*										
Less than 1000	-	-	-	-	-	3	1	1	1	1
Less than 1500	1	-	1	1	1	13	9	4	2	6
Less than 2000	18	3	4	5	6	30	30	16	10	19
Less than 2500	33	19	10	15	17	61	60	39	30	44
Less than 3000	53	42	31	32	37	82	79	63	59	68
Less than 3500	86	65	51	46	58	94	94	85	80	86
Less than 4000	93	86	77	66	78	100	100	95	92	96
Less than 4500	99	92	89	82	89			99	99	99
All	100	100	100	100	100			100	100	100
Base	*108*	*219*	*253*	*253*	*833*	*104*	*210*	*318*	*259*	*891*
Mean (average value)	2847	3286	3485	3553	3371	2364	2398	2734	2885	2655
Median	2935	3194	3472	3566	3304	2385	2383	2692	2829	2620
Lower 2.5 percentile	1630	1951	1833	1853	1783	923	1148	1194	1502	1186
Upper 2.5 percentile	4397	5331	5770	5571	5504	3756	3719	4291	4342	4183
Standard deviation	712.9	1012.9	910.8	998.2	968.9	688.9	655.4	759.5	731.3	747.9
	cum %	cum %	cum %	cum %	cum %	cum %	cum %	cum %	cum %	cum %
(b) Intakes from *food sources*										
Less than 1000	-	-	-	-	-	3	1	1	1	1
Less than 1500	1	-	2	1	1	13	9	4	2	6
Less than 2000	18	3	5	5	6	30	30	16	10	19
Less than 2500	33	19	10	15	17	62	60	39	30	44
Less than 3000	53	42	31	32	37	82	79	63	59	68
Less than 3500	86	65	51	46	58	94	94	85	80	87
Less than 4000	93	86	77	66	78	100	100	95	92	96
Less than 4500	99	92	89	82	89			99	99	99
All	100	100	100	100	100			100	100	100
Base	*108*	*219*	*253*	*253*	*833*	*104*	*210*	*318*	*259*	*891*
Mean (average value)	2841	3284	3481	3552	3367	2362	2397	2731	2884	2653
Median	2935	3194	3472	3566	3301	2385	2383	2692	2828	2619
Lower 2.5 percentile	1630	1948	1798	1853	1774	923	1148	1194	1502	1186
Upper 2.5 percentile	4397	5331	5770	5571	5504	3756	3719	4291	4342	4183
Standard deviation	708.1	1000.4	915.7	997.4	966.5	687.9	654.4	759.0	731.2	747.3

Table 3.28

Average daily intake of potassium as a percentage of Reference Nutrient Intake (RNI) by sex and age of respondent

Percentages

Sex and age of respondent	Average daily intake as % of RNI*							
	(a) All sources			Base	(b) Food sources			Base
	Mean	Median	sd		Mean	Median	sd	
Men aged (years):								
19–24	81	84	20.4	108	81	84	20.2	108
25–34	94	91	28.9	219	94	91	28.6	219
35–49	100	99	26.0	253	99	99	26.2	253
50–64	102	102	28.5	253	101	102	28.5	253
All	96	94	27.7	833	96	94	27.6	833
Women aged (years):								
19–24	68	68	19.7	104	67	68	19.7	104
25–34	69	68	18.7	210	68	68	18.7	210
35–49	78	77	21.7	318	78	77	21.7	318
50–64	82	81	20.9	259	82	81	20.9	259
All	76	75	21.4	891	76	75	21.4	891

Note: * Intake as a percentage of RNI was calculated for each respondent. The values for all respondents in each age group were then pooled to give a mean, median and sd.

Table 3.29

Percentage contribution of food types to average daily intake of potassium by sex and age of respondent

Percentages

Type of food	Men aged (years):				All men	Women aged (years):				All women	All
	19–24	25–34	35–49	50–64		19–24	25–34	35–49	50–64		
	%	%	%	%	%	%	%	%	%	%	%
Cereals & cereal products	14	14	13	14	14	12	13	13	13	13	13
of which:											
white bread	4	4	4	3	3	4	3	3	2	3	3
wholemeal bread	1	1	1	2	1	0	1	1	1	1	1
soft grain and other bread	1	1	1	1	1	2	1	1	1	1	1
breakfast cereals	1	3	3	3	3	2	2	3	4	3	3
Milk & milk products	10	13	13	13	13	13	14	15	15	15	13
of which:											
whole milk	1	3	3	2	2	3	3	3	2	2	2
semi-skimmed milk	6	6	7	6	6	5	6	7	7	7	6
skimmed milk	0	2	1	1	1	2	1	2	3	2	2
Eggs & egg dishes	1	1	1	1	1	1	1	1	1	1	1
Fat spreads	0	0	0	0	0	0	0	0	0	0	0
Meat & meat products	19	17	16	14	16	15	13	13	11	13	15
of which:											
beef, veal & dishes	4	4	4	3	4	4	3	3	3	3	3
chicken, turkey & dishes including coated	6	6	6	4	5	6	5	5	4	5	5
Fish & fish dishes	2	2	3	4	3	2	2	3	4	3	3
Vegetables (excluding potatoes)	8	8	9	10	9	9	13	11	11	11	10
Potatoes & savoury snacks	25	19	17	16	18	27	20	17	16	18	18
of which:											
potato chips	13	8	7	5	7	11	8	6	4	6	7
savoury snacks	4	3	2	1	2	4	3	2	1	2	2
Fruit & nuts	2	5	7	8	6	5	7	9	12	9	7
Sugars, preserves & confectionery	2	1	1	1	1	1	1	1	1	1	1
Drinks*	15	17	18	17	17	12	12	14	13	13	15
of which:											
fruit juice	2	2	2	2	2	3	3	2	2	2	2
beer & lager	6	6	5	5	5	2	1	1	0	1	3
coffee	3	4	5	4	4	2	3	4	4	4	4
tea	2	2	3	4	3	2	3	4	4	3	3
Miscellaneous**	3	3	2	2	2	2	3	3	3	3	2
Average daily intake (mg)	2841	3284	3481	3552	3367	2362	2397	2731	2884	2653	2998
Total number of respondents	108	219	253	253	833	104	210	318	259	891	1724

Note: * Includes soft drinks, alcoholic drinks, tea, coffee and water.

  ** Includes powdered beverages (except tea and coffee), soups, sauces, condiments and artificial sweeteners.

Table 3.30

Average daily intake of zinc (mg) by sex and age of respondent

Cumulative percentages

Zinc (mg)	Men aged (years):				All men	Women aged (years):				All women
	19–24	25–34	35–49	50–64		19–24	25–34	35–49	50–64	
	cum %	cum %	cum %	cum %	cum %	cum %	cum %	cum %	cum %	cum %
(a) Intakes from *all sources*										
Less than 4.0	1	-	1	1	1	5	5	3	3	4
Less than 5.5	7	2	4	3	4	24	25	13	14	18
Less than 6.0	9	4	6	5	6	35	37	20	17	25
Less than 6.5	17	7	8	7	9	45	46	30	23	33
Less than 7.0	17	15	10	9	12	57	58	38	29	42
Less than 8.0	35	23	16	17	21	74	73	55	47	59
Less than 9.0	46	35	26	29	32	82	86	73	66	75
Less than 9.5	57	47	35	38	42	84	88	80	73	80
Less than 10.0	63	52	43	46	49	86	92	85	80	85
Less than 12.5	94	79	79	75	80	98	96	94	91	94
Less than 15.0	99	91	91	91	92	98	97	97	95	97
All	100	100	100	100	100	100	100	100	100	100
Base	*108*	*219*	*253*	*253*	*833*	*104*	*210*	*318*	*259*	*891*
Mean (average value)	9.2	10.7	11.4	10.8	10.7	7.1	7.1	8.2	8.6	7.9
Median	9.2	9.8	10.3	10.3	10.1	6.6	6.6	7.8	8.1	7.4
Lower 2.5 percentile	4.2	5.6	4.4	5.0	4.9	3.0	3.3	3.4	3.6	3.3
Upper 2.5 percentile	13.7	21.4	23.0	20.2	19.6	11.0	15.1	21.6	19.4	17.3
Standard deviation	2.49	4.36	8.41	4.22	5.75	3.17	2.88	3.79	3.66	3.54
	cum %	cum %	cum %	cum %	cum %	cum %	cum %	cum %	cum %	cum %
(b) Intakes from *food sources*										
Less than 4.0	1	-	1	1	1	5	5	4	3	4
Less than 5.5	7	2	4	3	4	24	25	14	15	18
Less than 6.0	9	4	6	6	6	35	38	20	18	26
Less than 6.5	17	7	8	8	9	45	46	32	25	35
Less than 7.0	17	15	11	11	13	58	60	39	33	45
Less than 8.0	35	23	17	20	22	75	77	58	53	63
Less than 9.0	46	37	27	32	34	82	89	78	73	79
Less than 9.5	57	49	36	41	43	85	92	84	80	85
Less than 10.0	67	58	44	49	52	87	95	90	86	89
Less than 12.5	98	82	80	77	82	100	99	99	97	99
Less than 15.0	100	92	93	93	94		100	100	100	100
All		100	100	100	100					
Base	*108*	*219*	*253*	*253*	*833*	*104*	*210*	*318*	*259*	*891*
Mean (average value)	9.0	10.2	10.6	10.3	10.2	6.8	6.7	7.6	7.8	7.4
Median	9.2	9.6	10.2	10.1	9.9	6.6	6.6	7.6	7.9	7.3
Lower 2.5 percentile	4.2	5.6	4.3	5.0	4.8	3.0	3.3	3.4	3.6	3.3
Upper 2.5 percentile	12.7	19.1	18.1	15.8	17.1	10.9	10.6	11.9	12.9	11.9
Standard deviation	2.28	3.60	3.45	2.83	3.21	2.11	1.89	2.04	2.20	2.11

Table 3.31

Average daily intake of zinc as a percentage of Reference Nutrient Intake (RNI) by sex and age of respondent

Percentages

Sex and age of respondent	Average daily intake as % of RNI*							
	(a) All sources			Base	(b) Food sources			Base
	Mean	Median	sd		Mean	Median	sd	
Men aged (years):								
19–24	96	97	26.2	108	95	97	24.0	108
25–34	112	103	45.9	219	108	101	37.9	219
35–49	120	108	88.6	253	111	108	36.3	253
50–64	114	108	44.4	253	109	106	29.8	253
All	113	106	60.5	833	107	104	33.8	833
Women aged (years):								
19–24	102	95	45.3	104	98	95	30.1	104
25–34	102	95	41.2	210	96	95	26.9	210
35–49	117	111	54.1	318	108	109	29.2	318
50–64	123	116	52.3	259	112	113	31.5	259
All	113	106	50.5	891	105	104	30.1	891

Note: * Intake as a percentage of RNI was calculated for each respondent. The values for all respondents in each age group were then pooled to give a mean, median and sd.

Table 3.32

Percentage contribution of food types to average daily intake of zinc by sex and age of respondent

Percentages

Type of food	Men aged (years):				All men	Women aged (years):				All women	All
	19–24	25–34	35–49	50–64		19–24	25–34	35–49	50–64		
	%	%	%	%	%	%	%	%	%	%	%
Cereals & cereal products	25	26	24	24	25	24	27	25	26	26	25
of which:											
pizza	5	3	1	1	2	3	2	1	1	2	2
white bread	7	6	7	6	7	7	6	5	5	6	6
wholemeal bread	1	3	3	3	3	1	3	3	3	3	3
soft grain and other bread	2	2	2	3	2	3	3	2	2	3	2
breakfast cereals	3	5	4	5	4	3	4	5	7	6	5
Milk & milk products	13	16	16	17	16	16	19	19	19	19	17
of which:											
whole milk	1	2	2	2	2	3	3	2	2	2	2
semi-skimmed milk	5	5	6	6	5	4	6	6	7	6	6
skimmed milk	0	1	1	1	1	2	1	2	3	2	2
cheese	5	6	6	6	6	5	7	5	6	6	6
Eggs & egg dishes	3	3	3	3	3	3	2	3	3	3	3
Fat spreads	0	0	0	0	0	0	0	0	0	0	0
Meat & meat products	43	37	36	34	36	36	29	31	29	30	34
of which:											
bacon & ham	4	4	4	4	4	2	3	3	3	3	3
beef, veal & dishes	13	12	12	11	12	13	9	12	10	11	11
chicken, turkey & dishes including coated	6	6	6	4	5	7	6	6	5	6	5
burgers & kebabs	9	5	3	1	4	7	3	2	1	2	3
Fish & fish dishes	1	2	4	3	3	2	3	3	4	3	3
Vegetables (excluding potatoes)	4	5	5	5	5	6	8	6	6	6	6
Potatoes & savoury snacks	6	5	5	5	5	7	6	5	5	5	5
Fruit & nuts	0	2	2	2	2	2	2	2	3	3	2
Sugars, preserves & confectionery	2	1	1	1	1	1	1	1	1	1	1
Drinks*	1	2	3	4	3	1	2	2	2	2	2
Miscellaneous**	1	1	1	2	2	1	2	2	2	2	2
Average daily intake (mg)	**9.0**	**10.2**	**10.6**	**10.3**	**10.2**	**6.8**	**6.7**	**7.6**	**7.8**	**7.4**	**8.7**
Total number of respondents	**108**	**219**	**253**	**253**	**833**	**104**	**210**	**318**	**259**	**891**	**1724**

Note: *   Includes soft drinks, alcoholic drinks, tea, coffee and water.

** Includes powdered beverages (except tea and coffee), soups, sauces, condiments and artificial sweeteners.

Table 3.33

Average daily intake of copper (mg) by sex and age of respondent

Cumulative percentages

Copper (mg)	Men aged (years):				All men	Women aged (years):				All women
	19–24	25–34	35–49	50–64		19–24	25–34	35–49	50–64	
	cum %	cum %	cum %	cum %	cum %	cum %	cum %	cum %	cum %	cum %
(a) Intakes from *all sources*										
Less than 0.5	-	-	1	0	0	8	4	3	3	4
Less than 0.6	4	0	1	2	2	16	10	8	6	9
Less than 0.7	6	2	3	4	4	35	19	14	12	17
Less than 0.8	12	9	7	5	7	45	31	23	22	27
Less than 0.9	19	16	12	10	13	54	46	33	32	38
Less than 1.0	36	20	17	14	19	70	57	45	48	52
Less than 1.2	59	39	32	32	38	78	73	72	68	72
Less than 1.4	78	60	52	49	56	87	87	83	81	84
Less than 1.6	91	74	66	68	72	88	92	91	89	90
Less than 1.8	93	83	78	76	80	93	95	93	93	94
Less than 2.0	97	88	84	83	87	95	97	96	95	96
All	100	100	100	100	100	100	100	100	100	100
Base	*108*	*219*	*253*	*253*	*833*	*104*	*210*	*318*	*259*	*891*
Mean (average value)	1.16	1.43	1.58	1.56	1.48	0.97	1.02	1.11	1.11	1.07
Median	1.14	1.30	1.36	1.41	1.32	0.84	0.94	1.03	1.01	0.99
Lower 2.5 percentile	0.53	0.70	0.63	0.63	0.65	0.31	0.45	0.47	0.47	0.45
Upper 2.5 percentile	2.09	2.91	3.56	3.33	3.20	3.00	2.10	3.02	2.24	2.25
Standard deviation	0.338	0.673	0.972	0.882	0.820	0.523	0.416	0.514	0.433	0.473
	cum %	cum %	cum %	cum %	cum %	cum %	cum %	cum %	cum %	cum %
(b) Intakes from *food sources*										
Less than 0.5	-	-	1	0	0	8	4	4	3	4
Less than 0.6	4	0	2	2	2	16	10	9	6	9
Less than 0.7	6	2	4	4	4	35	19	15	12	17
Less than 0.8	12	9	7	6	8	45	32	23	22	27
Less than 0.9	19	16	12	11	14	54	47	34	33	39
Less than 1.0	39	22	17	15	20	71	57	46	50	53
Less than 1.2	62	40	33	34	39	78	74	74	70	73
Less than 1.4	78	61	53	51	58	92	88	86	83	86
Less than 1.6	91	76	67	70	73	93	93	94	91	93
Less than 1.8	95	85	79	77	82	97	97	97	95	96
Less than 2.0	100	90	86	84	88	98	99	99	97	98
All		100	100	100	100	100	100	100	100	100
Base	*108*	*219*	*253*	*253*	*833*	*104*	*210*	*318*	*259*	*891*
Mean (average value)	1.14	1.37	1.53	1.51	1.43	0.91	1.00	1.05	1.07	1.03
Median	1.08	1.30	1.36	1.39	1.32	0.84	0.94	1.03	1.00	0.98
Lower 2.5 percentile	0.53	0.70	0.63	0.63	0.64	0.31	0.45	0.47	0.47	0.45
Upper 2.5 percentile	1.89	2.54	3.30	2.94	2.93	1.81	1.82	1.88	2.01	1.92
Standard deviation	0.316	0.517	0.864	0.751	0.705	0.376	0.374	0.375	0.376	0.378

Table 3.34

Average daily intake of copper as a percentage of Reference Nutrient Intake (RNI) by sex and age of respondent

Percentages

Sex and age of respondent	Average daily intake as % of RNI*							
	(a) All sources			Base	(b) Food sources			Base
	Mean	Median	sd		Mean	Median	sd	
Men aged (years):								
19–24	97	95	28.1	108	95	90	26.3	108
25–34	119	108	56.1	219	114	108	43.1	219
35–49	131	113	81.0	253	128	113	72.0	253
50–64	130	117	73.5	253	126	116	62.6	253
All	123	110	68.4	833	119	110	58.7	833
Women aged (years):								
19–24	81	70	43.5	104	76	70	31.4	104
25–34	85	79	34.7	210	83	78	31.2	210
35–49	93	86	42.8	318	88	86	31.3	318
50–64	92	84	36.1	259	89	83	31.3	259
All	89	82	39.4	891	86	81	31.5	891

Note: * Intake as a percentage of RNI was calculated for each respondent. The values for all respondents in each age group were then pooled to give a mean, median and sd.

Table 3.35

Percentage contribution of food types to average daily intake of copper by sex and age of respondent

Percentages

Type of food	Men aged (years):				All men	Women aged (years):				All women	All
	19–24	25–34	35–49	50–64		19–24	25–34	35–49	50–64		
	%	%	%	%	%	%	%	%	%	%	%
Cereals & cereal products	36	34	30	29	31	34	33	32	31	32	31
of which:											
pasta	4	3	2	2	3	5	3	3	2	3	3
pizza	8	4	2	1	3	4	3	2	1	2	3
white bread	10	9	8	8	8	10	7	7	6	7	8
wholemeal bread	2	3	3	3	3	1	3	3	3	3	3
soft grain and other bread	2	3	2	3	3	5	3	3	3	3	3
breakfast cereals	3	4	4	4	4	4	4	5	6	5	4
biscuits, buns, cakes & pastries	4	4	5	5	5	3	5	5	6	5	5
Milk & milk products	5	6	5	5	5	5	6	5	5	5	5
Eggs & egg dishes	2	2	1	2	2	1	1	1	2	2	2
Fat spreads	0	0	0	0	0	0	0	0	0	0	0
Meat & meat products	17	16	19	17	17	15	12	13	12	12	15
of which:											
beef, veal & dishes	3	3	2	2	2	3	2	2	2	2	2
chicken, turkey & dishes including coated	4	4	4	3	4	4	4	4	3	4	4
liver, liver products & dishes	0	2	7	6	5	2	1	2	2	2	3
burgers & kebabs	3	1	1	0	1	2	1	0	0	1	1
Fish & fish dishes	2	3	4	3	3	3	3	3	3	3	3
Vegetables (excluding potatoes)	4	6	6	6	6	6	9	7	6	7	6
Potatoes & savoury snacks	15	10	9	9	10	16	11	10	9	11	10
of which:											
potato chips	9	5	4	3	5	8	5	4	3	4	5
Fruit & nuts	4	7	9	11	9	9	11	11	15	12	10
of which:											
fruit	4	5	7	10	7	7	9	10	14	10	9
Sugars, preserves & confectionery	5	4	4	3	4	4	4	4	3	4	4
Drinks*	6	8	11	12	10	5	7	9	9	8	9
of which:											
tea	2	2	3	4	3	2	3	4	5	4	3
Miscellaneous**	4	3	3	4	3	3	4	4	4	4	4
Average daily intake (mg)	1.14	1.37	1.53	1.51	1.43	0.91	1.00	1.05	1.07	1.03	1.22
Total number of respondents	108	219	253	253	833	104	210	318	259	891	1724

Note: * Includes soft drinks, alcoholic drinks, tea, coffee and water.
      ** Includes powdered beverages (except tea and coffee), soups, sauces, condiments and artificial sweeteners.

Table 3.36

Average daily intake of iodine (μg) by sex and age of respondent

Cumulative percentages

Iodine (μg)	Men aged (years):				All men	Women aged (years):				All women
	19–24	25–34	35–49	50–64		19–24	25–34	35–49	50–64	
	cum %	cum %	cum %	cum %	cum %	cum %	cum %	cum %	cum %	cum %
(a) Intakes from *all sources*										
Less than 70	2	1	2	1	2	12	5	4	1	4
Less than 100	17	7	5	3	6	28	21	13	13	17
Less than 120	33	12	9	7	12	45	35	23	20	28
Less than 140	41	16	17	12	18	61	53	37	27	41
Less than 150	50	19	21	14	22	67	56	43	34	46
Less than 200	70	49	41	36	45	84	85	76	60	74
Less than 250	86	71	67	62	69	94	96	88	81	88
Less than 300	93	84	83	80	84	96	99	94	94	95
Less than 350	100	90	92	91	92	100	99	97	97	98
All		100	100	100	100		100	100	100	100
Base	*108*	*219*	*253*	*253*	*833*	*104*	*210*	*318*	*259*	*891*
Mean (average value)	167	223	226	235	220	136	148	171	190	167
Median	152	202	217	227	209	129	138	157	180	155
Lower 2.5 percentile	65	80	79	91	80	40	57	65	75	58
Upper 2.5 percentile	314	432	444	442	428	309	267	360	382	340
Standard deviation	70.1	122.4	93.0	85.0	99.1	62.3	65.4	78.4	84.2	77.8
	cum %	cum %	cum %	cum %	cum %	cum %	cum %	cum %	cum %	cum %
(b) Intakes from *food sources*										
Less than 70	2	1	2	1	2	12	5	4	1	4
Less than 100	21	7	5	3	7	28	22	13	14	17
Less than 120	33	13	9	7	13	45	37	24	21	29
Less than 140	41	16	17	12	18	63	56	38	31	43
Less than 150	50	19	21	14	22	68	58	46	38	49
Less than 200	70	51	42	37	46	88	87	79	66	78
Less than 250	86	75	68	64	71	99	96	91	88	92
Less than 300	93	88	83	83	86	99	99	96	96	97
Less than 350	100	93	94	93	94	100	99	99	99	99
All		100	100	100	100		100	100	100	100
Base	*108*	*219*	*253*	*253*	*833*	*104*	*210*	*318*	*259*	*891*
Mean (average value)	166	216	221	230	215	130	145	162	178	159
Median	152	196	215	223	205	129	135	155	171	151
Lower 2.5 percentile	65	80	74	91	80	40	57	63	75	58
Upper 2.5 percentile	314	432	407	405	405	233	263	312	326	305
Standard deviation	70.9	119.6	84.3	80.2	94.3	51.2	64.1	63.7	73.7	67.4

Table 3.37

Average daily intake of iodine as a percentage of Reference Nutrient Intake (RNI) by sex and age of respondent

Percentages

Sex and age of respondent	Average daily intake as % of RNI*							
	(a) All sources			Base	(b) Food sources			Base
	Mean	Median	sd		Mean	Median	sd	
Men aged (years):								
19–24	119	109	50.1	108	119	109	50.6	108
25–34	159	144	87.4	219	154	140	85.4	219
35–49	161	155	66.5	253	158	154	60.2	253
50–64	168	162	60.7	253	164	160	57.3	253
All	157	149	70.8	833	154	147	67.3	833
Women aged (years):								
19–24	97	92	44.5	104	93	92	36.6	104
25–34	106	99	46.7	210	103	96	45.8	210
35–49	122	112	56.0	318	116	111	45.5	318
50–64	136	129	60.1	259	127	122	52.7	259
All	119	111	55.5	891	114	108	48.1	891

Note: * Intake as a percentage of RNI was calculated for each respondent. The values for all respondents in each age group were then pooled to give a mean, median and sd.

Table 3.38

Percentage contribution of food types to average daily intake of iodine by sex and age of respondent

Percentages

Type of food	Men aged (years):				All men	Women aged (years):				All women	All
	19–24	25–34	35–49	50–64		19–24	25–34	35–49	50–64		
	%	%	%	%	%	%	%	%	%	%	%
Cereals & cereal products	14	12	11	12	12	12	12	12	11	12	12
of which:											
bread	4	3	3	3	3	4	3	3	2	3	3
biscuits, buns, cakes & pastries	3	2	3	4	3	2	3	3	4	3	3
Milk & milk products	29	36	37	35	35	40	41	44	42	42	38
of which:											
whole milk	3	8	7	7	7	9	10	8	5	7	7
semi-skimmed milk	17	16	20	17	18	16	18	20	19	19	18
skimmed milk	2	5	3	4	3	5	4	7	8	6	5
cheese	2	2	2	2	2	3	3	2	2	2	2
yogurt	2	2	3	3	3	3	4	4	5	4	3
Eggs & egg dishes	5	5	5	5	5	5	4	5	5	5	5
Fat spreads	3	2	2	2	2	2	2	2	2	2	2
Meat & meat products	10	7	7	6	7	9	6	6	5	6	7
Fish & fish dishes	7	7	10	14	10	8	10	11	15	12	11
of which:											
coated & fried white fish	5	4	5	6	5	5	4	5	7	5	5
other white fish	1	1	2	4	2	1	3	3	5	4	3
oily fish	0	1	2	3	2	2	2	2	3	2	2
Vegetables (excluding potatoes)	2	2	2	2	2	2	3	2	2	2	2
Potatoes & savoury snacks	4	2	2	2	2	4	3	2	2	3	3
Fruit & nuts	0	1	2	2	1	1	2	2	3	2	2
Sugars, preserves & confectionery	2	1	1	1	1	2	1	2	1	1	1
Drinks*	22	22	19	17	19	12	10	9	8	9	15
of which:											
beer & lager	19	18	14	12	15	8	4	3	1	3	10
Miscellaneous**	2	2	2	2	2	3	5	3	4	4	3
Average daily intake (μg)	166	216	221	230	215	130	145	162	178	159	186
Total number of respondents	108	219	253	253	833	104	210	318	259	891	1724

Note: * Includes soft drinks, alcoholic drinks, tea, coffee and water.

   ** Includes powdered beverages (except tea and coffee), soups, sauces, condiments and artificial sweeteners.

Table 3.39

Average daily intake of manganese (mg) by sex and age of respondent

Cumulative percentages

Manganese (mg)	Men aged (years):				All men	Women aged (years):				All women
	19–24	25–34	35–49	50–64		19–24	25–34	35–49	50–64	
	cum %	cum %	cum %	cum %	cum %	cum %	cum %	cum %	cum %	cum %
(a) Intakes from *all sources*										
Less than 1.0	1	0	1	0	1	7	2	3	2	3
Less than 1.4	6	4	5	3	4	20	9	9	6	9
Less than 1.6	14	5	7	4	6	27	18	12	9	14
Less than 2.0	33	19	15	7	16	46	34	26	19	28
Less than 2.4	53	28	25	15	27	67	54	39	32	44
Less than 2.8	70	44	39	27	40	81	73	54	46	60
Less than 3.2	81	56	49	39	52	86	81	68	60	71
Less than 3.6	88	67	62	52	64	91	91	76	72	80
Less than 4.0	91	77	71	64	73	93	93	85	81	87
Less than 4.5	99	84	81	74	82	95	94	91	87	91
Less than 5.0	99	89	87	86	89	97	97	94	91	94
All	100	100	100	100	100	100	100	100	100	100
Base	*108*	*219*	*253*	*253*	*833*	*104*	*210*	*318*	*259*	*891*
Mean (average value)	2.48	3.22	3.63	3.77	3.42	2.19	2.48	2.86	3.11	2.77
Median	2.37	3.00	3.22	3.54	3.12	2.02	2.31	2.67	2.88	2.55
Lower 2.5 percentile	1.14	1.38	1.31	1.34	1.34	0.69	1.05	0.93	1.07	0.98
Upper 2.5 percentile	4.15	6.24	7.75	8.11	7.06	5.22	5.47	6.07	6.05	5.63
Standard deviation	0.840	1.342	3.080	1.513	2.074	1.009	1.030	1.249	1.456	1.278
	cum %	cum %	cum %	cum %	cum %	cum %	cum %	cum %	cum %	cum %
(b) Intakes from *food sources*										
Less than 1.0	1	0	1	0	1	7	2	3	2	3
Less than 1.4	6	4	5	3	4	22	9	9	6	9
Less than 1.6	14	5	7	5	7	29	18	13	9	15
Less than 2.0	33	19	15	8	16	48	34	27	19	29
Less than 2.4	57	30	26	16	28	67	55	39	32	44
Less than 2.8	70	44	39	29	41	81	74	55	47	60
Less than 3.2	83	57	50	39	53	89	81	68	60	72
Less than 3.6	90	70	62	52	65	94	91	77	74	81
Less than 4.0	91	78	72	65	74	96	94	87	82	88
Less than 4.5	99	85	82	76	83	98	95	93	89	93
Less than 5.0	99	90	88	87	90	100	98	96	93	96
All	100	100	100	100	100		100	100	100	100
Base	*108*	*219*	*253*	*253*	*833*	*104*	*210*	*318*	*259*	*891*
Mean (average value)	2.45	3.18	3.42	3.70	3.32	2.12	2.45	2.79	3.01	2.69
Median	2.29	2.97	3.21	3.53	3.10	2.02	2.30	2.66	2.88	2.55
Lower 2.5 percentile	1.14	1.38	1.30	1.34	1.33	0.69	1.05	0.91	1.07	0.95
Upper 2.5 percentile	4.15	6.24	6.90	7.79	6.83	4.50	4.89	5.40	5.44	5.31
Standard deviation	0.827	1.326	1.524	1.434	1.423	0.892	0.980	1.110	1.136	1.102

Table 3.40

Percentage contribution of food types to average daily intake of manganese by sex and age of respondent

Percentages

Type of food	Men aged (years):				All men	Women aged (years):				All women	All
	19–24	25–34	35–49	50–64		19–24	25–34	35–49	50–64		
	%	%	%	%	%	%	%	%	%	%	%
Cereals & cereal products	49	53	52	50	51	47	49	48	48	48	50
of which:											
pasta	4	3	2	1	2	5	3	2	1	2	2
white bread	16	13	13	11	12	14	11	9	8	9	11
wholemeal bread	5	10	10	10	9	3	9	9	9	8	9
soft grain and other bread	5	6	6	6	6	7	6	5	5	6	6
breakfast cereals	7	10	10	12	11	9	9	12	15	12	11
biscuits, buns, cakes & pastries	4	4	5	6	5	4	5	5	6	5	5
Milk & milk products	0	1	0	0	0	1	1	1	1	1	1
Eggs & egg dishes	0	0	0	0	0	0	0	0	0	0	0
Fat spreads	0	0	0	0	0	0	0	0	0	0	0
Meat & meat products	10	8	6	5	7	8	5	5	4	5	6
Fish & fish dishes	1	1	1	1	1	1	1	1	1	1	1
Vegetables (excluding potatoes)	9	9	9	9	9	11	12	11	10	11	10
Potatoes & savoury snacks	10	6	6	5	6	10	7	6	5	6	6
Fruit & nuts	2	5	7	7	6	5	6	7	10	8	7
Sugars, preserves & confectionery	3	2	1	1	2	2	2	2	1	2	2
Drinks*	12	14	16	19	16	14	15	19	19	18	17
of which:											
tea	8	10	11	15	12	9	11	14	14	13	12
Miscellaneous**	2	2	2	2	2	1	2	2	2	2	2
Average daily intake (mg)	**2.45**	**3.18**	**3.42**	**3.70**	**3.32**	**2.12**	**2.45**	**2.79**	**3.01**	**2.69**	**2.99**
Total number of respondents	**108**	**219**	**253**	**253**	**833**	**104**	**210**	**318**	**259**	**891**	**1724**

Note: * Includes soft drinks, alcoholic drinks, tea, coffee and water.
      ** Includes powdered beverages (except tea and coffee), soups, sauces, condiments and artificial sweeteners.

Table 3.41

Average daily intake of minerals by sex of respondent and region

Mineral (unit of measurement)	Sex of respondent and region											
	Men											
	Scotland			Northern			Central, South West and Wales			London and the South East		
	Mean	Median	sd	Mean	Median	sd	Mean	Median	sd	Mean	Median	sd
All sources												
Total iron (mg)	13.9	12.8	5.82	12.9	12.3	4.81	14.9	13.2	13.06	14.2	13.2	6.28
Haem iron (mg)	1.0	0.9	0.58	0.8	0.7	0.51	0.8	0.7	0.51	0.8	0.7	0.50
Non-haem iron (mg)	12.9	11.9	5.68	12.0	11.6	4.67	14.1	12.2	12.99	13.5	12.4	6.24
Calcium (mg)	1066	1044	397.3	997	966	347.3	1050	1003	524.0	979	957	381.9
Phosphorus (mg)	1586	1498	442.6	1469	1431	426.7	1537	1514	652.2	1470	1448	389.3
Magnesium (mg)	306	291	99.3	305	301	96.2	315	300	113.1	312	306	97.2
Sodium (mg)*	3462	3312	1132.9	3337	3268	981.5	3385	3277	1095.3	3184	3160	908.8
Chloride (mg)*	5197	4994	1641.3	5029	4973	1458.3	5134	5011	1807.2	4815	4805	1365.0
Potassium (mg)	3416	3225	1028.0	3332	3292	963.1	3407	3329	1010.7	3351	3304	908.1
Zinc (mg)	11.4	11.1	4.39	10.3	10.1	3.32	10.9	10.1	7.27	10.8	9.9	5.83
Copper (mg)	1.44	1.24	0.981	1.37	1.27	0.503	1.52	1.33	0.738	1.54	1.35	1.074
Iodine (µg)	252	240	94.4	218	205	100.2	221	209	109.5	214	204	83.6
Manganese (mg)	3.28	3.08	1.417	3.18	3.09	1.308	3.61	3.11	2.865	3.45	3.21	1.615
Base		65			234			294			240	
Food sources												
Total iron (mg)	13.2	12.6	4.90	12.6	12.2	4.46	13.3	12.9	5.22	13.5	13.1	4.56
Haem iron (mg)	1.0	0.9	0.58	0.8	0.7	0.51	0.8	0.7	0.51	0.8	0.7	0.50
Non-haem iron (mg)	12.3	11.4	4.74	11.7	11.4	4.31	12.5	11.9	5.07	12.7	12.3	4.51
Calcium (mg)	1063	1044	394.1	993	953	348.2	1039	1001	486.6	965	954	367.3
Phosphorus (mg)	1584	1498	438.7	1466	1431	427.8	1518	1514	524.0	1465	1446	390.4
Magnesium (mg)	304	291	94.5	303	301	96.9	311	297	109.0	309	306	89.2
Sodium (mg)*	3462	3312	1132.9	3337	3268	981.9	3369	3268	1082.9	3182	3160	913.4
Chloride (mg)*	5196	4994	1639.8	5028	4973	1458.7	5072	5008	1610.3	4813	4805	1369.3
Potassium (mg)	3415	3225	1026.9	3331	3292	962.8	3402	3308	1001.4	3348	3304	912.4
Zinc (mg)	10.7	10.7	3.01	10.1	10.0	3.04	10.2	9.8	3.31	10.2	9.8	3.32
Copper (mg)	1.39	1.24	0.929	1.35	1.27	0.486	1.45	1.33	0.586	1.50	1.33	0.914
Iodine (µg)	245	239	88.0	214	201	95.3	216	206	106.2	208	202	76.6
Manganese (mg)	3.23	3.00	1.378	3.14	3.08	1.242	3.41	3.06	1.496	3.40	3.18	1.496
Base		65			234			294			240	

*Note: * Data in this table are for intakes from food and dietary supplements only and do not include further additions of salt in cooking or at the table.*

												Mineral (unit of measurement)
Women												
Scotland			Northern			Central, South West and Wales			London and the South East			
Mean	Median	sd	Mean	Median	sd	Mean	Median	sd	Mean	Median	sd	
												All sources
12.1	10.8	14.89	11.1	9.9	8.33	12.2	9.9	22.25	11.3	10.1	5.48	Total iron (mg)
0.7	0.5	0.62	0.5	0.4	0.47	0.5	0.5	0.37	0.5	0.4	0.35	Haem iron (mg)
11.4	10.3	14.88	10.6	9.4	8.23	11.7	9.3	22.26	10.8	9.7	5.43	Non-haem iron (mg)
773	709	251.9	817	778	349.6	808	769	285.9	812	762	329.0	Calcium (mg)
1095	1056	270.2	1119	1115	333.7	1115	1095	276.6	1121	1120	308.6	Phosphorus (mg)
218	216	65.5	230	225	72.9	232	221	75.7	241	228	86.6	Magnesium (mg)
2424	2361	618.1	2352	2271	720.9	2301	2223	647.1	2234	2249	703.7	Sodium (mg)*
3653	3562	943.7	3554	3489	1046.5	3459	3345	956.2	3408	3425	1064.1	Chloride (mg)*
2583	2509	669.3	2656	2621	794.7	2661	2666	707.4	2665	2587	775.5	Potassium (mg)
8.0	7.1	3.78	7.5	7.4	2.87	7.9	7.4	3.43	8.3	7.8	4.06	Zinc (mg)
1.06	0.96	0.477	1.02	0.94	0.446	1.08	0.97	0.485	1.12	1.07	0.476	Copper (mg)
168	156	76.8	169	159	81.9	164	150	74.5	169	157	78.6	Iodine (μg)
2.61	2.45	0.982	2.67	2.43	1.239	2.78	2.56	1.235	2.87	2.67	1.416	Manganese (mg)
	66			229			327			268		*Base*
												Food sources
10.2	10.5	2.94	9.9	9.5	4.07	9.8	9.5	3.46	10.2	9.8	3.67	Total iron (mg)
0.7	0.5	0.62	0.5	0.4	0.47	0.5	0.5	0.37	0.5	0.4	0.35	Haem iron (mg)
9.5	9.9	2.72	9.4	8.9	3.87	9.3	9.0	3.39	9.7	9.4	3.59	Non-haem iron (mg)
766	707	248.6	786	766	285.8	779	758	257.5	769	743	272.9	Calcium (mg)
1093	1052	269.3	1117	1115	333.1	1111	1090	275.5	1115	1112	306.0	Phosphorus (mg)
216	216	64.3	228	224	71.0	228	220	66.8	233	225	73.6	Magnesium (mg)
2424	2361	618.1	2351	2271	720.7	2299	2220	645.9	2232	2249	705.1	Sodium (mg)*
3653	3562	943.7	3553	3489	1046.1	3457	3345	956.1	3406	3425	1063.9	Chloride (mg)*
2582	2509	669.3	2654	2621	793.9	2659	2666	707.6	2663	2584	774.3	Potassium (mg)
7.2	6.9	1.99	7.3	7.3	2.24	7.4	7.3	1.99	7.4	7.4	2.17	Zinc (mg)
1.01	0.96	0.353	0.98	0.94	0.380	1.03	0.96	0.370	1.08	1.06	0.390	Copper (mg)
160	148	66.2	161	157	66.7	157	147	67.0	159	152	69.1	Iodine (μg)
2.56	2.45	0.872	2.60	2.42	1.071	2.71	2.55	1.113	2.78	2.65	1.162	Manganese (mg)
	66			229			327			268		*Base*

Table 3.42

Average daily intake of minerals as a percentage of the Reference Nutrient Intake (RNI) and proportion of respondents with intakes below the Lower Reference Nutrient Intake (LRNI) by sex of respondent and region

Percentages

Mineral (unit of measurement)	Sex of respondent and region							
	Men				Women			
	Scotland*	Northern	Central, South West and Wales	London and the South East	Scotland*	Northern	Central, South West and Wales	London and the South East
All sources								
Total iron (mg)**								
mean daily intake as % RNI	160	148	171	164				
19 to 50 years					78	70	83	75
over 50 years					[16]	150	137	133
% with intakes below LRNI	-	1	1	1				
19 to 50 years					28	37	34	27
over 50 years					[0]	6	-	3
Calcium (mg)								
mean daily intake as % RNI	152	142	150	140	110	117	115	116
% with intakes below LRNI	-	2	2	3	3	6	3	7
Phosphorus (mg)								
mean daily intake as % RNI	288	267	279	267	199	204	203	204
% with intakes below LRNI	-	-	-	-	-	0	-	0
Magnesium (mg)								
mean daily intake as % RNI	102	102	105	104	81	85	86	89
% with intakes below LRNI	6	9	10	8	12	15	11	14
Sodium (mg)***								
mean daily intake as % RNI	216	209	212	199	151	147	144	140
% with intakes below LRNI	-	-	-	0	-	0	0	0
Chloride (mg)***								
mean daily intake as % RNI	208	201	205	193	146	142	138	136
% with intakes below LRNI	-	-	-	0	-	0	-	0
Potassium (mg)								
mean daily intake as % RNI	98	95	97	96	74	76	76	76
% with intakes below LRNI	4	5	6	8	17	22	19	18
Zinc (mg)								
mean daily intake as % RNI	120	109	114	113	114	108	113	119
% with intakes below LRNI	2	4	4	3	-	6	3	4
Copper (mg)****								
mean daily intake as % RNI	120	114	127	129	89	85	90	93
Iodine (µg)								
mean daily intake as % RNI	180	156	158	153	120	121	117	121
% with intakes below LRNI	-	3	2	1	-	6	4	4

Table 3.42 continued

Average daily intake of minerals as a percentage of the Reference Nutrient Intake (RNI) and proportion of respondents with intakes below the Lower Reference Nutrient Intake (LRNI) by sex of respondent and region

Percentages

Mineral (unit of measurement)	Sex of respondent and region							
	Men				Women			
	Scotland*	Northern	Central, South West and Wales	London and the South East	Scotland*	Northern	Central, South West and Wales	London and the South East
Food sources								
Total iron (mg)**								
mean daily intake as % RNI	152	144	153	155				
19 to 50 years					65	64	64	68
over 50 years					[16]	125	125	121
% with intakes below LRNI	-	1	1	1				
19 to 50 years					30	39	36	28
over 50 years					[0]	6	-	3
Calcium (mg)								
mean daily intake as % RNI	152	142	148	138	109	112	111	110
% with intakes below LRNI	-	2	2	3	3	7	3	7
Phosphorus (mg)								
mean daily intake as % RNI	288	267	276	266	199	203	202	203
% with intakes below LRNI	-	-	-	-	-	0	-	0
Magnesium (mg)								
mean daily intake as % RNI	101	101	104	103	80	84	84	86
% with intakes below LRNI	6	9	11	8	12	15	11	14
Sodium (mg)***								
mean daily intake as % RNI	216	209	211	199	151	147	144	140
% with intakes below LRNI	-	-	-	0	-	0	0	0
Chloride (mg)***								
mean daily intake as % RNI	208	201	203	193	146	142	138	136
% with intakes below LRNI	-	-	-	0	-	0	-	0
Potassium (mg)								
mean daily intake as % RNI	98	95	97	96	74	76	76	76
% with intakes below LRNI	4	5	6	8	17	22	19	18
Zinc (mg)								
mean daily intake as % RNI	113	106	107	107	103	104	106	106
% with intakes below LRNI	2	5	4	4	1	6	3	4
Copper (mg)****								
mean daily intake as % RNI	116	113	121	125	84	82	86	90
Iodine (µg)								
mean daily intake as % RNI	175	153	155	148	114	115	112	113
% with intakes below LRNI	-	3	2	1	-	6	4	5
Base – respondents aged 19 to 50 years	*44*	*178*	*209*	*173*	*50*	*158*	*245*	*196*
Base – respondents aged over 50 years	*21*	*56*	*84*	*67*	*16*	*71*	*83*	*73*

Note: * Square brackets enclosing numbers denote the actual number of cases, when the base is fewer than 30. The number of women aged over 50 years living in Scotland is less than 30 and mean values and percentages are not, therefore, presented for total iron.

  ** For total iron, the RNI and LRNI values are for men of all ages; for women, the RNI and LRNI values are different for 19 to 50 year olds and over 50 year olds.

  *** Data in this table are for intakes from food and dietary supplements only and do not include further additions of salt in cooking or at the table.

  **** There is no LRNI for copper.

Table 3.43

Average daily intake of minerals by sex of respondent and whether someone in the respondent's household was receiving certain benefits

Mineral (unit of measurement)	Sex of respondent and whether receiving benefits											
	Men						**Women**					
	Receiving benefits			**Not receiving benefits**			**Receiving benefits**			**Not receiving benefits**		
	Mean	Median	sd	Mean	Median	sd	Mean	Median	sd	Mean	Median	sd
All sources												
Total iron (mg)	11.8	11.3	5.04	14.4	13.1	9.42	9.7	8.4	10.53	12.0	10.4	15.71
Haem iron (mg)	0.8	0.7	0.50	0.8	0.7	0.52	0.6	0.4	0.59	0.5	0.5	0.37
Non-haem iron (mg)	11.0	10.5	4.91	13.6	12.2	9.35	9.2	7.9	10.47	11.5	9.8	15.70
Calcium (mg)	889	865	326.1	1035	1001	441.4	699	669	287.0	831	784	314.7
Phosphorus (mg)	1307	1260	401.3	1532	1491	519.2	976	976	317.6	1145	1134	289.6
Magnesium (mg)	257	232	92.5	319	307	101.9	199	191	71.7	240	231	77.3
Sodium (mg)*	3065	2867	1043.2	3358	3275	1009.5	2143	2029	789.1	2335	2274	655.5
Chloride (mg)*	4557	4323	1547.5	5087	5000	1578.0	3198	3071	1149.5	3540	3464	974.3
Potassium (mg)	2939	2710	931.8	3436	3361	958.2	2292	2217	703.2	2729	2700	735.5
Zinc (mg)	9.6	9.5	3.46	10.9	10.2	6.00	6.7	6.3	2.67	8.2	7.6	3.63
Copper (mg)	1.23	1.17	0.522	1.52	1.34	0.851	0.91	0.82	0.437	1.11	1.02	0.473
Iodine (µg)	185	161	97.6	226	214	98.3	139	126	68.1	173	159	78.4
Manganese (mg)	2.92	2.64	1.417	3.49	3.21	2.147	2.30	2.12	1.262	2.86	2.65	1.261
Base		*110*			*723*			*150*			*741*	
Food sources												
Total iron (mg)	11.4	11.2	4.39	13.4	12.9	4.82	8.8	8.2	3.96	10.3	10.0	3.54
Haem iron (mg)	0.8	0.7	0.50	0.8	0.7	0.52	0.6	0.4	0.59	0.5	0.5	0.37
Non-haem iron (mg)	10.7	10.4	4.23	12.6	12.0	4.71	8.2	7.7	3.72	9.8	9.5	3.44
Calcium (mg)	883	852	327.4	1025	996	419.5	685	666	264.5	795	765	265.9
Phosphorus (mg)	1302	1260	405.8	1522	1488	456.3	974	976	316.1	1140	1129	288.4
Magnesium (mg)	254	231	92.7	316	306	97.4	197	190	70.2	235	230	68.0
Sodium (mg)*	3061	2867	1051.7	3352	3272	1004.0	2141	2029	789.5	2334	2274	655.3
Chloride (mg)*	4551	4323	1555.5	5062	4989	1488.5	3196	3071	1149.4	3539	3464	974.1
Potassium (mg)	2931	2710	939.1	3434	3356	953.9	2290	2217	702.3	2727	2700	735.1
Zinc (mg)	9.3	9.3	3.19	10.3	10.0	3.20	6.5	6.3	2.35	7.5	7.4	2.02
Copper (mg)	1.21	1.17	0.482	1.47	1.33	0.727	0.88	0.82	0.361	1.06	1.01	0.375
Iodine (µg)	179	161	85.3	221	210	94.4	137	126	61.5	163	153	67.7
Manganese (mg)	2.82	2.61	1.254	3.39	3.17	1.432	2.26	2.12	1.123	2.78	2.64	1.078
Base		*110*			*723*			*150*			*741*	

*Note: * Data in this table are for intakes from food and dietary supplements only and do not include further additions of salt in cooking or at the table.*

Table 3.44

Average daily intake of minerals as a percentage of the Reference Nutrient Intake (RNI) and proportion of respondents with intakes below the Lower Reference Nutrient Intake (LRNI) by sex of respondent and whether someone in the respondent's household was receiving certain benefits

Percentages

Mineral (unit of measurement)	Sex of respondent and whether receiving benefits			
	Men		Women	
	Receiving benefits	Not receiving benefits	Receiving benefits*	Not receiving benefits
All sources				
Total iron (mg)**				
mean daily intake as % RNI	136	165		
19 to 50 years			66	80
over 50 years			[25]	144
% with intakes below LRNI	2	1		
19 to 50 years			50	28
over 50 years			[3]	2
Calcium (mg)				
mean daily intake as % RNI	127	148	100	119
% with intakes below LRNI	5	2	12	4
Phosphorus (mg)				
mean daily intake as % RNI	238	279	178	208
% with intakes below LRNI	-	-	1	0
Magnesium (mg)				
mean daily intake as % RNI	86	106	74	89
% with intakes below LRNI	26	7	26	10
Sodium (mg)***				
mean daily intake as % RNI	192	210	134	146
% with intakes below LRNI	1	-	1	0
Chloride (mg)***				
mean daily intake as % RNI	182	204	128	142
% with intakes below LRNI	1	-	1	-
Potassium (mg)				
mean daily intake as % RNI	84	98	65	78
% with intakes below LRNI	15	5	34	16
Zinc (mg)				
mean daily intake as % RNI	101	115	95	117
% with intakes below LRNI	9	3	10	2
Copper (mg)****				
mean daily intake as % RNI	103	126	76	92
Iodine (μg)				
mean daily intake as % RNI	132	161	100	123
% with intakes below LRNI	5	1	11	3

121

Table 3.44 continued

Average daily intake of minerals as a percentage of the Reference Nutrient Intake (RNI) and proportion of respondents with intakes below the Lower Reference Nutrient Intake (LRNI) by sex of respondent and whether someone in the respondent's household was receiving certain benefits

Percentages

Mineral (unit of measurement)	Sex of respondent and whether receiving benefits			
	Men		Women	
	Receiving benefits	Not receiving benefits	Receiving benefits*	Not receiving benefits
Food sources				
Total iron (mg)**				
mean daily intake as % RNI	131	154		
19 to 50 years			58	67
over 50 years			[25]	126
% with intakes below LRNI	2	1		
19 to 50 years			53	29
over 50 years			[3]	2
Calcium (mg)				
mean daily intake as % RNI	126	147	98	114
% with intakes below LRNI	6	2	12	4
Phosphorus (mg)				
mean daily intake as % RNI	237	277	177	207
% with intakes below LRNI	-	-	1	0
Magnesium (mg)				
mean daily intake as % RNI	85	105	73	87
% with intakes below LRNI	27	7	27	10
Sodium (mg)***				
mean daily intake as % RNI	191	209	134	146
% with intakes below LRNI	1	-	1	0
Chloride (mg)***				
mean daily intake as % RNI	182	202	128	142
% with intakes below LRNI	1	-	1	-
Potassium (mg)				
mean daily intake as % RNI	84	98	65	78
% with intakes below LRNI	16	5	34	16
Zinc (mg)				
mean daily intake as % RNI	98	109	93	108
% with intakes below LRNI	10	3	10	2
Copper (mg)****				
mean daily intake as % RNI	100	122	74	88
Iodine (μg)				
mean daily intake as % RNI	128	158	98	117
% with intakes below LRNI	6	1	11	3
Base – respondents aged 19 to 50 years	87	518	125	523
Base – respondents aged over 50 years	23	206	25	218

Note: *   *Square brackets enclosing numbers denote the actual number of cases, when the base is fewer than 30. The number of women aged over 50 years living in benefit households is less than 30 and mean values and percentages are not, therefore, presented for total iron.*

       **   *For total iron, the RNI and LRNI values was for men of all ages; for women, the RNI and LRNI values are different for 19 to 50 year olds and over 50 year olds.*

      *** *Data in this table are for intakes from food and dietary supplements only and do not include further additions of salt in cooking or at the table.*

    **** *There is no LRNI for copper.*

Table 3.45

Comparison of average daily mineral intakes from food sources* by respondents in two surveys: 1986/87 Adults Survey; 2000/01 NDNS Adults aged 19–64 years (present survey)

Mineral (unit of measurement)	Age and sex of respondent									
	1986/87 Adults survey**				All	2000/01 NDNS				All
	16–24	25–34	35–49	50–64		19–24	25–34	35–49	50–64	
Men										
Total iron (mg)										
mean	12.6	13.8	14.2	13.9	13.7	11.4	13.0	13.7	13.6	13.2
median	12.4	13.2	13.3	13.7	13.2	11.2	12.5	13.1	13.3	12.6
se/sd***	0.29	0.36	0.26	0.28	0.15	4.40	5.13	4.75	4.58	4.81
Calcium (mg)										
mean	894	931	960	949	937	860	1017	1040	1027	1007
median	858	908	956	947	917	825	934	1014	1002	979
se/sd***	23.1	20.0	16.5	16.3	9.3	316.4	564.8	351.9	323.9	411.2
Copper (mg)										
mean	1.40	1.56	1.68	1.63	1.59	1.14	1.37	1.53	1.51	1.43
median	1.37	1.45	1.55	1.52	1.48	1.08	1.30	1.36	1.39	1.32
se/sd***	0.03	0.05	0.05	0.04	0.02	0.316	0.517	0.864	0.751	0.705
Iodine (μg)										
mean	225	238	248	231	237	166	216	221	230	215
median	217	235	235	216	225	152	196	215	223	205
se/sd***	6.6	5.7	6.4	5.2	3.1	70.9	119.6	84.3	80.2	94.3
Base – number of respondents	214	254	346	273	1087	108	219	253	253	833
Women										
Total iron (mg)										
mean	9.8	10.2	11.0	10.6	10.5	8.8	9.2	10.2	10.9	10.0
median	9.1	9.4	10.2	10.1	9.8	9.1	9.0	10.1	10.6	9.6
se/sd***	0.28	0.25	0.25	0.23	0.13	3.12	3.37	3.58	3.91	3.65
Calcium (mg)										
mean	675	699	760	739	726	694	731	796	823	777
median	656	689	737	731	716	661	709	777	810	752
se/sd***	19.4	17.4	13.8	12.9	7.8	256.8	228.9	271.9	287.2	268.7
Copper (mg)										
mean	1.09	1.15	1.31	1.28	1.23	0.91	1.00	1.05	1.07	1.03
median	1.01	1.08	1.17	1.17	1.12	0.84	0.94	1.03	1.00	0.98
se/sd***	0.04	0.03	0.03	0.03	0.02	0.376	0.374	0.375	0.376	0.378
Iodine (μg)										
mean	158	166	180	174	171	130	145	162	178	159
median	144	157	168	164	161	129	135	155	171	151
se/sd***	4.6	4.8	3.8	4.4	2.2	51.2	64.1	63.7	73.7	67.4
Base – number of respondents	189	253	385	283	1110	104	210	318	259	891

Note: * Data on intakes from food sources were only available for comparison from the 1986/87 Adults Survey for the minerals presented.

** Gregory JR et al. The Dietary and Nutritional Survey of British Adults. HMSO (London, 1990).

*** The 1986/87 survey reported standard errors; the present survey reports standard deviations.

Table 3.46(a)

Comparison of average daily mineral intakes from all sources by respondents in two surveys: 1986/87 Adults Survey; 2000/01 NDNS Adults aged 19–64 years (present survey): men

Mineral (unit of measurement)	Age and sex of respondent									
	1986/87 Adults survey*				All	2000/01 NDNS				All
	16–24	25–34	35–49	50–64		19–24	25–34	35–49	50–64	
Total iron (mg)										
mean	13.0	14.1	14.5	14.1	14.0	11.5	13.9	14.1	15.2	14.0
median	12.5	13.3	13.4	13.7	13.2	11.3	12.8	13.2	13.6	12.9
se/sd**	0.35	0.37	0.32	0.30	0.17	4.60	7.50	5.63	13.21	9.00
Calcium (mg)										
mean	899	933	961	952	940	867	1030	1049	1035	1016
median	863	908	959	947	919	825	951	1017	1002	987
se/sd**	22.9	20.4	16.5	16.4	9.4	324.6	606.3	358.7	331.0	430.7
Sodium (mg)***										
mean	3432	3327	3459	3272	3376	3342	3366	3340	3249	3320
median	3430	3309	3406	3232	3320	3356	3187	3312	3077	3255
se/sd**	78.2	61.2	51.9	51.8	29.8	1090.3	1077.5	1007.6	943.6	1018.2
Chloride (mg)***										
mean	5245	5125	5296	5029	5179	4921	5135	5052	4923	5018
median	5252	5052	5216	4991	5115	5157	4870	5011	4739	4965
se/sd**	115.4	91.1	78.8	78.0	44.6	1554.9	1879.6	1498.5	1385.8	1583.3
Potassium (mg)										
mean	3018	3237	3279	3155	3187	2847	3286	3485	3553	3371
median	3006	3223	3197	3089	3143	2935	3194	3472	3566	3304
se/sd**	60	50	45	43	25	712.9	1012.9	910.8	998.2	968.9
Magnesium (mg)										
mean	304	325	336	317	323	260	311	322	320	311
median	298	317	321	308	312	251	300	310	314	300
se/sd**	6.8	5.9	5.8	5.8	3.1	72.8	104.8	106.3	102.8	102.9
Phosphorus (mg)										
mean	1382	1454	1492	1456	1452	1341	1550	1524	1508	1502
median	1360	1421	1473	1435	1429	1287	1485	1500	1499	1474
se/sd**	28.2	24.3	20.8	20.9	11.6	318.9	727.4	429.1	402.8	510.7
Copper (mg)										
mean	1.41	1.57	1.82	1.63	1.63	1.16	1.43	1.58	1.56	1.48
median	1.37	1.45	1.56	1.52	1.49	1.14	1.30	1.36	1.41	1.32
se/sd**	0.03	0.05	0.17	0.04	0.06	0.338	0.673	0.972	0.882	0.820
Zinc (mg)										
mean	10.7	11.3	11.7	11.5	11.4	9.2	10.7	11.4	10.8	10.7
median	10.4	11.0	11.1	11.1	10.9	9.2	9.8	10.3	10.3	10.1
se/sd**	0.24	0.21	0.24	0.21	0.11	2.49	4.36	8.41	4.22	5.75
Iodine (μg)										
mean	233	240	251	243	243	167	223	226	235	220
median	218	235	236	217	226	152	202	217	227	209
se/sd**	8.8	5.8	6.7	9.8	3.9	70.1	122.4	93.0	85.0	99.1
Base - number of respondents	214	254	346	273	1087	108	219	253	253	833

Note: * Gregory JR et al. The Dietary and Nutritional Survey of British Adults. HMSO (London, 1990).

** The 1986/87 survey reported standard errors; the present survey reports standard deviations.

*** Data in this table are for intakes from food and dietary supplements only and do not include further additions of salt in cooking or at the table.

Table 3.46(b)

Comparison of average daily mineral intakes from all sources by respondents in two surveys: 1986/87 Adults Survey; 2000/01 NDNS Adults aged 19–64 years (present survey): women

Mineral (unit of measurement)	Age and sex of respondent									
	1986/87 Adults survey*				All	2000/01 NDNS				All
	16–24	25–34	35–49	50–64		19–24	25–34	35–49	50–64	
Total iron (mg)										
mean	11.8	11.1	12.9	12.9	12.3	10.0	9.8	12.9	12.3	11.6
median	9.5	9.6	10.3	10.3	10.0	9.3	9.0	10.5	11.0	10.0
se/sd**	0.95	0.42	0.69	0.78	0.36	4.88	5.98	23.30	8.00	14.99
Calcium (mg)										
mean	675	700	764	747	730	706	736	814	903	809
median	656	692	739	732	717	669	718	789	850	763
se/sd**	19.4	17.4	13.9	13.5	7.9	263.9	232.6	292.8	381.7	314.0
Sodium (mg)***										
mean	2334	2372	2389	2294	2351	2304	2325	2317	2267	2303
median	2291	2345	2356	2259	2313	2247	2283	2241	2243	2247
se/sd**	49.1	43.4	33.8	42.4	20.5	721.3	666.4	707.5	652.3	683.1
Chloride (mg)***										
mean	3572	3601	3615	3490	3573	3412	3479	3514	3474	3482
median	3497	3575	3552	3485	3536	3342	3433	3451	3443	3425
se/sd**	74.0	64.5	50.4	63.3	30.7	1013.8	985.1	1051.6	991.9	1013.3
Potassium (mg)										
mean	2259	2324	2562	2476	2434	2364	2398	2734	2885	2655
median	2228	2297	2510	2418	2410	2385	2383	2692	2829	2620
se/sd**	45	43	37	43	21	688.9	655.4	759.5	731.3	747.9
Magnesium (mg)										
mean	215	232	250	238	237	208	211	241	252	233
median	208	225	233	226	226	206	203	234	241	223
se/sd**	5.2	5.0	4.5	4.7	2.5	69.9	64.9	79.3	82.4	77.9
Phosphorus (mg)										
mean	986	1032	1121	1099	1072	1050	1045	1134	1180	1116
median	943	1017	1114	1103	1054	1057	1017	1124	1174	1107
se/sd**	21.5	19.7	15.5	16.7	9.1	298.8	278.9	296.4	309.0	301.0
Copper (mg)										
mean	1.10	1.16	1.31	1.29	1.23	0.97	1.02	1.11	1.11	1.07
median	1.01	1.08	1.18	1.17	1.13	0.84	0.94	1.03	1.01	0.99
se/sd**	0.04	0.03	0.03	0.03	0.02	0.523	0.416	0.514	0.433	0.473
Zinc (mg)										
mean	7.6	8.2	8.7	8.6	8.4	7.1	7.1	8.2	8.6	7.9
median	7.5	7.8	8.5	8.3	8.2	6.6	6.6	7.8	8.1	7.4
se/sd**	0.16	0.17	0.13	0.14	0.08	3.17	2.88	3.79	3.66	3.54
Iodine (µg)										
mean	161	168	184	181	176	136	148	171	190	167
median	146	158	172	171	163	129	138	157	180	155
se/sd**	4.7	5.0	3.9	5.0	2.3	62.3	65.4	78.4	84.2	77.8
Base – number of respondents	189	253	385	283	1110	104	210	318	259	891

Note: * Gregory JR et al. The Dietary and Nutritional Survey of British Adults. HMSO (London, 1990).

** The 1986/87 survey reported standard errors; the present survey reports standard deviations.

*** Data in this table are for intakes from food and dietary supplements only and do not include further additions of salt in cooking or at the table.

4   Urinary analytes

4.1 Introduction

This chapter presents data based on the analysis of the samples taken from the 24-hour urine collection made by respondents in the survey.

As described in Appendix P of the Technical Report[1] the main reason for collecting a urine sample was to provide an indirect estimate of sodium intakes. It is not possible to obtain accurate estimates of dietary intake of sodium from weighed food intake information, mainly because it is not possible to assess accurately the amount of salt added to food in cooking or at the table. Estimates of sodium and potassium intakes can be obtained by measuring their urinary excretion, assuming the body is in balance for these minerals. Since the rate of excretion of both sodium and potassium varies with intake, the best estimate of intake is obtained from the analysis of a urine sample taken from a complete 24-hour collection, which allows for the fluctuations in intake over the collection period. A spot urine sample is not sufficiently representative to provide a valid measurement of sodium and potassium excretion.

Appendix P also describes the procedure for the 24-hour urine collection (including the administration of para-aminobenzoic acid (PABA)), the taking of the sub-samples, the processing of the urine samples and quality control procedures. The response rate for the urine sample is given in Chapter 1 of this report.

4.1.1 Para-aminobenzoic acid (PABA)

The collection of a complete 24-hour urine sample is a demanding task, and previous experience has shown that samples are frequently incomplete. Therefore, an additional procedure, 'PABA-check', has been devised. This is designed to monitor the completeness of the collection by asking respondents to take three 80mg tablets of para-aminobenzoic acid (PABA) at intervals during the 24-hour collection period. Measurement of the PABA concentration and total volume of the collected sample permits the calculation of the percentage recovery of the administered PABA, which in turn is a measure of completeness of the 24-hour urine collection.

The use of this procedure in this survey was approved by the Multi-centre and Local Research Ethics Committees and was successfully piloted in the feasibility study. It was included in part of Wave 1 of the mainstage survey. One respondent in Wave 1 exhibited an acute allergic reaction soon after taking the three PABA doses. Although this occurrence may have been a chance association, the survey doctor decided, after seeking external advice, to recommend the discontinuation of the PABA-check procedure as a precaution[2]. From part-way through Wave 1 until the end of the survey, all subsequent 24-hour urines were collected without PABA-check.

Analysis was carried out on urine samples for respondents in Wave 1 who completed the PABA-check. There were 29 respondents where PABA was taken and measured and where the result obtained was within the acceptable limits for PABA recovery of 108mg to 198mg[3]. Mean estimated 24-hour excretion of sodium, potassium and creatinine was calculated for this subset and the remaining respondents who provided a urine sample. The data suggest that the samples unvalidated by PABA contained slightly more of these analytes than the PABA-validated samples, suggesting on average a slight, but non-significant, over-collection of urine. Therefore, the mean excretion per 24 hours of sodium and potassium from the survey data seem unlikely to be underestimates.

4.1.2 Plasma creatinine

Following the removal of the PABA-check from the survey procedures, an alternative method of checking the completeness of the 24-hour urine collections was used. Measuring plasma creatinine concentration, which is relatively constant for individuals over time, allows the calculation of each respondent's theoretical 24-hour creatinine excretion rate and this can be compared with the measured excretion rate from the urine samples[4]. An acceptable range of values for creatinine that would be expected in a complete 24-hour urine sample was calculated for each respondent who completed this component and compared with the observed amounts of creatinine in the urine samples. Half of all respondents for whom this could be done fell within the acceptable limits, 32% gave creatinine recoveries that appeared to be too low, and 18% recoveries that appeared too high.

Mean 24-hour sodium and potassium excretion rates of the 50% who fell within the acceptable range for creatinine excretion were compared with the mean values for all respondents who reported making a 24-hour urine collection and were found to be no more than 2% higher. The errors that are likely to have arisen as a result of the lack of the PABA-check confirmation of completeness of the 24-hour urine collections are considered to have been relatively small and probably resulted in a small downward bias in the results.

4.2 Results used in the analysis

A total of 1,495 respondents made a 24-hour urine collection. From this, 1,459 samples were analysed; 36 samples were either not received or received in an unsuitable condition for analysis and have been excluded from the urine analysis results. A number of respondents, 298 (20%), from whom a urine sample was obtained and analysed, reported failing to collect at least one void during the 24-hour period[5].

The samples were analysed for concentrations of urinary sodium, urinary potassium, urinary urea, urinary fluoride and urinary creatinine. By measuring urinary creatinine in the samples a comparison can be made between groups based on ratios of urinary sodium to urinary creatinine. The ratios quoted with creatinine as the denominator will enable comparisons to be made with other datasets where only spot urine samples were collected and the analyte results expressed as a ratio with creatinine. The use of creatinine ratios also makes it possible to include those results from the present survey where a full 24-hour collection was not achieved.

Data from the present survey were converted to mmol/24h based on the weight of the full collection in kg and a conversion factor of 1kg being equal to 1 litre[6]. In 18 cases the complete urine collection could not be weighed due to technical problems so excretion per 24 hours cannot be calculated.

Data on excretion per 24 hours are presented only for complete 24-hour collections which were weighed (1,153 unweighted). Partial collections, where at least one void was missed, have been excluded. Ratios of urinary analytes are presented including data for incomplete collections as well as for complete collections (1,458 unweighted).

4.3 Urinary sodium

The main purpose for measuring urinary sodium excretion was to provide an indirect estimate of sodium intake. It is not possible to measure intake directly as the amount of salt added to food in cooking or at the table cannot be accurately assessed.

Table 4.1 presents data on mean urinary sodium excretion per 24 hours for men and women by age. The mean urinary sodium excretion per 24 hours for men was 187.4mmol, significantly higher than for women, 138.5mmol (p<0.01). Men had significantly higher mean urinary sodium excretion per 24 hours than women in each age group except those aged 19 to 24 years (p<0.01). There were no significant age differences in mean urinary sodium excretion per 24 hours for men or women. Urinary sodium excretion (mmol/24h) can be compared with dietary intakes of sodium (mg/day), where 1mmol is equal to 23mg. Mean values for sodium calculated from total urinary sodium excretion were 4310mg/day for men and 3186mg/day for women. This compares with a mean daily intake of dietary sodium of 3320mg/day for men and 2303mg/day for women (*see* Chapter 3, section 3.6), indicating that the dietary measurement is underestimating intake by 25% to 30% largely due to exclusion of salt added in cooking and at the table from the dietary sodium estimates.

Urinary sodium excretion can be converted to provide an estimate of salt intake, where 1g salt contains 17.1mmol sodium. This assumes that dietary intake of sodium is equal to the urinary output, and that all sodium in the diet comes from salt. In the Report on Nutritional Aspects of Cardiovascular Disease, the Committee on Medical Aspects of Food Policy (COMA) recommended an intake of salt of 6g/day or less[7]. This recommendation was endorsed by the Scientific Advisory Committee on Nutrition in its recent report on Salt and Health[8]. Mean salt intakes calculated from urinary sodium excretion, shown in Table 4.2, were 11.0g/day for men in this survey and 8.1g/day for women[9] (p<0.01). For all age/sex groups mean salt intakes were higher than the COMA recommendation of 6g/day. There were no significant differences in mean salt intakes by age for men or women. Overall, 85% of men and 69% of women had salt intakes of more than 6g/ day (p<0.01). A significantly higher proportion of the youngest group of men had intakes of salt of more than 6g/day, than men in any other age group (p<0.01). For example, 98% of men aged 19 to 24 years had an estimated salt intake of more than 6g/day compared with 82% of those aged 50 to 64 years. The youngest group of women were significantly more likely to have salt intakes of more than 6g/day, 83%, than those aged 50 to 64 years, 62% (p<0.05).

(Tables 4.1 and 4.2)

4.4 Urinary potassium

Table 4.3 shows that the mean urinary potassium excretion per 24 hours for men was 80.7mmol, significantly higher than that for women, 67.5mmol (p<0.01). Men had significantly higher mean urinary potassium excretion than women in all age groups except those aged 19 to 24 years (25 to 34: p<0.05; 35 to 64: p<0.01).

The youngest group of men had significantly lower mean excretion of potassium than men in any other age group (p<0.05). For example, men aged 19 to 24 years had a mean urinary potassium excretion of 65.8mmol/24h compared with 84.5mmol/24h for men aged 25 to 34 years. There were no significant differences by age for women.

Urinary potassium excretion (mmol/24h) can be compared with dietary intakes of potassium (mg/ day), where 1mmol is equal to 39mg. Mean values for potassium calculated from total urinary potassium excretion were 3147mg/day for men and 2632mg/day for women. This compares with a mean daily intake of dietary potassium of 3371mg for men and 2655mg for women (see Chapter 3, section 3.7), and shows good agreement between the urinary and the dietary data.

(Table 4.3)

4.5 Urinary fluoride

The main sources of fluoride in the diet are fluoridated water, and other natural sources, tea and toothpaste. The concentration of fluoride in the

water supplies varies, with about 10% of the UK population receiving a water supply which has either been fluoridated or has a naturally occurring fluoride content at or around 1ppm (53μmol/l). Tea contains high concentrations of fluoride and provides about 70% of the average fluoride intake[10]. Safe intakes of fluoride for adults are 0.05mg/kg body weight/day[10].

Table 4.4 presents data on mean urinary fluoride excretion per 24 hours for respondents who made a full 24-hour urine collection. Mean urinary fluoride excretion per 24 hours was 70.3μmol for men, and 66.3μmol for women (ns). Men and women aged 19 to 24 years had significantly lower mean urinary fluoride excretion than those in any other age group (25 to 34: p<0.05; all others: p<0.01). For example, men and women aged 19 to 24 years had a mean urinary fluoride excretion of 45.2μmol/24h and 35.3μmol/24h respectively, compared with 82.7μmol/24h for men and 81.4μmol/24h for women aged 50 to 64 years. Men and women aged 25 to 34 years had significantly lower mean urinary fluoride excretion than the oldest group of men and women (men: p<0.05; women: p<0.01). In addition, women aged 25 to 34 years had significantly lower mean urinary fluoride excretion than those aged 35 to 49 years (p<0.05).

The distribution of values for urinary fluoride was skewed with median values about 20% lower than mean values.

Safe intakes of fluoride for adults are 0.05mg/kg/ day (or 3μmol/kg/day)[10]. Overall, 1% of men and 3% of women had a urinary fluoride excretion per 24 hours that suggest intakes of fluoride above the safe level[12] (table not shown). This proportion ranged from none of those aged 19 to 24 years to 2% of men and 6% of women aged 50 to 64 years. Fluoride comes from a range of sources including tap water, toothpaste and dietary supplements. The level of fluoride in the tap water samples provided by respondents and in toothpaste are yet to be analysed. Respondents were asked at the dietary interview if they were taking any dietary supplements. One per cent of men and less than 0.5% of women who reported taking supplements said that they were taking fluoride supplements.

(Table 4.4)

4.6 Urinary urea

The mean urinary urea excretion per 24 hours was 375.1mmol for men, and for women was, significantly lower, 273.0mmol (p<0.01). As for urinary sodium and urinary potassium, men had significantly higher mean urinary urea excretion than women in all age groups except those aged 19 to 24 years (p<0.01). There were no significant age differences in mean urinary urea excretion for men or women.

(Table 4.5)

4.7 Urinary sodium to urinary creatinine ratio

The ratio of urinary sodium to urinary creatinine is given for all those respondents who made the 24-hour urine collection, and includes those who reported failing to collect at least one void during the 24-hour collection period.

In adults, creatinine excretion is generally higher for men than women; this is associated with the higher proportion of lean body tissue in men. Urinary concentrations of sodium relative to urinary concentrations of creatinine are therefore generally lower for men than women. This general pattern was reflected in the results of the current survey (Table 4.6). The mean urinary sodium to urinary creatinine ratio was 10.6mol/mol for men, significantly lower than the value for women, 12.4mol/mol (p<0.01). The mean urinary sodium to urinary creatinine ratio was significantly lower for men than women in each age group except 19 to 24 years (25 to 34: p<0.05; 35 to 64: p<0.01). There were no significant differences in the mean ratio for men or women by age.

(Table 4.6)

4.8 Variation in urinary analyte levels

Tables 4.7 and 4.8 show the mean excretion per 24 hours for the four urinary analytes measured and the urinary ratio of sodium to creatinine for men and women according to the region[12] in which they lived, and whether someone in the respondent's household was receiving benefits[13] (see caveat to section 2.7).

For region, there were very few clear patterns in the data or significant differences between sub-groups. Men in Scotland had a significantly higher mean urinary sodium excretion per 24 hours and a higher urinary sodium to urinary creatinine ratio than men living in Central and South West regions of England and in Wales or in London and the South East (both: p<0.05). Men and women living in Central and South West regions of England and in Wales had a significantly higher mean urinary fluoride excretion per 24 hours than those living in Scotland (p<0.05). This difference may be

attributable in part to regional differences in the fluoridation of water. About 10% of the UK population receive a water supply which has either been fluoridated or has a naturally occurring fluoride content at or around 1ppm (53μmol/l). Major fluoridation schemes are in operation in Birmingham and throughout the West Midlands and also in Tyneside[14].

There were no significant differences in any of the urinary analytes associated with household receipt of benefits for men or women.

(Tables 4.7 and 4.8)

4.9 Comparisons of urinary analytes between 1986/87 Adults Survey and present NDNS

Table 4.9 compares data from this survey with data on urinary sodium and urinary potassium from the Dietary and Nutritional Survey of British Adults aged 16 to 64 years carried out in 1986/87 (1986/87 Adults Survey)[15]. Data are presented for those respondents in this survey who made a full 24-hour urine collection. In the 1986/87 Adults Survey, respondents who failed to collect one or more voiding, and all cases where the period of collection was less than 18 hours or greater than 30 hours were excluded from the analysis[16]. It should be noted that in the 1986/87 Adults Survey the youngest age group was adults aged 16 to 24 years, while in the current NDNS the youngest age group is adults aged 19 to 24 years. This should be borne in mind where there are differences between these groups. A summary of the methodology and findings from the 1986/87 Adults Survey is given in Appendix S of the Technical Report[1].

There were few significant differences in mean urinary sodium and potassium excretion per 24 hours between the two surveys. Overall, men in the present survey had significantly higher mean urinary sodium excretion per 24 hours than men in the 1986/87 Adults Survey, 187mmol compared with 173mmol (p<0.05). There were no significant differences in mean urinary sodium excretion between the two surveys for women, or by age for both sexes.

When urinary sodium excretion data are converted to salt intake, the mean intake for men in the present survey was 11.0g/day and for women 8.1g/day compared with 10.1g/day for men and 7.7g/day for women in the 1986/87 Adults Survey (data not shown; significance of differences not calculated).

Overall, women in the present survey had significantly higher mean urinary potassium excretion per 24 hours than women in the 1986/87 Adults Survey, 68mmol and 62mmol respectively (p<0.05). The only other significant difference in mean urinary potassium excretion between the two surveys was for women aged 50 to 64 years, with those in the present survey having a higher mean excretion than those in the 1986/87 Adults Survey (p<0.05). This is not surprising given that women overall, and those aged 50 to 64 years, had significantly higher mean daily potassium intakes in the present survey than in the 1986/87 Adults Survey (see Chapter 3, section 3.10).

(Table 4.9)

References and endnotes

[1] The Technical Report is available online at http://www.food.gov.uk/science.

[2] A challenge test performed in July 2001 concluded that PABA was not the cause of the respondent's allergic symptoms. By this stage fieldwork had been completed.

[3] Bates CJ, Thurnham DI, Bingham SA, Margetts BM, Nelson M. Biochemical markers of nutrient intake. In: Margetts BM, Nelson M, eds. Design Concepts in Nutritional Epidemiology. 2nd Edition. Open University Press (Oxford, 1997): 170-240.

[4] There are no generally accepted values for expected creatinine excretion rates and plasma clearance values in the literature. The following reference was used in calculating expected excretion rates: Tietz NW, ed. Clinical Guide to Laboratory Tests. 2nd Edition. W.B.Saunders (Philadelphia, 1990): pp174-176. The acceptable range for the amount of creatinine expected to be excreted in the urine in 24 hours can be calculated in terms of the number of millilitres of plasma that is completely cleared of creatinine per minute for a standard 1.73 square metres of body surface area (Tietz, 1990). This is specified as 90-139ml for men aged 15 to 40 years and 80 to 125ml for women aged 15 to 40 years. For each year of age above this the values decrease by 0.65ml. Actual surface area (for adjustment) is calculated from weight and height, and excretion rates are converted to millimoles per 24 hours. Thus the measured plasma creatinine concentration is converted to an acceptable range of urinary excretion of creatinine in a 24-hour period. If the observed urinary creatinine excretion (concentration times volume) is less than the lower limit of this range, the urine collection is likely to have been incomplete. If higher than the upper limit, the collection may have been extended for more than 24 hours.

[5] The assessment of completeness of collection using plasma creatinine suggested that in 32% of cases the creatinine recoveries appeared to be too low. This contrasts with 20% of cases where the respondent reported missing at least one collection during the 24 hours. These findings are not incompatible. The plasma creatinine assessment relies on published 'normal ranges' and these may not be exactly appropriate for the sample in this survey, for example, because of different assay methods or differences in the characteristics of the population examined.

[6] The interviewer weighed the full 24-hour urine collection twice, prior to taking any sub-samples, and the mean weight is taken.

[7] Department of Health. Report on Health and Social Subjects: 46. Nutritional Aspects of Cardiovascular Disease. HMSO (London, 1994).

[8] Scientific Advisory Committee on Nutrition. Salt and Health. TSO (London, 2003). The Scientific Advisory Committee on Nutrition found no basis for a revision of the 1994 COMA recommendation for a target salt intake of 6g/day (2.4g/100mmol sodium) for the adult population. Six grams is higher than the Reference Nutrient Intake (RNI) and substantially greater than the salt intake required to maintain the sodium content of the body.

[9] Values were calculated for all respondents who reported making a full 24-hour urine collection.

[10] Department of Health. Report on Health and Social Subjects: 41. Dietary Reference Values for Food Energy and Nutrients for the United Kingdom. HMSO (London, 1991).

[11] Safe levels of intake were calculated for each respondent based on their body weight (kg) and 3μmol/kg/day. Calculated safe levels of intake were compared with fluoride excretion levels.

[12] The areas included in each of the four analysis 'regions' are given in the response chapter, Chapter 2 of the Technical Report, online at http://www.food.gov.uk/science. Definitions of 'regions' are given in the glossary (see Appendix C).

[13] Households receiving benefits are those where someone in the respondent's household was currently receiving Working Families Tax Credit or had, in the previous 14 days, drawn Income Support or (Income-related) Job Seeker's Allowance. Definitions of 'household' and 'benefits (receiving)' are given in the glossary (see Appendix C).

[14] Medical Research Council. Water Fluoridation and Health. Medical Research Council (London, 2002).

[15] Gregory J, Foster K, Tyler H, Wiseman M. The Dietary and Nutritional Survey of British Adults. HMSO (London, 1990).

[16] Excluding those with collections less than 18 hours in the 1986/87 Adults Survey is equivalent to excluding all partial collections from the analyses in the present survey. Excluding respondents to the present survey where the period of urine collection was greater than 30 hours made little difference to overall mean values and no difference to the significance of differences between the two surveys. The 1986/87 Adults Survey did not include PABA-check and the completeness of the 24-hour collections made by respondents was not validated.

Table 4.1

Percentage distribution of total urinary sodium (mmol/24h)by sex and age of respondent

Respondents who reported making a full 24-hour urine collection*

Cumulative percentages

Total urinary sodium (mmol/24h)	Men aged (years):				All men	Women aged (years):				All women
	19–24	25–34	35–49	50–64		19–24	25–34	35–49	50–64	
	cum %	cum %	cum %	cum %	cum %	cum %	cum %	cum %	cum %	cum %
Less than 60	-	6	2	8	5	4	7	5	12	8
Less than 90	-	12	9	15	11	17	25	20	28	24
Less than 120	9	27	19	27	23	34	41	43	50	44
Less than 150	33	33	36	42	37	65	57	67	68	65
Less than 180	46	48	51	54	51	70	74	80	84	79
Less than 210	60	59	60	67	62	84	85	87	92	88
Less than 240	75	70	74	77	74	88	91	92	94	92
Less than 270	96	78	82	85	84	90	95	97	98	96
All	100	100	100	100	100	100	100	100	100	100
Base	62	152	170	183	567	60	129	203	187	580
Mean (average value)	188.5	194.7	189.9	178.7	187.4	155.7	148.2	137.0	128.0	138.5
Median	180.9	185.5	175.1	173.5	177.5	130.2	136.8	128.4	119.4	129.3
Lower 2.5 percentile	103.1	37.3	41.8	35.9	41.0	29.4	33.3	43.7	39.2	39.0
Upper 2.5 percentile	284.2	381.6	378.2	361.8	370.1	397.2	380.2	277.7	268.1	282.7
Standard deviation	58.38	99.03	82.55	84.61	85.80	79.09	78.83	58.40	58.92	66.42

Note: * This excludes 298 cases where the respondent reported missing at least one collection.

Table 4.2

Percentage distribution of salt intake (g/day) estimated from total urinary sodium by sex and age of respondent

Respondents who reported making a full 24-hour urine collection*

Cumulative percentages

Salt intake (g/d)	Men aged (years):				All men	Women aged (years):				All women
	19–24	25–34	35–49	50–64		19–24	25–34	35–49	50–64	
	cum %	cum %	cum %	cum %	cum %	cum %	cum %	cum %	cum %	cum %
3 or less	-	5	2	5	4	4	6	5	7	6
6 or less	2	20	13	18	15	17	29	31	38	31
9 or less	37	34	39	42	39	66	59	68	69	66
12 or less	60	57	58	65	60	84	81	85	91	86
15 or less	81	73	80	83	79	90	92	96	96	95
18 or less	100	89	91	91	91	92	97	100	99	98
All		100	100	100	100	100	100		100	100
Base	62	152	170	183	567	60	129	203	187	580
Mean (average value)	11.0	11.4	11.1	10.5	11.0	9.1	8.7	8.0	7.5	8.1
Median	10.6	10.9	10.2	10.1	10.4	7.6	8.0	7.5	7.0	7.6
Lower 2.5 percentile	6.0	2.2	2.4	2.1	2.4	1.7	1.9	2.6	2.3	2.3
Upper 2.5 percentile	16.6	22.3	22.1	21.2	21.6	23.2	22.2	16.2	15.7	16.5
Standard deviation	3.41	5.79	4.83	4.95	5.02	4.62	4.61	3.42	3.45	3.88

Note: * This excludes 298 cases where the respondent reported missing at least one collection.

Table 4.3

Percentage distribution of total urinary potassium (mmol/24h) by sex and age of respondent

Respondents who reported making a full 24-hour urine collection*   Cumulative percentages

Total urinary potassium (mmol/24h)	Men aged (years):				All men	Women aged (years):				All women
	19–24	25–34	35–49	50–64		19–24	25–34	35–49	50–64	
	cum %	cum %	cum %	cum %	cum %	cum %	cum %	cum %	cum %	cum %
Less than 20	-	2	1	2	1	6	3	1	2	2
Less than 30	9	4	3	5	5	9	12	3	5	6
Less than 40	12	9	7	8	8	23	17	8	15	14
Less than 50	22	20	14	15	17	44	35	21	22	27
Less than 60	34	29	24	23	26	57	51	38	37	43
Less than 70	49	42	37	36	40	65	67	54	57	59
Less than 80	84	51	52	50	54	79	78	70	71	73
Less than 90	88	63	65	64	66	86	87	84	81	84
Less than 100	93	72	74	71	75	92	93	90	89	90
Less than 120	100	83	87	89	88	97	97	95	94	96
Less than 140		92	97	96	96	100	97	99	99	99
All		100	100	100	100		100	100	100	100
Base	62	152	170	184	568	60	129	203	187	580
Mean (average value)	65.8	84.5	81.4	82.0	80.7	59.8	64.3	70.2	69.2	67.5
Median	70.6	78.4	78.1	81.0	76.7	53.8	58.5	67.5	66.5	65.2
Lower 2.5 percentile	23.4	23.0	28.6	20.7	24.3	9.3	19.2	29.7	20.2	22.4
Upper 2.5 percentile	108.6	164.8	145.0	151.4	152.1	132.4	140.1	127.1	124.4	127.0
Standard deviation	21.28	40.62	29.70	32.33	33.42	27.12	39.60	26.16	27.94	30.41

Note: * This excludes 298 cases where the respondent reported missing at least one collection.

Table 4.4

Percentage distribution of total urinary fluoride (μmol/24h) by sex and age of respondent

Respondents who reported making a full 24-hour urine collection*   Cumulative percentages

Total urinary fluoride (μmol/24h)	Men aged (years):				All men	Women aged (years):				All women
	19–24	25–34	35–49	50–64		19–24	25–34	35–49	50–64	
	cum %	cum %	cum %	cum %	cum %	cum %	cum %	cum %	cum %	cum %
Less than 10	4	1	0	2	1	1	5	2	-	2
Less than 20	15	7	7	4	7	30	16	11	10	14
Less than 30	34	17	18	15	18	52	40	22	23	30
Less than 40	51	27	32	30	32	69	50	30	29	38
Less than 50	63	40	45	41	44	78	61	42	38	48
Less than 60	82	55	53	49	56	86	68	50	48	57
Less than 70	87	64	62	58	64	88	74	61	61	67
Less than 80	90	71	67	63	69	95	77	66	68	72
Less than 90	91	81	73	69	76	96	80	73	73	77
Less than 100	91	85	77	72	79	99	85	78	76	81
Less than 120	96	93	87	78	86	99	90	86	81	86
All	100	100	100	100	100	100	100	100	100	100
Base	62	152	170	184	568	60	129	203	187	580
Mean (average value)	45.2	64.2	71.6	82.7	70.3	35.3	54.5	69.2	81.4	66.3
Median	37.4	55.9	52.6	62.7	54.9	27.8	39.0	59.9	61.0	52.2
Lower 2.5 percentile	4.5	13.2	16.3	11.7	13.1	11.5	6.5	10.9	13.8	10.7
Upper 2.5 percentile	122.7	178.2	205.2	241.3	205.2	93.1	172.6	186.8	339.1	199.6
Standard deviation	28.64	40.15	52.07	62.14	51.99	23.04	43.16	46.11	78.32	58.22

Note: * This excludes 298 cases where the respondent reported missing at least one collection.

Table 4.5

Percentage distribution of total urinary urea (mmol/24h) by sex and age of respondent

Respondents who reported making a full 24-hour urine collection*

Cumulative percentages

Total urinary urea (mmol/24h)	Men aged (years):				All men	Women aged (years):				All women
	19–24	25–34	35–49	50–64		19–24	25–34	35–49	50–64	
	cum %	cum %	cum %	cum %	cum %	cum %	cum %	cum %	cum %	cum %
Less than 100	4	2	1	2	2	-	7	1	4	4
Less than 150	6	5	3	4	4	13	15	8	12	11
Less than 200	13	12	10	8	10	27	28	18	22	22
Less than 250	18	23	18	17	19	40	53	39	42	43
Less than 300	30	30	32	31	31	53	71	60	66	64
Less than 350	42	41	45	48	45	82	82	79	80	80
Less than 400	63	55	62	62	60	91	95	90	90	91
Less than 450	78	69	75	75	74	94	97	96	96	96
Less than 500	90	82	83	84	84	94	97	97	99	97
All	100	100	100	100	100	100	100	100	100	100
Base	62	152	170	184	568	60	129	203	187	580
Mean (average value)	362.0	387.7	368.3	375.3	375.1	284.9	256.3	281.9	271.1	273.0
Median	375.6	388.4	362.8	353.1	366.2	283.6	244.9	272.5	263.6	262.3
Lower 2.5 percentile	59.3	117.2	134.4	109.1	115.5	123.1	79.5	113.1	83.1	83.1
Upper 2.5 percentile	695.4	817.7	653.0	698.3	702.5	607.8	580.8	519.5	475.5	514.5
Standard deviation	136.36	164.47	132.60	157.02	149.93	116.02	109.09	96.46	100.60	103.07

Note: * This excludes 298 cases where the respondent reported missing at least one collection.

Table 4.6

Percentage distribution of urinary sodium: urinary creatinine ratio (mol/mol) by sex and age of respondent

Respondents who made 24-hour urine collection*

Cumulative percentages

Urinary sodium: urinary creatinine ratio (mol/mol)	Men aged (years):				All men	Women aged (years):				All women
	19–24	25–34	35–49	50–64		19–24	25–34	35–49	50–64	
	cum %	cum %	cum %	cum %	cum %	cum %	cum %	cum %	cum %	cum %
Less than 5.0	7	7	5	5	6	6	6	2	2	3
Less than 7.5	20	21	17	23	20	18	19	18	14	17
Less than 10.0	54	50	45	48	48	33	41	39	33	37
Less than 12.5	70	73	72	72	72	54	59	60	57	58
Less than 15.0	84	91	88	86	88	64	75	74	72	73
Less than 17.5	89	94	97	93	94	87	87	88	84	86
All	100	100	100	100	100	100	100	100	100	100
Base	92	186	214	213	704	88	178	269	219	754
Mean (average value)	10.9	10.5	10.7	10.6	10.6	12.8	12.4	12.0	12.6	12.4
Median	9.3	10.1	10.2	10.2	10.1	12.1	11.5	11.5	11.7	11.6
Lower 2.5 percentile	2.7	3.6	4.3	3.2	3.7	4.2	3.8	5.0	5.1	4.5
Upper 2.5 percentile	23.1	21.3	18.0	21.1	20.4	26.4	27.8	24.6	23.0	25.4
Standard deviation	4.48	4.19	3.49	4.34	4.07	5.43	6.02	4.94	5.11	5.32

Note: * This includes respondents who reported making a full 24-hour urine collection and those who made a partial collection, that is, recorded missing at least one collection during the 24 hours.

Table 4.7

Urinary analytes by sex of respondent and region

Sex of respondent and urinary analyte (unit of measurement)	Region															
	Scotland				Northern				Central, South West and Wales				London and the South East			
	Mean	Median	sd	Base	Mean	Median	sd	Base	Mean	Median	sd	Base	Mean	Median	sd	Base
Men																
Urinary sodium (mmol/24h)*	229.2	239.7	80.46	50	186.9	163.0	95.75	156	184.3	181.2	80.98	200	178.7	166.7	79.87	161
Urinary potassium (mmol/24h)*	79.6	73.6	32.33	50	77.5	74.8	32.69	156	79.9	77.1	30.86	201	85.2	80.7	37.17	161
Urinary fluoride (μmol/24h)*	53.5	41.5	34.93	50	65.4	52.6	48.03	156	79.4	58.1	58.97	201	69.1	56.0	49.12	161
Urinary urea (mmol/24h)*	414.6	407.7	153.60	50	361.2	349.6	169.84	156	373.0	366.0	122.58	201	378.8	385.5	158.04	161
Urinary sodium: urinary creatinine ratio (mol/mol)**	12.1	11.6	3.83	56	11.1	11.0	3.98	192	10.2	9.6	3.78	258	10.3	9.9	4.47	198
Women																
Urinary sodium (mmol/24h)*	142.4	130.0	72.53	44	136.6	125.7	63.37	158	137.1	128.1	70.88	203	141.0	133.8	62.52	175
Urinary potassium (mmol/24h)*	58.5	55.6	26.79	44	68.1	65.3	27.86	158	65.3	62.4	35.03	203	71.7	68.9	27.01	175
Urinary fluoride (μmol/24h)*	44.6	26.9	49.82	44	64.1	47.0	60.14	158	72.6	56.5	66.41	203	66.5	58.2	45.94	175
Urinary urea (mmol/24h)*	269.9	252.1	114.39	44	268.4	256.5	109.87	158	262.1	255.6	98.89	203	290.6	285.3	96.97	175
Urinary sodium: urinary creatinine ratio (mol/mol)**	12.8	12.9	5.09	51	12.3	12.0	5.12	202	12.5	11.6	5.47	270	12.2	11.3	5.38	230

Note: * Results are for those who completed a full 24-hour collection only, that is, where the respondent reported not missing any collection during the 24 hours. There were an additional 298 cases where the respondent reported missing at least one collection during the 24 hours, these cases have been excluded from this analysis.

** Urinary sodium:creatinine ratio is given for all respondents who made a urine collection, irrespective of whether they reported making a full or partial collection.

Table 4.8

Urinary analytes by sex of respondent and whether someone in the respondent's household was receiving certain benefits

Sex of respondent and urinary analyte (unit of measurement)	Whether receiving benefits							
	Receiving benefits				Not receiving benefits			
	Mean	Median	sd	Base	Mean	Median	sd	Base
Men								
Urinary sodium (mmol/24h)*	185.9	177.3	85.97	77	187.7	177.8	85.85	490
Urinary potassium (mmol/24h)*	74.3	73.3	31.89	77	81.7	77.3	33.58	491
Urinary fluoride (μmol/24h)*	77.3	63.1	59.49	77	69.2	53.2	50.70	491
Urinary urea (mmol/24h)*	344.5	381.1	145.98	77	379.8	366.0	150.12	491
Urinary sodium: urinary creatinine ratio (mol/mol)**	11.2	11.1	4.33	98	10.5	10.1	4.03	606
Women								
Urinary sodium (mmol/24h)*	136.1	125.6	77.80	107	139.1	130.2	63.64	472
Urinary potassium (mmol/24h)*	61.3	54.4	42.34	107	68.9	66.7	26.84	472
Urinary fluoride (μmol/24h)*	55.8	43.2	46.73	107	68.7	56.0	60.31	472
Urinary urea (mmol/24h)*	249.4	233.0	110.57	107	278.4	265.1	100.65	472
Urinary sodium: urinary creatinine ratio (mol/mol)**	12.2	11.6	5.14	137	12.4	11.6	5.36	617

Note: * Results are for those who completed a full 24-hour collection only, that is, where the respondent reported not missing any collection during the 24 hours. There were an additional 298 cases where the respondent reported missing at least one collection during the 24 hours, these cases have been excluded from this analysis.

** Urinary sodium:creatinine ratio is given for all respondents who made a urine collection, irrespective of whether they reported making a full or partial collection.

Table 4.9

Comparison of total urinary sodium and potassium (mmol/24h) by respondents in two surveys: 1986/87 Adults Survey; 2000/01 NDNS Adults aged 19 to 64 years (present survey)

Sex of respondent and urinary analyte (unit of measurement)	Age (years) of respondent									
	1986/87 Adults survey*				All	2000/01 NDNS**				All
	16–24	25–34	35–49	50–64		19–24	25–34	35–49	50–64	
Men										
Urinary sodium (mmol/24h)										
mean	179	175	175	166	173	188	195	190	179	187
median	171	167	166	164	166	181	186	174	174	178
se/sd***	7.30	5.48	4.47	4.29	2.58	58.38	99.03	82.55	84.61	85.80
Base	*144*	*193*	*280*	*225*	*842*	*62*	*152*	*170*	*183*	*567*
Urinary potassium (mmol/24h)										
mean	79	79	79	73	77	66	84	81	82	81
median	75	78	74	71	74	71	78	78	81	77
se/sd***	3.5	2.0	2.3	2.0	1.2	21.3	40.6	29.7	32.3	33.4
Base	*144*	*193*	*280*	*225*	*842*	*62*	*152*	*170*	*184*	*568*
Women										
Urinary sodium (mmol/24h)										
mean	136	131	135	124	132	156	148	137	128	138
median	126	129	131	119	126	130	137	128	119	129
se/sd***	5.05	3.51	3.23	2.96	1.78	79.09	78.83	58.40	58.92	66.42
Base	*136*	*213*	*293*	*223*	*865*	*60*	*129*	*203*	*187*	*580*
Urinary potassium (mmol/24h)										
mean	62	62	66	58	62	60	64	70	69	68
median	58	59	62	56	60	54	58	68	66	65
se/sd***	2.1	1.8	1.5	1.3	0.8	27.1	39.6	26.2	27.9	30.4
Base	*136*	*213*	*293*	*223*	*865*	*60*	*129*	*203*	*187*	*580*

Note: * Gregory JR et al. The Dietary and Nutritional Survey of British Adults. HMSO (London, 1990).

 ** Data for the 2000/01 NDNS is presented for those respondents who made a full 24-hour urine collection only that is, did not report missing any collections. Data for the 1986/87 Adults Survey is presented for those who did not report missing any collections, and for those where the period of collection was at least 18 hours and no more than 30 hours.

 *** 1986/87 survey reported standard errors; present survey reports standard deviations.

Appendix A   Sampling errors and statistical methods

1   Sampling errors

This section examines the sources of error associated with survey estimates and presents sampling errors of survey estimates, referred to as standard errors, and design factors for a number of key variables shown in this volume. It should be noted that tables showing standard errors in the main part of this volume have assumed a simple random sample design. In testing for the significance of the differences between two survey estimates, proportions or means, the standard error calculated as for a simple random sample design was multiplied by an assumed, conservative, design factor of 1.5 to allow for the complex sample design.

The estimates presented in the main part of this volume are based on data weighted to correct for differential sampling probability and for differential non-response. The sampling errors presented in this appendix were calculated after applying a weight to compensate for differential sampling probability and differential non-response. The sample was also post-stratified, so that it matched the population distribution in terms of age, sex and region[1].

1.1   The accuracy of survey results

Survey results are subject to various sources of error. The total error in a survey estimate is the difference between the estimate derived from the data collected and the true value for the population. It can be thought of as being comprised of random and systematic errors, and each of these two main types of error can be subdivided into error from a number of different sources.

1.1.1 Random error

Random error is the part of the total error which would be expected to average zero if a number of repeats of the same survey were carried out based on different samples from the same population.

An important component of random error is sampling error, which arises because the estimate is based on a survey rather than a census of the population. The results of this or any other survey would be expected to vary from the true population values. The amount of variation depends on both the size of the sample and the sample design.

Random error may also arise from other sources such as the respondent's interpretation of the questions. As with all surveys carried out by the Social Survey Division (SSD), considerable efforts were made on this survey to minimise these effects through interviewer training and through feasibility work; however, it is likely some will remain that are not possible to quantify.

1.1.2 Systematic error

Systematic error, or bias, applies to those sources of error that will not average to zero over a number of repeats of the survey. The category includes, for example, bias due to omission of certain parts of the population from the sampling frame, or bias due to interviewer or coder variation. A substantial effort is put into avoiding systematic errors but it is likely that some will remain.

Non-response bias is a systematic error that is of particular concern. It occurs if non-respondents to the survey, or to particular elements of the survey, differ significantly in some respect from respondents, so that the responding sample is not representative of the total population. Non-response can be minimised by training interviewers in how to deal with potential refusals and in strategies to minimise non-contacts. However, a certain level of non-response is inevitable in any voluntary survey. The resulting bias is, however, dependent not only on the absolute level of non-response, but on the extent to which non-respondents differ from respondents in terms of the measures that the survey aims to estimate.

Although respondents were encouraged to take part in all components of the survey, some refused certain components. Chapter 2 of the Technical Report[2] examines the characteristics of groups responding to the different parts of the survey package. The analysis of the region, sex and age profile of respondents compared with population estimates showed evidence of some response bias. In particular, there was an under representation of men and of people aged 19 to 24 years. The data for the main part of this volume (and all volumes in the series) were therefore weighted for differential non-response by sex, age and region.

1.2   Standard errors for estimates for the NDNS of adults aged 19 to 64 years

As described in Chapter 1 and Appendix D of the Technical Report[2], this survey used a complex sample design, which involved both clustering and stratification. In considering the accuracy of estimates, standard errors calculated on the basis of a simple random sample design will be incorrect because of the complex sample design.

This dietary survey sample was clustered using postcode sectors as primary sampling units (PSUs). Clustering can increase standard errors if there is a lot of variation in characteristics between the PSUs, but little variation within them. By contrast, stratification tends to reduce standard errors especially where the stratification factors are correlated to the survey estimate. Stratifying the sample ensures that certain sections of the population are represented in the sample. The main stratifier used on this survey was Standard Statistical Region (SSR). The PSUs were further stratified by population density, socio-economic group and car ownership (see Appendix D of the Technical Report[2]).

In a complex sample design, the size of the standard error of any estimate depends on how the characteristic of interest is spread within and between PSUs and strata: this is taken into account by pairing up adjacent PSUs from the same strata. The squared differences in the estimates between successive PSUs from the same strata are calculated and summed to produce the standard error.

The majority of estimates in this survey take the form of ratio estimates, either means or proportions. The formula to calculate the standard error of these is:

$$se\ (r) = \frac{1}{x}\ [var(y) + r^2\ var\ (x) - 2r\ cov(y,x)]^{1/2}$$

where the ratio $r = y/x$.

The method explicitly allows for the fact that the percentages and means are actually ratios of two survey estimates, both of which are subject to random error. The value $se\ (r)$ is the estimate of the standard error of the ratio, r, expressed in terms of $se(y)$ and $se(x)$ which are the estimated standard errors of y and x, and $cov(y, x)$ which is their estimated covariance. The resulting estimate is slightly biased and only valid if the denominator is not too variable[3]. The ratio means for age groups have standard errors equal to zero for the full sample because both the numerator and the denominator have been set to equal the population totals and thus cannot vary for any selected sample.

The method of standard error estimation compares the successive differences between totals of the characteristic of interest for adjacent PSUs (postal sectors)[4]. The characteristic is the numerator (for example the average daily intake of vitamin C), and the sample size is the denominator in the ratio estimate[5]. The ordering of PSUs reflects the ranking of postal sectors on the stratifiers used in the sample design.

Tables A1 and A4 give standard errors, taking account of the complex sample design used on this survey, for the key variables presented in this volume. For selected vitamins and minerals and urinary analytic estimates are shown by sex and age. Standard errors for estimates of socio-demographic subgroups, such as household benefit status and region, are shown separately for men and women to reflect the way they are presented in the main part of the report. Standard errors are presented for the diary sample only.

1.3 Estimating standard errors for other survey estimates

Although standard errors can be calculated readily by computer, there are practical problems in presenting a large number of survey estimates. One solution is to calculate standard errors for selected variables and, from these, identify design factors appropriate for the specific survey design and for different types of survey variable. The standard error of other survey measures can then be estimated using an appropriate design factor, together with the sampling error assuming a simple random sample.

1.3.1 The Design Factor (deft)

The effect of a complex sample design can be quantified by comparing the observed variability in the sample with the expected variability had the survey used a simple random sample. The most commonly used statistic is the design factor (deft), which is calculated as a ratio of the standard error for a survey estimate allowing for the full complexity of the sample design (including weighting), to the standard error assuming that the result has come from a simple random sample. The deft can be used as a multiplier to the standard error based on a simple random sample, $se(p)_{srs}$, to give the standard error of the complex design, se(p), by using the following formula:

$$se(p) = deft \times se(p)_{srs}$$

Tables A1 to A3 show deft values for certain measures for those who completed a seven-day dietary record, and Table A4 for those who made a 24-hour urine collection. The level of deft varies between survey variables, reflecting the degree to which the characteristic is clustered within PSUs or is distributed between strata. Variables which are highly correlated to the post-strata should also have reduced deft values. For a single variable, the level of the deft can also vary according to the size of the subgroup on which the estimate is based because smaller subgroups can be less affected by clustering.

Table A1 shows the deft values for a range of socio-demographic variables for the diary sample, Tables A2 for selected vitamins, Table A3 for selected minerals and Table A4 for urinary analytes. For the socio-demographic variables, where geographic clustering would be expected, six out of ten of the design factors for men and eight out of ten for women are less than 1.2. Design factors of this order are considered to be small and they indicate that, in this survey, the characteristic is not markedly clustered geographically. For two of the ten

socio-demographic variables deft values are above 1.5 for both sexes.

For women, 77% of the design factors presented in Tables A2 to A4 are less than 1.2, while for men 71% are less than 1.2. For women, none of the deft values are greater than 1.5, while for men, 3% are greater than 1.5.

(Tables A1 to A4)

1.3.2 Testing differences between means and proportions

Standard errors can be used to test whether an observed difference between two proportions or means in the sample is likely to be entirely due to sampling error. An estimate for the standard error of a difference between percentages assuming a simple random sample is:

$$se_1(p_1 - p_2) = \sqrt{[(p_1 q_1 / n_1) + (p_2 q_2 / n_2)]}$$

where p_1 and p_2 are the observed percentages for the two subsamples, q_1 and q_2 are respectively $(100 - p_1)$ and $(100 - p_2)$, and n_1 and n_2 are the subsample sizes.

The equivalent formula for the standard error of the difference between the means for subsamples 1 and 2 is:

$$se_2(diff) = \sqrt{(se_1^2 + se_2^2)}$$

Allowance for the complex sample design is then made by multiplying the standard errors se_1 and se_2 from the above formula by the appropriate deft values.

In this volume the calculation of the difference between proportions and means assumed a deft value of 1.5 across all survey estimates. The calculation of complex sampling errors and design factors for key characteristics show that this was a conservative estimate for some characteristics for some age and sex groups, but was an optimistic estimate for other characteristics. Therefore there will be some differences in sample proportions and means that are not commented on in the text, but that are significantly different, at least at the p<0.05 level. Equally, there will be some differences that are described as significant in the text, but that are not significantly different when the complex sampling design is taken into account. An indication of the characteristics for which significance tests are likely to provide false-positives or false-negatives can be gained by looking at the size of the deft values in the tables in this appendix.

Confidence intervals can be calculated around a survey estimate using the standard error for that estimate. For example, the 95% confidence interval is calculated as 1.96 times the standard error on either side of the estimated proportion or mean value. At the 95% confidence level, over many repeats of the survey under the same conditions, 95% of these confidence intervals would contain the population estimate. However, when assessing the results of a survey, it is usual to assume that there is only a 5% chance that the true population value will fall outside the 95% confidence interval calculated for the survey estimate.

References and endnotes

[1]   Weighting for different sampling probabilities results in larger sampling errors than for an equal-probability sample without weights. However, using population totals to control for differential non-response tends to lead to a reduction in the errors. The method used to calculate the sampling errors identifies the weighting for unequal sampling probabilities and to the population separately, and adjusts the sampling errors accordingly.

[2]   The Technical Report, including its Appendices, is available online at http://www.food.gov.uk/science.

[3]   This variability of the denominator can be measured by the coefficient of variation of x, denoted by $cv(x)$, which is the standard error of x expressed as a proportion of x

$$cv(x) = \frac{se(x)}{x}$$

It has been suggested that the ratio estimator should not be used if $cv(x)$ is greater than 0.2. For the standard errors produced here, the denominators for the ratios were 'number of men' and 'number of women'. Both of these totals were constant, determined by the post-stratification and, therefore, there is no variation in these denominators and hence the cv of the denominator will be zero.

[4]   The calculation of standard errors and design factors for this survey used the software package Stata. For further details of the method of calculation see: Elliot D. A comparison of software for producing sampling errors on social surveys. *Survey Methodology Bulletin* 1999; **44**: 27–36.

[5]   For a survey of this kind the sample size is subject to random fluctuation, both within each PSU and overall. This is because the number of adults identified in each PSU is dependent on which households are sampled and there will be differing amounts of non-response. There is more control in the (weighted) sample sizes of subgroups such as age and sex since these variables were used as post-stratifiers.

Table A1

True standard errors and design factors for socio-demographic characteristics of the diary sample by sex of respondent

Diary sample   Numbers

	Men			Women		
	% (p)	Standard error of p*	Design factor	% (p)	Standard error of p*	Design factor
Age group						
19–24 years	13	0.00	0.00	12	0.00	0.00
25–34 years	26	0.00	0.00	24	0.00	0.00
35–49 years	30	0.00	0.00	36	0.00	0.00
50–64 years	30	0.00	0.00	29	0.00	0.00
Region						
Scotland	8	0.92	0.98	7	0.86	0.98
Northern	28	1.14	0.73	26	0.96	0.65
Central, South West and Wales	35	2.54	1.54	37	2.62	1.62
London and the South East	29	2.48	1.58	30	2.57	1.67
Household receipt of benefits						
Receiving benefits	13	1.47	1.25	17	1.47	1.17
Not receiving benefits	87	1.47	1.25	83	1.47	1.17
Sample size		833			891	

Note: * The ratio means for age groups for the diary sample have standard errors equal to zero because both the numerator and the denominator have been set to equal the population totals and thus cannot vary for any selected sample.

Table A2

True standard errors and design factors for average daily intake of selected vitamins from food sources by sex and age of respondent

Diary sample   Numbers

Vitamin (unit of measurement)	Age (years):								
	19–24			25–34			35–49		
	Mean r	Standard error of r	Design factor	Mean r	Standard error of r	Design factor	Mean r	Standard error of r	Design factor
Men									
Total carotene (β-carotene equivalents) (μg)	1469	128.6	1.38	1801	114.1	1.35	2077	87.1	1.09
Vitamin A (retinol equivalents) (μg)	560	45.5	1.35	724	52.3	1.48	989	79.8	0.94
Thiamin (mg)	1.60	0.071	1.34	2.08	0.172	1.13	2.04	0.102	1.00
Riboflavin (mg)	1.68	0.105	1.41	2.12	0.077	1.04	2.19	0.060	1.08
Niacin equivalents (mg)	39.4	1.31	1.20	46.2	1.41	1.15	45.9	0.87	1.04
Vitamin B$_6$ (mg)	2.6	0.12	1.29	3.0	0.09	1.09	2.9	0.07	1.08
Vitamin B$_{12}$ (μg)	4.4	0.22	1.39	5.9	0.28	1.24	7.0	0.35	1.02
Folate (μg)	301	13.2	1.27	346	10.5	1.22	343	7.4	0.99
Vitamin C (mg)	64.9	6.97	1.40	74.1	3.97	1.21	88.4	3.97	1.10
Vitamin D (μg)	2.9	0.19	1.32	3.5	0.18	1.25	3.7	0.13	0.91
Vitamin E (α-tocopherol equivalents) (mg)	9.8	0.48	1.25	10.5	0.33	1.09	10.8	0.30	1.11
Women									
Total carotene (β-carotene equivalents) (μg)	1294	133.7	1.42	1712	92.5	1.09	2015	92.3	1.08
Vitamin A (retinol equivalents) (μg)	467	41.0	1.21	587	47.3	0.99	675	29.6	1.04
Thiamin (mg)	1.45	0.099	1.30	1.55	0.075	0.84	1.52	0.050	0.92
Riboflavin (mg)	1.39	0.076	1.23	1.44	0.036	0.95	1.66	0.037	1.07
Niacin equivalents (mg)	29.5	1.20	1.28	28.8	0.73	1.16	31.5	0.57	1.13
Vitamin B$_6$ (mg)	2.0	0.09	1.22	1.9	0.05	1.09	2.0	0.04	1.04
Vitamin B$_{12}$ (μg)	4.0	0.25	1.29	4.0	0.17	1.11	4.9	0.18	1.26
Folate (μg)	229	10.7	1.19	233	6.3	1.13	255	4.3	0.88
Vitamin C (mg)	67.9	4.84	1.18	72.3	3.69	1.13	80.0	2.72	0.98
Vitamin D (μg)	2.3	0.19	1.23	2.4	0.12	1.04	2.8	0.14	1.19
Vitamin E (α-tocopherol equivalents) (mg)	7.9	0.56	1.26	7.9	0.22	0.95	8.2	0.16	0.87
Sample sizes									
Men		*108*			*219*			*253*	
Women		*104*			*210*			*318*	

Numbers

50–64			All			Vitamin (unit of measurement)
Mean r	Standard error of r	Design factor	Mean r	Standard error of r	Design factor	
						Men
2459	118.2	1.08	2041	54.2	1.09	Total carotene (β-carotene equivalents) (μg)
1145	88.7	1.11	911	37.4	1.00	Vitamin A (retinol equivalents) (μg)
2.07	0.095	1.20	2.00	0.061	1.08	Thiamin (mg)
2.20	0.064	1.20	2.11	0.032	0.99	Riboflavin (mg)
44.6	0.92	1.09	44.7	0.51	1.01	Niacin equivalents (mg)
2.8	0.07	1.12	2.9	0.04	1.08	Vitamin B_6 (mg)
7.3	0.37	1.10	6.5	0.16	1.00	Vitamin B_{12} (μg)
361	10.6	1.23	344	4.3	0.99	Folate (μg)
94.5	3.70	1.09	83.4	2.12	1.12	Vitamin C (mg)
4.2	0.14	0.93	3.7	0.08	1.05	Vitamin D (μg)
11.0	0.43	1.27	10.6	0.21	1.29	Vitamin E (α-tocopherol equivalents) (mg)
						Women
2205	74.3	0.86	1914	49.8	1.07	Total carotene (β-carotene equivalents) (μg)
816	45.1	0.95	671	20.5	0.97	Vitamin A (retinol equivalents) (μg)
1.60	0.045	0.83	1.54	0.032	0.96	Thiamin (mg)
1.75	0.047	1.11	1.60	0.024	1.11	Riboflavin (mg)
32.3	0.58	1.06	30.9	0.38	1.24	Niacin equivalents (mg)
2.1	0.05	1.14	2.0	0.03	1.13	Vitamin B_6 (mg)
5.7	0.20	1.01	4.8	0.11	1.21	Vitamin B_{12} (μg)
268	7.2	1.21	251	3.1	1.03	Folate (μg)
94.5	3.19	0.99	81.0	1.79	1.07	Vitamin C (mg)
3.5	0.15	1.01	2.8	0.08	1.21	Vitamin D (μg)
8.2	0.25	1.28	8.1	0.11	1.00	Vitamin E (α-tocopherol equivalents) (mg)
						Sample sizes
	253			833		*Men*
	259			891		*Women*

Table A3

True standard errors and design factors for average daily intake of selected minerals from food sources by sex and age of respondent

Diary sample

Numbers

Mineral (unit of measurement)	Age (years):								
	19–24			25–34			35–49		
	Mean r	Standard error of r	Design factor	Mean r	Standard error of r	Design factor	Mean r	Standard error of r	Design factor
Men									
Total iron (mg)	11.4	0.62	1.47	13.0	0.38	1.11	13.7	0.28	0.95
Calcium (mg)	860	46.5	1.54	1017	36.4	0.96	1040	23.0	1.04
Phosphorus (mg)	1335	40.9	1.36	1527	42.0	1.08	1520	28.2	1.05
Magnesium (mg)	258	8.9	1.32	308	7.7	1.12	318	6.0	0.98
Sodium (mg)	3342	146.5	1.40	3347	87.1	1.22	3337	65.4	1.03
Chloride (mg)	4921	208.9	1.40	5056	132.9	1.22	5047	97.5	1.03
Potassium (mg)	2841	90.9	1.34	3284	75.1	1.11	3481	57.2	0.99
Zinc (mg)	9.0	0.28	1.31	10.2	0.26	1.08	10.6	0.21	0.98
Copper (mg)	1.14	0.042	1.39	1.37	0.038	1.10	1.53	0.053	0.98
Iodine (µg)	166	9.2	1.35	216	9.5	1.18	221	5.2	0.99
Manganese (mg)	2.45	0.107	1.35	3.18	0.104	1.17	3.42	0.093	0.97
Women									
Total iron (mg)	8.8	0.38	1.26	9.2	0.25	1.08	10.2	0.18	0.90
Calcium (mg)	694	32.7	1.31	731	15.3	0.97	796	17.3	1.14
Phosphorus (mg)	1046	39.1	1.35	1041	21.8	1.15	1130	16.8	1.02
Magnesium (mg)	205	7.7	1.20	209	5.0	1.17	235	3.6	0.94
Sodium (mg)	2303	90.1	1.28	2324	42.7	0.93	2316	36.2	0.91
Chloride (mg)	3409	126.5	1.28	3478	65.8	0.97	3512	53.5	0.91
Potassium (mg)	2362	85.6	1.28	2397	54.2	1.20	2731	41.8	0.98
Zinc (mg)	6.8	0.28	1.36	6.7	0.14	1.07	7.6	0.11	1.00
Copper (mg)	0.91	0.044	1.19	1.00	0.026	1.02	1.05	0.018	0.86
Iodine (µg)	130	6.5	1.31	145	4.6	1.05	162	3.5	0.98
Manganese (mg)	2.12	0.108	1.24	2.45	0.074	1.10	2.79	0.050	0.80
Sample sizes:									
Men		*108*			*219*			*253*	
Women		*104*			*210*			*318*	

Numbers

50–64			All			Mineral (unit of measuremnet)
Mean r	Standard error of r	Design factor	Mean r	Standard error of r	Design factor	
						Men
13.6	0.32	1.11	13.2	0.17	1.04	Total iron (mg)
1027	24.1	1.18	1007	13.2	0.92	Calcium (mg)
1505	28.4	1.12	1493	15.4	0.98	Phosphorus (mg)
318	7.0	1.09	308	3.5	1.01	Magnesium (mg)
3248	62.4	1.05	3313	38.7	1.10	Sodium (mg)
4922	93.4	1.07	4995	56.7	1.09	Chloride (mg)
3552	70.5	1.13	3367	36.0	1.08	Potassium (mg)
10.3	0.19	1.07	10.2	0.10	0.94	Zinc (mg)
1.51	0.050	1.07	1.43	0.023	0.95	Copper (mg)
230	6.4	1.28	215	3.8	1.17	Iodine (µg)
3.70	0.095	1.06	3.32	0.049	1.00	Manganese (mg)
						Women
10.9	0.23	0.96	10.0	0.12	1.01	Total iron (mg)
823	18.5	1.04	777	11.0	1.22	Calcium (mg)
1176	20.9	1.09	1112	12.5	1.25	Phosphorus (mg)
246	4.8	1.06	229	2.6	1.12	Magnesium (mg)
2266	41.8	1.03	2302	23.3	1.02	Sodium (mg)
3474	62.2	1.01	3481	34.2	1.01	Chloride (mg)
2884	54.2	1.19	2653	30.4	1.21	Potassium (mg)
7.8	0.15	1.07	7.4	0.09	1.25	Zinc (mg)
1.07	0.029	1.22	1.03	0.014	1.08	Copper (mg)
178	4.9	1.07	159	2.4	1.08	Iodine (µg)
3.01	0.079	1.12	2.69	0.040	1.09	Manganese (mg)
						Sample sizes:
	253			833		*Men*
	259			891		*Women*

Table A4

True standard errors and design factors for urinary analytes by sex and age of respondent

Diary sample

Urinary analytes (unit of measurement)*	Age (years):											
	19–24				25–34				35–49			
	Mean r	Standard error of r	Design factor	Base	Mean r	Standard error of r	Design factor	Base	Mean r	Standard error of r	Design factor	Base
Men												
Urinary sodium (mmol/24h)	188.5	11.13	1.51	62	194.6	11.32	1.42	152	189.9	5.98	0.94	170
Urinary potassium (mmol/24h)	65.8	3.84	1.43	62	84.4	4.25	1.30	152	81.5	2.05	0.90	170
Urinary fluoride (μmol/24h)	45.2	5.39	1.49	62	64.4	5.03	1.55	152	71.4	4.23	1.06	170
Urinary urea (mmol/24h)	362.0	26.95	1.57	62	387.8	16.76	1.26	152	368.2	9.92	0.98	170
Urinary sodium: urinary creatinine ratio (mol/mol)	10.9	0.71	1.52	92	10.5	0.43	1.40	186	10.7	0.21	0.88	214
Women												
Urinary sodium (mmol/24h)	154.4	13.08	1.31	60	148.8	7.41	1.07	129	137.0	4.08	1.00	203
Urinary potassium (mmol/24h)	59.0	4.83	1.39	60	64.7	3.86	1.11	129	70.2	1.85	1.01	203
Urinary fluoride (μmol/24h)	35.1	3.07	1.06	60	54.7	4.05	1.06	129	69.2	3.30	1.02	203
Urinary urea (mmol/24h)	283.2	19.22	1.31	60	256.8	11.45	1.19	129	281.9	6.80	1.01	203
Urinary sodium: urinary creatinine ratio (mol/mol)	12.7	0.76	1.32	88	12.4	0.53	1.18	178	12.1	0.30	0.99	269

Note: * Full 24-hour collection is where the respondent reported not missing any collection during the 24 hours. There were an additional 298 cases where the respondent reported missing at least one collection during the 24 hours, these cases have been excluded from the analysis of urinary sodium, potassium, fluoride and urea but included for the urinary creatinine: urinary sodium ratio.

50–64				All				**Urinary analytes (unit of measurement)***
Mean r	Standard error of r	Design factor	Base	Mean r	Standard error of r	Design factor	Base	
								Men
178.7	5.53	0.89	183	187.4	4.66	1.29	567	Urinary sodium (mmol/24h)
82.0	2.42	1.02	184	80.7	1.85	1.32	568	Urinary potassium (mmol/24h)
82.7	5.22	1.14	184	70.3	2.88	1.32	568	Urinary fluoride (μmol/24h)
375.3	10.31	0.89	184	375.1	7.44	1.18	568	Urinary urea (mmol/24h)
10.6	0.30	1.02	213	10.6	0.18	1.16	704	Urinary sodium: urinary creatinine ratio (mol/mol)
								Women
128.0	3.59	0.84	187	138.5	2.98	1.08	580	Urinary sodium (mmol/24h)
69.2	2.30	1.13	187	67.5	1.37	1.08	580	Urinary potassium (mmol/24h)
81.4	6.59	1.15	187	66.3	2.61	1.08	580	Urinary fluoride (μmol/24h)
271.1	6.66	0.91	187	273.0	4.74	1.11	580	Urinary urea (mmol/24h)
12.6	0.36	1.04	219	12.4	0.20	1.05	754	Urinary sodium: urinary creatinine ratio (mol/mol)

Appendix B   Unweighted base numbers

Table B1

Unweighted base numbers: dietary interview, seven-day dietary record and 24-hour urine collection by sex of respondent

	Dietary interview	Seven-day weighed intake dietary record	24-hour urine collection*	
			Full collection	All
Age				
Men aged (years):				
19–24	86	61	31	44
25–34	219	160	103	126
35–49	394	303	221	277
50–64	309	242	183	209
All men	1008	766	538	655
Women aged (years):				
19–24	109	78	44	61
25–34	277	211	131	175
35–49	487	379	244	325
50–64	370	290	204	242
All women	1243	958	623	803
Region				
Men				
Scotland	80	53	41	46
Northern	267	195	137	165
Central, South West and Wales	337	274	190	241
London and the South East	324	244	170	203
Women				
Scotland	111	70	42	51
Northern	341	256	177	226
Central, South West and Wales	436	350	223	289
London and the South East	355	282	181	237
Household receipt of benefits**				
Men				
Receiving benefits	145	106	75	95
Not receiving benefits	863	660	463	561
Women				
Receiving benefits	283	199	135	174
Not receiving benefits	960	759	488	629
All	2251	1724	1161	1459

Note: *   Unweighted bases are given for those who made a full 24-hour collection, that is, where the respondent reported not missing any
          collection during the 24 hours; and for all those from whom a urine sample was obtained, that is including partial cases where the
          respondent reported missing at least one collection during the 24 hours.

       ** Receipt of benefits was asked of the respondent about themselves, their partner or anyone else in the household. Benefits asked
          about were Working Families Tax Credit, Income Support and (Income-related) Job Seeker's Allowance.

Appendix C   Glossary of abbreviations, terms and survey definitions

Benefits (receiving)	Receipt of Working Families Tax Credit by the respondent or anyone in their household at the time of the interview, or receipt of Income Support, or (Income-related) Job Seeker's Allowance by the respondent or anyone in their household in the 14 days prior to the date of interview.
COMA	The Committee on Medical Aspects of Food and Nutrition Policy.
CAPI	Computer-assisted personal interviewing.
CASI	Computer-assisted self-interviewing. The respondent is given the opportunity to enter their responses directly on to a laptop computer. This technique is used to collect data of a sensitive or personal nature, for example, contraception.
Cum %	Cumulative percentage (of a distribution).
Deft	Design factor; *see* Notes to Tables and Appendix A.
DH	The Department of Health.
Diary sample	Respondents for whom a seven-day dietary record was obtained.
Doubly labelled water (DLW)	A method for assessing total energy expenditure, used to validate dietary assessment methods by comparison with estimated energy intake. The respondent drinks a measured dose of water labelled with the stable isotopes $^2H_2$ and ^{18}O and collects urine samples over the next 10 to 15 days. Energy expenditure is calculated from the excretion rates of the isotopes.
dna	Does not apply.
DRV	Dietary Reference Value. The term used to cover LRNI, EAR, RNI and safe intake. (*See* Department of Health. Report on Health and Social Subjects: 41. *Dietary Reference Values for Food Energy and Nutrients for the United Kingdom.* HMSO (London, 1991).)
EAR	The Estimated Average Requirement of a group of people for energy or protein or a vitamin or mineral. About half will usually need more than the EAR, and half less.
HNR	Medical Research Council Human Nutrition Research, Cambridge.

Household	The standard definition used in most surveys carried out by the Social Survey Division, ONS, and comparable with the 1991 Census definition of a household was used in this survey. A household is defined as a single person or group of people who have the accommodation as their only or main residence and who either share one main meal a day or share the living accommodation. *See* McCrossan E. *A Handbook for interviewers.* HMSO (London, 1991).
HRP	Household Reference Person. This is the member of the household in whose name the accommodation is owned or rented, or is otherwise responsible for the accommodation. In households with a *sole* householder, that person is the household reference person; in households with *joint* householders, the person with the *highest income* is taken as the household reference person – if both householders have exactly the same income, the *older* is taken as the household reference person. This differs from Head of Household in that female householders with the highest income are now taken as the HRP and, in the case of joint householders, income then age (rather than sex then age) is used to define the HRP.
LRNI	The Lower Reference Nutrient Intake for a vitamin or mineral. An amount of nutrient that is enough for only the few people in the group who have low needs.
MAFF	The Ministry of Agriculture, Fisheries and Food.
Mean	The average value.
Median	*see* Percentiles.
MRC	The Medical Research Council.
na	Not available, not applicable.
NDNS	The National Diet and Nutrition Survey.
No.	Number (of cases).
ONS	Office for National Statistics.
PAF	Postcode Address File: the sampling frame for the survey.
Para-aminobenzoic acid (PABA) -check	Para-aminobenzoic acid (PABA) is actively absorbed and excreted, so can be used to check the 24-hour urine collection to verify completeness. The PABA-check validation requires the respondent to take three tablets of 80mg PABA with meals on the day of the 24-hour urine collection. Provided that at least 85% of the PABA dose is then recovered in the urine

	collection, this is deemed to be a valid 24-hour collection.
Percentiles	The percentiles of a distribution divide it into equal parts. The median of a distribution divides it into two equal parts, such that half the cases in the distribution fall (or have a value) above the median, and the other half fall (or have a value) below the median.
PSU	Primary Sampling Unit: for this survey, postcode sectors.
Region	Based on the 'Standard regions' and grouped as follows:

Scotland

Northern
North
Yorkshire and Humberside
North West

Central, South West and Wales
East Midlands
West Midlands
East Anglia
South West
Wales

London and the South East
London
South East

The regions of England are as constituted after local government reorganisation on 1 April 1974. The regions as defined in terms of counties are listed in Chapter 2 of the Technical report online at http://www.food.gov.uk/science.

Responding sample	Respondents who completed the dietary interview and may/may not have co-operated with other components of the survey.
RNI	The Reference Nutrient Intake for protein or a vitamin or a mineral. An amount of the nutrient that is enough, or more than enough, for about 97% of the people in a group. If average intake of a group is at the RNI, then the risk of deficiency in the group is small.
sd/Std Dev	Standard deviation. An index of variability that is calculated as the square root of the variance and is expressed in the same units used to calculate the *mean* (*see* mean).
se	Standard error. An indication of the reliability of an estimate of a population parameter, which is calculated by dividing the standard deviation of

	the estimate by the square root of the sample size (*see also* sd/Std Dev).
SSD	The Social Survey Division of the Office for National Statistics.
Wave; Fieldwork wave	The three-month period in which fieldwork was carried out.

> Wave 1: July to September 2000
> Wave 2: October to December 2000
> Wave 3: January to March 2001
> Wave 4: April to June 2001

WHO	World Health Organization.

Appendix D List of tables

4:   Urinary analytes

Tables

Appendix A: Sampling errors and statistical methods

Tables

Appendix B: Unweighted base numbers

Tables